The Variety of Dream Experience

SUNY series in Dream Studies
Robert L. Van de Castle, editor

THE VARIETY OF DREAM EXPERIENCE

SECOND EDITION

Expanding Our Ways of Working with Dreams

edited by

Montague Ullman
and
Claire Limmer

STATE UNIVERSITY OF NEW YORK PRESS

Published by
State University of New York Press, Albany

Printed in the United States of America

First edition published by The Continuum Publishing Company, © 1988.

For information, address State University of New York Press,
State University Plaza, Albany, N.Y., 12246

Production by Marilyn P. Semerad
Marketing by Nancy Farrell

Library of Congress Cataloging in Publication Data

The variety of dream experience : expanding our ways of working with
dreams / edited by Montague Ullman and Claire Limmer. — 2nd ed.
p. cm. — (SUNY series in dream studies)
Includes bibliographical references and index.
ISBN 0–7914–4255–1 (hardcover : alk. paper). — ISBN 0–7914–4256–X
(pbk. : alk. paper)
1. Dreams. 2. Dream interpretation. 3. Dreams—Therapeutic use.
I. Ullman, Montague. II. Limmer, Claire. III. Series.
BF1078.V36 1999
154.6′3—dc21 99–13194
CIP

10 9 8 7 6 5 4 3 2 1

CONTENTS

Introduction to the Second Edition

Much has changed in the dream scene in the decade since this book first appeared. Books about dreams addressed to the general public seem to be flooding the market. There is an ever-increasing network of dream workers stimulated by the efforts of Roberta Ossana, editor of *Dream Network: A Journal Exploring Dreams and Myth.* The Association for the Study of Dreams, an open membership organization, has fostered public and academic interest. Dream groups are proliferating across the country. While on the whole this burgeoning enthusiasm is to be welcomed, it confronts the uninitiated with a confusing array of thoughts about what dreams can do and why one should pay greater attention to them.

This book was initially written to show what some people with very different backgrounds have done with dreams. In addition to the chapters that have been retained, three new chapters have been added to illustrate how many of the features of experiential dream group work, as it evolved from the initial efforts of Nan Zimmerman and myself, can contribute to the practice of pastoral counseling, group psychotherapy, and individual psychotherapy. In the wake of the progress made in psychopharmacology, psychotherapy, in general, and dreams, in particular, seem to have taken a back seat.

A recent book of mine (*Appreciating Dreams*) was reviewed in a social work journal. The writer commented positively on the way the group process assures the safety and privacy of the dreamer. She spoke respectfully and with understanding about the process. She ended the review on so cautionary a note, however, that I doubt whether it would stimulate much interest on the part of social workers to engage in experiential dream group work.

While a certain amount of caution and responsibility is understandable in undertaking dream work, an overemphasis on the danger of dream work plays into the mystique that serious and effective dream work should be limited to the domain of the experts. This is a mystique that is gradually being put to rest as public awareness of and sophistication about dreams increases. Dream work belongs both in and beyond the consulting room. It is to this end that this book is addressed.

Montague Ullman
Ardsley, NY (1997)

Introduction to the First Edition

In *Working with Dreams,* a book Nan Zimmerman and I wrote a number of years ago, we posed the question, Can dream work be extended safely and effectively beyond the confines of the psychotherapist's consulting room? We felt that it could, and we described a group approach to working with dreams that could meet the standards of responsible dream work and could also be entrusted to an interested public.

Since that time I have been involved in exploring and extending the small group process we developed in two directions, one toward the furthering of dream work in the community and the other in the training of psychotherapists. I have pursued these goals through workshops and training sessions held in the United States and Scandinavia and through various writings. In the training of therapists my approach was intended to give the beginning therapist a "hands-on" feeling about dreams and the healing value of dream work. In the community, as dream groups were organized in homes, churches, and schools, I became convinced that group work, as we developed it, could be placed in the hands of the general public.

To say I was gratified with the results would be an understatement. It was more a feeling of elation at witnessing the positive response from both the public and the psychotherapists who were exposed to the process. What delighted me was the way that dream work touched on and opened up dormant areas of interest, liberated creative energies, and, in some instances, found new directions for those energies. My own understanding of dreams has been greatly enriched and revised because of this experience.

The past several decades have seen the emergence of many new ideas about dreams and the critical examination of old ones. The public is beginning to take a more active interest in its dream life, and a number of guides have appeared on the scene to further this endeavor. I am more and more convinced that by going beyond the privacy of the self, by sharing and working on dreams with others, we can have a most satisfying experience, one that meets a universal need to unload personal secrets in a safe environment and to meet others at deeper levels than in ordinary social intercourse.

This need is largely unmet in what we somewhat euphemistically regard as civilized society. When a supportive and stimulating structure is offered, it is amazing how responsive people are to dream work and how rapidly they acquire the skills needed to help the dreamer. Much more useful work can be done with dreams than we now are doing. We have failed to appreciate the resources in each of us that can be developed to achieve this goal. We have treated dream work as too specialized a task and have assigned it exclusively to the province of the psychoanalyst, or else we trivialize it by sweeping it under the rug, leaving people on their own to find some way of dealing with their dreams.

In short, we have the ability to be a healing influence for one another through dream work. In order for this to happen we must understand and respond to the two basic needs of the dreamer—first, to feel safe as he or she moves along this private path back into the intimate domain of the psyche, and second, to be helped to see what the dream images may be revealing that are difficult for the dreamer to see alone. I refer to the first as the Safety Factor and to the second as the Discovery Factor. For dream work to be effective, it has to meet both these needs. Anyone who is motivated enough can learn the necessary skills to accomplish this. It makes available a natural pathway toward emotional healing, toward becoming more of what we are capable of becoming. Every therapist is aware of how powerful a tool a dream is in the therapeutic process. The point is that dream work can also provide the basis for a healing experience outside the consulting room without the formal trappings of a therapeutic arrangement. It can be therapeutic without being therapy.

The path is not easy. There are booby traps all along the way. Those who wish to pursue dream work will have to disengage from certain widespread but false notions about the nature of our dream life. These have become so deeply entrenched that they have reached the status of prevailing myths which are not recognized as such. They include the belief that the necessary skills for dream work can come only from professional training and experience and that dream work therefore should remain exclusively in the hands of the expert, that it otherwise carries a certain danger and, finally, that dream work carried on by nonprofessionals is apt to remain at a superficial level.

My experience in group dream work points in a different direction. I am convinced that it need not remain a specialized tool in the hands of the expert but that it can develop into a culturally sanctioned, generally available approach to a deeper understanding of the emotional side of our lives. The skills involved can be identified, learned, and applied by anyone interested enough to do so. They are not the exclusive result of training in psychotherapy, although one object of such training should be to develop such skills.

Is dream work dangerous? There is the possibility of danger, but it is not intrinsic to the dream or to what the dream says to the dreamer. The danger does not come from that source. It can come from a wrong approach to the dreamer. By a wrong approach I mean one that is intrusive, one that does not respect the limits set by the dreamer, one that is conducted from an authoritarian stance, one that superimposes interpretations.

A dreamer who awakens with a dream is potentially ready to be confronted by the information in that dream. However, the dreamer awake is not prepared to be quite as honest with himself as he was while dreaming. He views himself more cautiously. In dream work outside a clinical setting he is not seeking professional help but is testing his own ability to allow himself to relate to all the information embedded in the dream imagery instead of screening out whatever might not feel comfortable for his waking ego. He is there to learn to use the dream itself as a healing instrument. The ability to do this depends on how secure he is made to feel by the way the group process is structured; this, in turn, depends on how respectful the group is of the dreamer's right to manage his own defenses. In practice the factor of safety in combination with the natural curiosity of the dreamer and the support and stimulation from the group all have the effect of minimizing defensive operations and, in turn, allow meanings in the dream to come into clearer focus.

Many years as a practicing analyst have left me with some idea of what can and what cannot be achieved with dream work in individual therapy. It is true that defensive operations come into play during dream work and therapy does address that question. It is also true, however, that those operations are not immutable and that, as people experience trust in the dream group process, they also change in relation to the importance they place on maintaining their defenses. I have seen remarkable and sometimes rapid changes in this respect. In many instances they occur sooner than they might in individual therapy where the very situation both creates as well as makes it possible to analyze resistances. The result is that profound conflicts and the deep levels of one's psyche are exposed, experienced, and worked upon. As I extend my efforts to do dream work with a broader population, I find the notion of superficiality simply does not hold. Criticism on that basis is without merit.

Certain real problems are encountered when an effort is made to extend serious dream work beyond the arena of therapy. Questions of safety do arise. Any process, regardless of how intrinsically safe it may be, can be misused. It seems to me that the rewards gained by educating the public to the significance of dreams and the way to work with them in a supportive social context far exceed the risk involved. People who start at the same level of experience and are aware of the precautionary measures to be observed will do productive work. There will always be some who overestimate their capacity and present themselves as leaders without a sound grounding in leadership skills. In other words, when groups are organized at a peer level the problems that arise can generally be handled by the group. If, on the other hand, one organizes dream groups on a professional basis, taking on all comers, so to speak, it is incumbent upon that person to have had sufficient leadership training. It is then no longer a peer group but one that looks to the leader for help in gaining mastery over the process.

I do feel that mental health professionals have an important role in the extension of dream work into the community. Sweden offers a model in this respect. Since working intensively with such professionals there for over ten years, I have reached many more than I do in this country. If dream work is to extend into the community, it will depend in large measure on the attitude and willingness of therapists to appreciate the need and to lend their skills to the task of educating and training others in the skills necessary to do dream work. I stress the fact that they are skills that can be shared, and a start has to be made somewhere. Since Sweden is a small country it proved to be an ideal testing ground. Psychoanalysis came late to Sweden, and there is less of an entrenched notion that the only approach to dreams is via the analytic couch. The myth of the expert was not so strongly entrenched, particularly in relation to dreams. Professionals have been more open to participating in dream groups. In most instances they have remained involved in leadership training to the point of feeling confident of their own mastery of the dream group process. Included among these are psychiatrists, psychologists and social workers, nurses, priests engaged in pastoral counseling, and teachers interested in counseling or guidance. As a result, dream groups have been organized in hospital settings, training centers, churches, schools (gymnasia or junior college level), and in addition, in the community with partial funding from the government. In a small country the fallout from this activity is quite visible. Interest in dreams is increasing, and dream groups have been formed in almost every major city. All this offers a glimpse of what might be possible in extending safe and effective dream work to within the reach of all who are curious about their own dream life. And that includes just about everyone.

In Working With Dreams Nan Zimmerman and I wrote:

> Nan and I have tried to pass on the message that more can be done with our dreams than most of us are doing. Our hope is that the process developed in this book will make its way into the systems that shape so many of our choices—into industry and institutions, into school programs at all educational levels. For parents and teachers who agonize over the distance between themselves and their children dreams offer a warm and honest connection. Dream work could find its place in halfway houses or prisons. It could open up something new for senior citizens at a time when society tends to disregard or discard them. Dream appreciation can become accessible to everyone in any setting where understanding and compassion are valued. (p. 319)

The present volume is a step in the direction of the fulfillment of these expectations. All the contributors have had exposure to the group process I use, and all have linked it to their own special areas of interest, areas as divergent as literature, the ministry, art, political science, computer science, anthropology, and the training of psychotherapists.

This book is addressed to both the interested layman and to the therapist who uses dreams in his practice. There has been no attempt to cover ground dealt with elsewhere, such as the experimental studies on dreaming. We have tried rather to pull together a number of threads to weave a pattern that reflects not only the growing interest in dreams but also the seminal effect that dream work can have in diverse fields. The contributors to this volume are trying to extend dream work in their own way into their specialized fields of interest. They cut across a number of disciplines and represent a number of emerging trends. Their range illustrates the diverse ramifications that dream work can take. What is unique is that the work presented is rooted in an experiential process that enriches the more abstract and theoretical levels of discourse. As it taps into the creative source in each of us, dream work spills over and opens other channels for creative expression. The ensuing chapters offer only a small sample of the possibilities we are tapping into. Our hope is that they will stimulate further exploration of the many constructive ramifications that dream work can have in our lives.

Claire Limmer has participated in dream workshops with me since the very first one I held in this country in 1976. She is a skilled dream worker. Because of a unique set of personal circumstances, she has also come to a deeply felt sense of what it means to link the notion of healing to dream work. Aspects of this are touched on in the chapter she contributed to this volume. As co-editor, she has helped shape the form and content of the book as well as taken over many of the more onerous tasks of an editor. I am profoundly grateful for her help and for the very generous way it was offered.

If we have succeeded in a small way in the rather formidable task of transforming oneirophobia (fear of dreams) into oneirophilia (love of dreams), we will have felt our efforts have been rewarded.

Montague Ullman
Ardsley, New York, (1987)

PART I

Group Dream Work

CHAPTER ONE

The Experiential Dream Group

MONTAGUE ULLMAN

This chapter outlines the rationale and structure of the experiential dream group process. All the contributors to this volume have at one time or another participated in this process. For those who had considerable prior experience with dreams it added a useful dimension to their knowledge and way of practicing and teaching dream work. For some it served as an introduction to dream work and provided them with a basis for moving into it on their own and exploring its usefulness in their own lives and/or in their own disciplines. The pursuit of dreams is a serious undertaking that requires a degree of both new learning and skill mastery. The point to be emphasized is that the knowledge and skills necessary can and should be available to everyone.[1]

My goal in this chapter is to describe a group approach to dream work oriented to connecting the dreamer to the dream in a way that is useful both in the training of psychotherapists and in making dreams accessible to the general public.

In working with dream groups I find it helpful to offer some preliminary orientation to the nature of the dream and the value of dream work. The first session is devoted to a description of the phenomenology of dreaming. For those who are new to dream work a clear distinction is drawn between dreaming and the dream. Although one is derivative of the other, they occur in two profoundly different states of being. Dreaming is a function of the sleeping organism and is a form of consciousness that occurs in repetitive cycles during the night, irrespective of recall. Its purposes are still under investigation and are by no means clearly understood despite the many theories that have been proposed. For those interested in an extended review of the various clinical approaches to dreams, see Fosshage and Loew (1987) and Shafton (1995). Psychoanalytic theories have ranged from the Freudian notion of the release of instinctual impulses to Jung's emphasis on communication and compensation. The experimental work on sleep and dreams over the past forty-five years has ushered in a number of new approaches, such as dreams serving a sentinel function (Snyder 1966), a vigilance function (Ullman 1958), an information processing function (Palumbo 1978), and a learning function (Greenberg and Pearlman 1974). For a recent review of the experimental contributions to our understanding of dreams, see Moffitt, Kramer, and Hoffmann (1993). For a presentation of the psychoanalytic approach to dreams most congruent with my own point of view, see Bonime (1962).

The dream is something quite different from the state of dreaming. It is a memory in the waking state of some aspect of the dreaming experience. Although clearly related to dreaming it lacks the spontaneous and immediate quality of the dreaming experience.

Dreaming consciousness differs from ordinary waking consciousness in both form and content. Dreaming consciousness is experienced in a predominantly sensory mode. While dreaming we are involuntary witnesses to a symbolic display of some aspect of our life, usually in the form of visual imagery but not exclusively so. Although borrowed from the world about us, the elements in the dream are not photographic reproductions of that world. Instead they come at us transformed into metaphorically expressive symbols that portray facets of a current life predicament in a highly specific and selective way. Everything in this form of consciousness is pressed into metaphorical usage—words, color, numbers, and other sensory impressions in addition to the visual.

Here are some examples of a "visual metaphor":

> A woman who has just been through a difficult period is looking forward to the future in a free and more expansive way. She dreams of a boat that succeeds in moving through a very narrow channel into the open sea.
>
> A young woman, rather shy about her initial presentation in a dream group, dreams of sitting on the toilet. To her surprise people keep opening the door to the bathroom, going in and out. What has heretofore been a most private experience (her dream) is now exposed to public viewing.

Punning is one way of getting across metaphorical meaning. Here is one about marital ties.

> A young man still in the throes of a difficult divorce has become seriously involved with another woman, and the issue of marriage has been raised. In his dream he sees himself leaving one hotel and walking in the street toward another hotel. While in the street he tries to put on his tie but discovers he is already wearing one.

So much for the form that dreaming consciousness takes. What about the content? There are vulnerable areas in each of us, vestiges from the past that have not been mastered, or aspects of our personality and resources about which we are ignorant. Encounters that touch on these areas set up a tension that we cannot resolve at the time. It is this tension that surfaces when we dream. The feeling residues associated with recent experiences of this kind shape the ensuing images. The feelings aroused point to some issue of current significance connected with our past but not yet fully set to rest. They serve as a guide into the past as we search out earlier experiences that, in a feeling way, are related to and shed some light on the present encounter. We transcend temporal relationships to bring together these emotionally related bits and pieces from our memory bank. In effect, we have embedded a current challenging context into its historical past. We dream about selected aspects of our lives because the issues involved have historical ramifications that are not clear to us at the moment. Our dreams thus have relevance to our present situation, enabling us to bring together information about the particular issue at hand in a way that is not easy to do when we are awake.

There is another feature of dreaming consciousness that makes the remembered dream so useful an instrument for getting to know who we really are and what we really feel. I refer to the intrinsic honesty with which events are registered in the imagery we create. We are completely alone while dreaming. With no one looking over our shoulder it is as if we risk taking an honest look at ourselves and allow ourselves to see just where our unique life history has brought us in relation to the issue we are dreaming about. I am not referring to seeing ourselves in a state of angelic bliss; rather, whatever deceits we are capable of are honestly displayed for us. The relevance of the dream to a still-active issue in our life, the mobilization of pertinent information from our past, and the ability of the dream to bring us closer to the truth are the three features of our dreaming experience that give value to the dream and render it a potentially healing resource.

The scenario of a dream often follows the structure of a three-act drama. The first act registers the impact of an intrusive experience on a preexisting status quo, the second explores the feelings aroused from a historical perspective, and the final act is devoted to an effort at resolution. Awakening occurs when there are accompanying feelings that are too intense or too disturbing to be resolved.

The dreamer, of course, has a problem. The remarkable images he has crafted often defy his understanding. He is not at ease with either the language of the dream or what it might be saying. No one has taught him much about the former, and the latter touches on aspects of his psyche that have not yet clearly emerged in consciousness. He needs help, and to get that help he must share the dream.

A small group (eight to ten people) can provide a most effective way of getting that help. Once the needs of the dreamer are understood, a process can be structured to meet those needs in a safe and effective way. What I am saying is that the task of helping a dreamer can be placed in the hands of anyone who is willing to take the trouble to learn what those needs are and how to work within a process designed to meet them.

To understand the needs of the dreamer let us look at his predicament more closely. In sharing his dream he is doing two things, neither of which is familiar or easy. He is exposing a most personal and vulnerable side of himself. He is also jumping into water the depth of which is not known to him. None of us knows in advance where dream work will take us. This double jeopardy defines the first and basic need of the dreamer, the need for safety. He has to be assured that the dream work he is to engage in will take place in a way that will provide the degree of safety he needs. In a general way this means that at every stage of the process, control will remain in the hands of the dreamer. The process will evolve in a nonintrusive way that respects the privacy of the dreamer and his authority over the dream. The dreamer can stop the process at any point. Concern with the Safety Factor then, is the first major determinant of the structure of the process within which the dream work will take place.

The group has to respond to another overriding need of the dreamer, namely, to be helped to make discoveries about himself that are difficult to make alone. I refer to this as the Discovery Factor and this, too, has to be built into the structure of the process.

The process Nan Zimmerman and I evolved for group dream work has been described in considerable detail elsewhere (Ullman and Zimmerman, 1979; Ullman, 1996). Here I will simply outline it, presenting briefly both the rationale and the way that each stage of the process meets both the Safety Factor and the Discovery Factor. The stages are outlined in the accompanying diagram. (See Figure 1.1)

Stage I

I A.

A dreamer *volunteers* a dream.

I B.

The group may ask questions to clarify the dream and to grasp it as clearly and as completely as possible. Any real characters in the dream are briefly identified.

The Safety Factor. The emphasis is on a dreamer volunteering to share a dream. This is a decision left completely in the hands of the dreamer. It is not a question of having to take turns.

The Discovery Factor. On occasion the simple act of relating a dream to others results in a sudden insight. The decision to share a dream is based on a readiness to lower one's defensive operations. Any lowering of defenses paves the way to greater insight.

Rationale. The presentation to the group is limited to the dream itself. The dreamer is asked to refrain from giving any associations or any ideas about the meaning of any element in the dream. This is important in relation to the next stage, where the group makes the dream their own. Were the dreamer to give associations or offer meanings, he would track the response of the group along the lines he is setting down for them and in that way limit the free play of their imagination.

Figure 1.1 Stages of the Dream Group Process

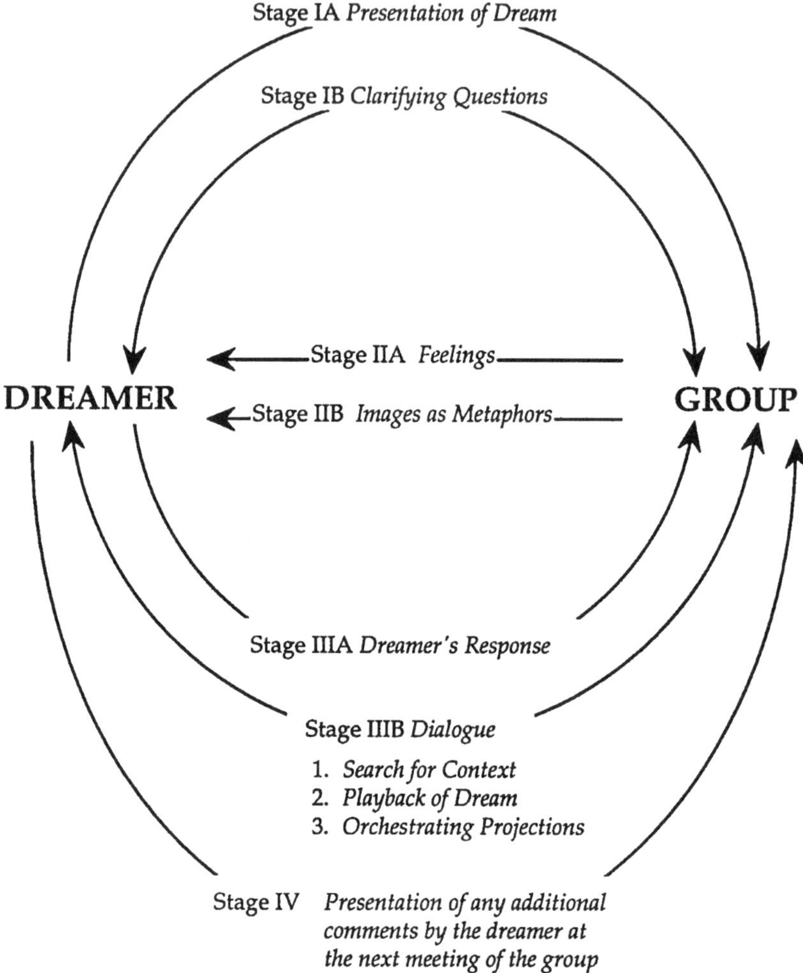

Stage II

This is a game or exercise that the group plays by making the dream their own. They will speak of it as their own dream, and what they offer to each other (they do not address the dreamer) will be their own projections. The dreamer is asked to listen without actively participating. He is free to accept or reject anything that comes from the group.

II A.

Group members share with one another any feelings or moods that the imagery conveys.

II B.

Next, the imagery is addressed and explored in its metaphorical potential. The task of the group is to use their imagination in an attempt to link the images in the dream to possible life situations or concerns suggested by the imagery. This is a random process offered in the hope that some of the group's responses will have meaning for the dreamer.

The Safety Factor. As members of the group address each other, they leave a clear space around the dreamer who then feels free to accept or reject anything coming from the group. He also remains in control of his thoughts and reactions to the input of the group and is under no obligation at a later stage to share more than he wishes.

The Discovery Factor. Despite the fact that, at this stage, the group is unaware of the events in the dreamer's life that shaped the dream, many of their projections do succeed in bringing the dreamer closer to his dream. Several factors are at work aside from anything the group has come up with that feels right to the dreamer. The dreamer responds to the group's interest in his dream, the sharing of themselves through their own projections, and the commonality of experiences as revealed by these projections. All have the effect of helping the dreamer move closer to the dream.

Rationale. At first glance it might seem unlikely that a group working on someone else's dream without knowing the dreamer's associations would come up with anything relevant to the plight of the dreamer. The fact is that they do. Even when the dreamer is a stranger, there are spontaneous and intuitive responses from the group members that touch the dreamer. In an ongoing group where there has been much sharing of dreams the projections offered by the group often get closer to the mark. Another factor, of course, is that there are a limited number of basic human issues (for example, issues around identity, authority, individuation, and so on) that touch us deeply enough to dream about. We may well relate to the metaphorical images of a dream the same way the dreamer did.

Stage III

III A.

The dream is returned to the dreamer who is then invited to respond to and share, to the extent he wishes, how far he has come in understanding the dream. He is free to shape his responses in any manner he wishes and is given as much time as he needs without interruption.

III B.

If further work is necessary, it proceeds in the form of a dialogue between the dreamer and the group. The various ways of helping the dreamer in the dialogue do not automatically follow after the dreamer's response. They are invoked only at the invitation of the dreamer. The purpose of the dialogue is to contextualize the dream; that is, to connect the dream to the set of waking life experiences that give rise to it. We do this by helping the dreamer explore his life context, beginning with recent events, until there is a felt sense of connection between dream image and waking reality. It is as if we are attempting to bring the two terms of the metaphor together to the point where a spark of understanding jumps the gap between them. Questions are put to the dreamer in an open-ended fashion. Their only purpose is to offer the dreamer an instrument to further explore his psyche. These are information-eliciting, not information-demanding questions. The dreamer can deal with the questions as he wishes. This includes the right not to answer.

III B 1.

Our first goal is to clarify the immediate life context that shaped the dream and defined the issue being dreamt about. The dreamer is helped to reconstruct an emotional diary of recent events in his life that may have been the impetus for the dream. The questions are simple and direct in an effort to recapture any felt residues to events of the night and day prior to the dream and even further back if his responses indicate some lingering preoccupations.

III B 2.

When we have elicited as much of the context as we can, we introduce, again at the invitation of the dreamer, another level of questioning now focused on the dream itself. We begin by having the dream read aloud to the dreamer scene by scene by one or more members of the group. The dreamer is asked to play back what he is now hearing against the background of all that he has shared thus far to see if any further thoughts occur to him about the images in that scene. The point is that as the dream is being read back he is now working with more information than before the dream work began (as a consequence of stage II and the search for the context) and so may be in a better position to say more about the imagery. There are many subtle ways of helping a dreamer focus in on images that remain puzzling—for example, helping the dreamer think about the image metaphorically rather than literally, or recalling for the dreamer anything said by him previously about the image (see Ullman 1996). As each scene is read in sequence, more and more of the associative matrix comes into view, making it more likely the dreamer will make felt connections between dream image and waking reality.

III B 3.

When the reading of the dream is completed, there may still be aspects of it that elude the dreamer. He has the option then of inviting the final phase of the dialogue where the group members offer what I have referred to as their "orchestrating" projections. This refers to the attempt by the members of the group to relate the imagery of the dream to what the dreamer has shared. If anyone feels they can shed light on an image, a scene, or on the entire dream, it can be offered to the dreamer as the group member's projection. If it doesn't, it remains a projection. The final arbiter of the fit is always the dreamer. The orchestrating projection differs from the projections offered in the second stage when the group made the dream their own. In contrast to the latter where the group members called upon their imagination and their own life experience, they now are offering a projection based on and limited by what has been shared by the dreamer.

The Safety Factor. In the dreamer's response (III A) the control remains in the dreamer's hands. She alone decides on the level of self-disclosure with which she is comfortable.

In the dialogue (III B 1 and 2) the dreamer remains in control by having the right to answer, or not answer, any questions put to her.

In the orchestration (III B 3) the dreamer is free to accept or reject any part of the orchestrating projection that has been offered.

The Discovery Factor. As she begins to respond, the dreamer will often come upon new ideas about the meaning of some of the imagery. When questioning (III B 1 and 2) is pursued in a nonintrusive way the dreamer is able to develop more of the waking-life context of the dream. With that comes a greater ease in seeing the way an image connects to a life situation. Often the dreamer is helped by an orchestration (III B 3) that highlights relationships not seen before.

Rationale. As a rule the dreamer has been able to come closer to the dream through the work done initially by the group (II). The dreamer generally has difficulty in fully contextualizing the dream on her own. By that I mean she may not know how to clarify the immediate relevant life events without the group posing the kind of questions that can elucidate the precipitating life circumstances (III B 1). She may have difficulty in accounting for various elements in the dream. Some elements may pose problems because they touch on sensitive areas. Others may simply have escaped the dreamer's attention. In either case she is in need of help from others who, with no ax to grind, can, in the course of reading the dream back (III B 2), call attention to whatever elements in the dream have not been adequately developed. As long as the dreamer remains in control of the process at each stage, there is a natural tendency to come forth with relevant data and to move further into the dream.

Stage IV

IV A.

The dreamer reviews the dream between the time the dream was presented and the next meeting of the group.

IV B.

The dreamer is invited to share any additional thoughts about the dream at the next meeting of the group.

With the completion of Stage IV the group dream work is ended.

The Safety Factor. It is the dreamer's choice to share anything more or not.

The Discovery Factor. Reviewing the dream alone in the light of the work done in the group, the dreamer sometimes is freer to see more than she could at the time she first shared the dream.

Rationale. While in the group the dreamer is often exposed to more input that she can handle at the time, input that may have touched her at many levels of her psyche without providing the time or opportunity to work through and clarify the feelings that have been set in motion. Furthermore, her position vis-à-vis the group, where she is constantly faced with the decision of how much to share, may limit to some extent her self-exploration. Reviewing the dream on her own, after the group's work, frees her from that constraint and provides her with the opportunity to examine some of the felt reactions set in motion by the group work.

Skills

We have referred to the fact that certain skills are needed. Since one of the basic skills is the art of knowing how to listen to the dreamer, therapists who come to group dream work may have this skill developed to a high degree. In that sense they may have an advantage. The point is that it is not a skill that is theirs exclusively; others who are interested enough can also master it. Let us look more closely at the skills involved.

There are two active ways in which the group offers help to the dreamer. Distinct skills can be identified with each of these ways.

In the second stage (II) the group makes the dream its own and works with projected feelings and meanings. The skills involved here are easily learned. There is no particular difficulty in picking up the mood and feeling tones evoked by the imagery. There is a good deal of freedom to proceed in any way one likes and to read whatever feelings one wishes into the individual pictures and the story they seem to be telling. To some extent one approaches the role of the dreamer as an actor might, bringing to that role the feelings he or she deems appropriate.

The transformation of the imagery of the dream into possible life contexts is a bit more difficult at first but, once the idea takes hold, there is generally no further difficulty. Here, again, the fact that one can give one's imagination free rein and that nothing offered is wrong as long as it is based on the dream, allows for plenty of room for coming up with possible life contexts that might be suggested by the images. The group members do have to divest themselves of waking prejudices about what might or might not be important to the dreamer. They try to address every element in the dream, every detail that has been given by the dreamer, for a possible reality reference that may be encoded in it.

There are two essential skills that come into play in the third stage. These skills can only be mastered through practice and experience. The first is learning how to listen to the dreamer once the dream is returned to the dreamer and she begins her response (III A). The second is the art of putting questions to the dreamer that are helpful without being intrusive (III B 1 and 2). The two skills work in concert. Without good listening, questioning can go astray.

As any therapist knows, the art of listening is not as simple as it appears. It involves, first of all, listening to everything the dreamer says about the dream, regardless of how convinced she may be that the dreamer will benefit from her view of the dream. Secondly, it involves listening without prejudging anything the dreamer has to say. Thirdly, it involves listening not only to what the dreamer says but also to what the dreamer does not say. While listening, she has to make a mental note of the extent to which the dreamer has clarified the current context. Has she done so to the point where the connection to the dream is obvious and where she now understands why she had the dream on that particular night and on no other? To what extent have all the elements in the dream been addressed and their connection to the life context, past and present, been noted? In short, the listener must listen attentively while keeping track of the extent to which the dream, in all its elements, has been contextualized.

The best preparation for questioning the dreamer in the dialogue is to keep in mind the two main goals, namely, to explore, to the extent possible, the recent emotional context that triggered the dream (III B 1) and to help the dreamer enrich the associative matrix of the dream by addressing those images that have not yet been contextualized or adequately contextualized (III B 2).

In dream work, where ideas about what the image may mean crowd in on the mind of the questioner, he has to avoid the tendency to ask a leading question. By a leading question I mean one based on an idea the questioner has of the possible meaning of the image, and where the question is asked in order to validate that idea. It is very tempting to ask leading or information-giving questions (an indirect way of offering an interpretive comment) rather than information-eliciting ones. Put in an open-ended way, the latter stimulates the dreamer to identify more of the associative context. When we do succeed in eliciting the relevant data, the dreamer herself is more apt to see the connection to the dream image. Asking leading questions or offering interpretive comments tends to complicate matters by puzzling the dreamer and possibly raising her anxiety level. She is deflected from the internal search to the task of evaluating connections someone else is inferring.

In the first phase of the dialogue (III B 1) the goal is to elicit as much as possible the feelings and concerns that impinged on the dreamer as she went to sleep on the night of the dream. If that goal is kept clearly in mind, the questions will follow more easily. The dreamer is simply invited to take a careful look at recent happenings that may provide a clue as to why the dream occurred at that particular night. It involves a systematic attempt through the use of simple and direct questions to focus the dreamer's attention on any aspect of the recent past that may have set off lingering feeling residues. Any thoughts or concerns that surface just prior to falling asleep can often be helpful. Anything in her personal life, her work life? Anything she read or anything she saw on TV, for example? This stage is essential as the dreamer is not apt to spontaneously offer as much about the recent emotional context when the dream is first returned to her (Stage III A) as can be elicited by further questioning.

Only after the elaboration of these thoughts and feelings does the group turn its attention to the task of confronting the dreamer with the dream by reading the dream back scene by scene. The task of questioning the dreamer is a bit more difficult when the dreamer hears her own dream being read back (III B 2). Here the goal is to enrich the associative matrix of the dream by addressing those images that have not yet been contextualized in the life of the dreamer or are not yet adequately contextualized. As a scene is read back the dreamer may or may not have more to add. When an image in that scene is not yet clear in its metaphorical meaning and it is specifically called to the dreamer's attention, additional associations are often forthcoming. A richer yield of associations at each step facilitates further associations (III B 2).

Several issues arise as questions are put to the dreamer:

1. Judging by the dreamer's response we need to ask ourselves if the dreamer seems interested in exploring the question further, or is it obvious that she prefers not to? In other words, is she inviting us in or inviting us out?
2. If the latter is the case, we don't pursue the matter.
3. If she seems interested in going further, then questioning continues to the extent further clarification can occur.
4. In confronting the dreamer with her own imagery it is important that the group takes into account every detail in the dream, not just the most striking ones.

Up to this point the group has been asking information-eliciting questions (not information-demanding ones). The questioning has been persistent without being insistent. Helping the dreamer externalize the information relevant to the dream can be all that is needed for the dreamer to see the connections of the dream to her life. In most instances, however, more is needed. This happens when all the relevant information the dreamer is capable of disclosing has come forth, but the essence of the dream still eludes the dreamer. One has to learn to recognize that this is so and that further questioning will simply result in repetition of answers already given. The response of the group now shifts to what I refer to as an integrating or orchestrating mode. On the basis of what the dreamer has shared with the group both in her initial response and in her answers to the questions in the dialogue, anyone in the group may have an idea how some of the material fits the metaphorical meaning of an image. Possible relationships of this kind are raised and addressed to the dreamer as questions. It is made clear that this is to be considered as the questioner's own projection unless it has meaning for the dreamer. This type of projection may be made in connection with the entire dream, or any part of it. Although the general idea can be grasped easily, the art of orchestrating is a skill that can come only with experience. It is easy to lose sight of the fact that dream imagery arises out of the unique life experiences of the dreamer and not out of the personal or theoretical predilections of the group member.

The basic skills to be learned in orchestrating are:

1. listening to everything the dreamer says, not only in her initial response but in all that she says during the dialogue;
2. while listening, looking for relationships between what the dreamer is saying and the metaphorical possibilities of the images of the dream;
3. learning how to stay with what has emerged from the dreamer and to avoid what may be a sheer and unwarranted projection on the part of the one offering the orchestration;
4. learning how to pick up more in the way of significant relationships between image and context by examining the sequential development of the imagery as the dream unfolds.

Problem Areas

There are a number of problem areas connected with this group approach.

In the second stage, when the group is working with the dream as its own, there is a tendency to lose sight of this fact and to discuss the dream in a way that leaves the impression that the group is offering interpretive comments to the dreamer and not really talking about the dream as its own.

The dialogue is the most difficult part of the process. It is not easy to contain what I refer to as the "interpretive impulse," namely, the compulsion on the part of the listener to spontaneously and inappropriately offer an interpretive comment. We have to disavow any conviction we may have as to where the dreamer should go with the dream. It is difficult at times to restrain the tendency to validate through our questions our own impression of what the dream means. To do so is a breach of the basic rule that we follow rather than lead the dreamer. We have to rely on the dreamer's ability to make discoveries on her own to the extent she feels ready to after we have elucidated the context. We need to base the questioning only on what is obvious to the dreamer, that is, on what is in the dream or on what the dreamer has shared. Any question that is not obvious to the dreamer but that is derived from something in the interrogator's mind, is apt to raise the anxiety level of the dreamer (what does the questioner know about my dream that I don't?) and is self-defeating.

The sole purpose of a question is to help the dreamer retrieve a bit more of the life context. Simple and direct questions can accomplish this most easily. Their aim is to elicit information from the dreamer in an unbiased way. If one is trying to clarify the current life context, a typical question might be: "Do you recall what feelings the day (prior to the dream) left you with?" If one is trying to help a dreamer do more with a particular image in the dream it often suffices to ask: "Why do you think such and such an image appeared in your dream that particular night?" Instead of staying with this simple information-eliciting approach there is an almost irresistible urge to test one's hunches about an image before the dreamer has provided a context that would bring a possible relationship out into the open. An inexperienced group will have trouble staying with a line of questioning, moving from the general to the specific, until a clear relation between context and image is established.

Sensing the proper point of closure can be difficult for beginners, who often probe more deeply than is either possible or appropriate in the group setting as it is structured.

A newcomer to the process who presents a dream for the first time may have difficulty seeing the imagery metaphorically and will tend to be unaware of the role that recent life events play in shaping the dream. It takes some experience before a dreamer feels at ease with the visual metaphorical language of the dream and what that language is expressing about present and past aspects of her life. There is a tendency to expect some sudden, spontaneous, exotic revelation from the dream. The dream yields its secret only after the slower but more rewarding work of gradually contextualizing the images.

Most people come to a dream group because they have a serious interest in learning more about their dreams. On rare occasions someone finds her way into the group with an agenda of her own, one that has nothing to do with dreams. The dream is simply a pretext for fulfilling some other compelling personal need, such as exhibitionism, dependency, or the like. Whatever the motive, unless checked, there will be an attempt to manipulate the group into fulfilling this need.

More common is the person who, having had a great deal of experience with other kinds of groups, has difficulty accepting the constraint that comes from the fact that the emphasis here is not on the interpersonal processes going on in the group but on the group's ability to be of help to the dreamer. The dreamer's needs come before those of any other group member. There may be attempts to transform the dream work into group therapy or an encounter type of situation where there is more freedom to confront each other. With time, most catch on to the basic difference between the experiential dream group and other groups. It does take time to get used to the idea of a group that is solely a support system, offering stimulation to the dreamer to the extent that the dreamer seeks and can use it. It is not there to focus on the needs of the other members of the group.

This approach stresses the importance of helping the dreamer recapture the emotional residues of the period immediately preceding the dream. This, of course, is done more easily with a fresh dream. In the case of a dream that is days or weeks old or older, if the dream is important to the dreamer, the group can often help the dreamer bring back enough of the context to make the effort worthwhile.

In the example given below some aspects of the process will be highlighted. In the actual workshop situation there is a sense of drama and tension as image and context gradually come together.

The dream that follows is that of Hal White, the Rector of an Episcopal church in a southern city on the occasion of a one-day workshop held in that church The dream was recalled on awakening on the morning of Saturday, April 12, 1997, the day of the workshop. Hal is sixty years old. I had met him on several earlier occasions on visits to a mutual friend, Nan Zimmerman, the co-author of our book "Working With Dreams." He and Nan had made the arrangements for the workshop. Hal was the first to volunteer a dream.

Stage I A: Volunteering a Dream

The Dream

I was in a house that had multiple levels, staircases, and rooms. The walls and ceilings kept moving into new configurations. I was attempting to pick up a few things in the house and go to another place. I was having a difficult time deciding on the things I wanted to take. There was a small child, a toddler, in a pink outfit that kept clinging to my leg so that it was difficult for me to go. Also I kept looking for what it was I was to take with me and couldn't find it. The other thing that happened was that I was not able to control a bowel movement, so I had this stuff in my pants. I was attempting to get to the bathroom, and at the same time I was frustrated because I needed to get to this other place, the first church I served thirty-two years ago. It had a new building attached to the old one in a geographical location near to the original.

Stage I B: Clarification of the Dream

Additional information was elicited during the questioning.

There were other people in the dream but not identified as known in waking life. They were in different rooms, and he felt as if he had to get past them. At first it was not clear whether the toddler was a boy or girl. The toddler clung to him for a long time and then disappeared.

His feelings were described as heavy and ponderous. He felt confused, as if he were in a maze. There were many rooms, some with marble walls and many staircases. He went from room to room. He felt as if he were looking for a sermon.

Stage II A: Working with Feelings[2]

Contributions from the Group

Things are out of control leaving me with a feeling of confusion and weightiness.

I feel lost, not knowing where to go. It makes me sad.

I was preoccupied with what to take with me.

I knew I had to be careful.

There were many things in this place I felt I hadn't seen.

I knew there was something I wanted to say, but it was too late to go back.

I felt I just had to find my sermon.

The child makes me feel I'm starting from the beginning.

I was overwhelmed by the kid's clinging when I had other things on my mind.

I felt like the only things I could say in the sermon were the things I had said to others and others have said to me.

Stage II B: Working with the Metaphors[3]

The contrast with the wood-brick church of thirty years ago makes me feel I'm going back thirty years to a stronger place made of stone.

The bowel movement was still in my underwear. It was not showing. No one else knew about my shit.

The old building was intact but in a different location. It was a wooden building. The new one was attached, about the same size and made of brick. In the dream I saw it in my mind's eye.

The frantic search was frustrating. I'm going about it all wrong. What I have to take is not a material thing.

I'm pushing through many obstacles, and nothing is going to stop me.

I'm a helpless and vulnerable child in this situation. It is overwhelming to deal with it all. It's not fun.

I feel guilty, letting the child down.

It's a joy to remember old things even though I could have dealt with them better.

The stronger building means that now I know who I am.

The house of wood conveys the story of the three little pigs.

I'm embarrassed, frustrated, pressured, and a little guilty.

I fear exposure.

The old, like the old house, is falling apart. It's tumbling down. But I feel consoled in the anticipation of a new structure.

Stage III A: The Dream is Returned to the Dreamer

At the invitation to Hal to respond he exclaimed:

"Whew! A month ago I resigned after twenty years in the job with no view of where I was going next. I thought about this workshop last night. I had not been remembering my dreams. I had my pen at my bedside all week in the hope I could record a dream, but there were no dreams. Then last night I had one. I guess it was the stimulation of coming here."

Hal then addressed the imagery in the dream.

"*The child*: It was a girl, a little tiny redhead. She wraps her arms around my legs, as if trying to hold me back. It's touching on the issue of my leaving my people and the new generation of children I will miss. Metaphorically it could be me, growing up, trying to find my sea legs. Or a self-image of my female self. The pink color may be my vulnerable female self trying to get my attention."

"The sermon I'm looking for is what I want to say to myself."

"The dream is about the difficulty I am having taking leave."

"*Bathroom*: I was looking for the bathroom. It was a place to hide my shame behind."

"*People*: There were people there but no one to help me. The people were in my way. I felt very isolated in the dream."

"*Leaving*: In recent years I felt I could make statements to others regardless of whether or not they would agree with me. Now I would like to have more control before I leave, over the leaving process. If I share my thoughts, what response would I get?"

"*People*: I didn't know the people in the dream. I've been in a consultative role with the vestry. I'm involved, but I feel I'm on the outside. My parishioners keep calling on me. I don't know who I am anymore. I'm giving help but not asking for what I need."

"*The shit*: The strange thing about it is that it doesn't stink. I assumed there would be enough time for it to be deposited in another place. It was good shit."

"*The buildings*: I'm involved with something that is familiar but adding something more substantial. What I've done with my life and what I'm going to do. I haven't started to get there yet."

(When he began to talk about the new annex there was a sudden outburst of sobbing.)

"It has to do with the losses I feel. It's about all the unraised children I'll miss."

(When the crying stopped he said it felt good to experience the sadness and the crying.)

"I have mixed feelings about sharing my feelings in public, about putting my shit out in public."

The sermon: "What nuggets do I want to leave behind for all those wonderful people? But there isn't a nugget to leave. All I can do is embrace them. I feel grief about leaving them. Part of me wants to still be part of their lives, but it's time to move on.

Comment

Hal's response to the work of the group was a very poignant one. He came close to tears as he moved more and more into the feelings about leaving until the final outburst noted above.

Hal invited the dialogue.

Stage III B: The Dialogue

Part I: The Context

(Hal had shared a good deal of what was on his mind during the period sometime before this dream occurred. What needed to be accounted for was why it occurred on this particular night.)

(What was on your mind just before falling asleep?)

"I was enjoying reading a novel. I was looking forward to today."

(Any particular feelings in connection with the novel?)

"It was *Coming Home*, by Rosamunde Pilcher. It was all about relationships and character development. I have done more reading recently than at any other time. I was thinking how nice it is to just sit and read and have more time to take care of myself. The book was a lot about giving and losing relationships."

(Any feelings last night in connection with the lecture?)[4]

"I was delighted to be with you (M.U.) and all the people who had gathered here. I was especially delighted that it was happening in this place (the church). I felt everyone was going to be fed."

(Were you aware of any other feelings?)

"No."

(Any other feeling residues from the day?)

"I had some feelings related to reading the novel. I take the day off on Friday. I would have liked to stay home Friday night and continue reading. I felt some resentment at having to give up the evening."

(Anything more about the resentment?)

"I had to come here and set things up for today. I'm tired of setting up chairs!"

(Anything more?)

"No. It didn't stay with me."

Hal then invited the playback.

Stage III B 2: The Dream is Read Back

The dream was read back to Hal ending at " . . . deciding on the things I wanted to take."

"The walls were movable and could be shifted. I had to take them down to get to the place I wanted to be. There were multiple levels with walls but no doors. It was a static scene. The spaces changed. Nothing stayed in place."

(Anything more?)

"I was concerned with the stability of that situation.

There was a door to the bathroom, and someone was in it. There were no doors elsewhere. It was something like beach houses."

(Any associations to that?)

"Reminded me of Sally's (Hal's wife, M.U.) beach house. I just remembered two walls in our house are falling in. We need an engineer."

(The next scene was read back to " . . . and couldn't find it.")

"The toddler on my leg was heavy. I had to drag my body along. I didn't want to hurt the toddler. How was I to move under these circumstances?"

(Anything more?)

"No."

(The remainder of the dream was read back.)

"It was very graphic! It looked like "cow pie".[5] It was solid, round and looked like it had been there a while. There were no flies in it."

"I saw the building. I could see the road winding up to it. But I was not there yet."

"I was frustrated. I needed to get rid of the shit before getting on the road. I was frustrated about not being able to find the sermon."

"It was more like cow dung. I remember as a child stepping in fresh cow shit. It was messy. Not very nice. As kids we used to take dried cow dung and toss it at each other."

"Early in the dream it was fresh stuff. Then it changed and it wasn't so bad."

Hal invited the orchestration.

Stage III B 3: Offering Orchestrating Projections

Before the group got started Hal had further thoughts about the cow dung.

"Cow pie is wonderful fertilizer. It's like a metaphor for growth. At the end it had structure as if it was a resolution of the whole conflict. I'll have to think more about that."

(Group member): "It may have to do with using what he knew in a new context. It changed from being smelly stuff that was hard to deal with."

Hal: "Yes."

(Group member): "The people there and the child were hanging on to you for dear life. You felt the responsibility as a burden."

Hal: "Yes."

(Group Member): "There was no chance to take care of your own response to change."

(Group Member): "You don't want the members of the parish to step in your cow dung."

Hal: "There is something to that at a deeper level. I hadn't wanted to look at that shit."

(Group Member): There is a contrast he knew, an amorphous unstable place and a lock solid building."

Hal: "I could see it in my mind's eye. I don't know what it is going to be like, but it was good to see it. I now feel some clarity of direction. I feel lighter since talking about it."

(Group Member): "The people were experienced as nagging obstacles. Recognizing that solidified your feelings."

Hal: "That was very perceptive. I felt that nagging. Yet I wanted everyone to feel happy."

(Group Member): "You were carrying your responsibility too far."

Hal: "You are probably right. I know I'm going to miss them, and I know I'll miss all those ankle biters."[6]

The above does not do justice to all that was offered by way of orchestrating projections. It was not possible to get down everything that was said while I was still struggling to work through my own thoughts. As far as I could recollect, what I had to say was along the following lines:

The dream seems to have brought together the mix of feelings you have on leaving a congregation you have worked with so intensely and so personally over a twenty-year period. In waking life you were blocked in the free display of these feelings, concerned as you were with the grief others felt about your leaving. You yourself felt a certain neediness in managing the mixed feelings about leaving the people you loved and missing out on being with the generations coming into being. You are struggling to free yourself of the pull they have on you and to more freely move to your own life. In that sense the people and the child are still presenting obstacles. There is an interesting transformation of the hidden messy shit into cow pie that you once as a child played with and that has fertile nurturing value. I think this connects to the feelings you had the day and evening before the dream. The reading of the novel, the leisurely time you took for yourself, made you more cognizant of your own need for greater freedom and self-recognition. Juxtaposed to this was the reassertion of your responsibility to others. That evening you had to return to the church and go back to the same old task of making arrangements for the benefit and comfort of others. The delightful bit of self-indulgence was terminated but not without a bit of resentment (messy shit) of the very people you loved and enjoyed helping. The ability to have the dream after an arid period of no dreams and to have it the night before this dream group confronted you with the opportunity to make the resentment public, including many of your own parishioners. It transformed private messy shit into something more public, cow pies, which lie in the open field and which can serve both playful and nurturing ends. The sermon you were looking for and couldn't find was the dream itself, a dream you wanted to have but didn't have until you had completed the act of dreaming it.

When the orchestrations were completed Hal was asked if there was anything he would like to say.

Hal: I feel I have been supported in opening up to the people I love and to tell them there are some things I've always wanted to do for myself.

At the end of the session the dreamer was thanked for sharing the dream and the work he did on it.

Since this dream was shared in the course of a single weekend of dream work, the follow-up Stage IV occurred by mail. Hal was asked if he had any other comments he wished to make. He wrote:

June 9, 1997. It has been about two months since Dr. Ullman worked with me on my "cow pie" dream. I have not thought a lot about the dream recently. However, on rereading my notes, I recall that several people projected onto my dream feelings which I did not feel. For instance, several thought the shit in my pants was very embarrassing and must have smelled badly. That was not my sense. I experienced the shit turning to cow pies as a useable, playful commodity which has since nurtured new growth and a hopeful picture of the future. The difficult, more morass-like feeling was going through the process of separating from the pink-clad toddler. Reflecting on this part of the dream since the workshop has helped me to experience my grief in leaving at an even deeper level.

Sharing openly with others the dream and my clear struggle with leave-taking opened us to each other at a deep level. Both they and I were enabled to say what we needed to say before I departed. Sharing the revelations of the dream and our responses enabled us to speak the truth in love and thereby experience healthier closure. I am most appreciative of Dr. Ullman's work with us around my dream and have had a first-hand experience of the power and healing nature of coming to understand one's dream in a trusting, supportive environment.

Comment

There were a number of unusual aspects to this presentation. Hal is a good friend of Nan Zimmerman, my co-author of "Working with Dreams." I had met Hal several times over the years on the occasion of my visits with the Zimmermans. The last occasion was about a year prior to the workshop. Subsequent to that Hal and Nan began to work together to arrange for this workshop. When he was the first and only one to volunteer to share a dream in his church where his parishioners were present I was, and I believe they too, were a bit surprised. Reflecting back on it I think our earlier contacts, casual as they were, and his prior knowledge of the process, accounted for the trust he felt that made him so openly share his feelings with those he was leaving.

The dream group gave him the opportunity to share with them the full range of feelings he was experiencing in connection with the move. The dream work evoked a depth and honesty of sharing that probably could not have come about in any other way. Sometimes dreams are dreamt for precisely that purpose. To be known and to feel accepted for who you are by significant others becomes as or even more important than any personal insights that may result. Dream work offers the opportunity to learn a bit more of the truth about oneself but also to see and feel acceptance and respect for the revelation of that truth.

The trust and level of sharing that Hal displayed in this first encounter with me in a dream group is more characteristic of what occurs in an ongoing group where the readiness to lower one's defensive system makes the message of the dream so much more accessible.

In a mystery story the plot unfolds bit by bit. So it is in group work with a dream. The search for context is often difficult and laborious. It takes the combined efforts of a dreamer and group to dislodge psychological blocks in order to examine the life that has been hidden from view. If the dreamer wants to unravel it and if he is made to feel safe as he struggles with it, then the group can provide enough leverage to do it. The end result is the product of an equation with many different contributory factors. When they work harmoniously there is movement into the dream, a feeling of relief, and a sense of doors being opened. That good feeling may be the result of encountering something new or feeling something more deeply and more truly than one has in the past.

In summary, a small-group process has been described, designed to be of help to the dreamer in a safe and nonintrusive way. The structure is protective of the privacy and authority of the dreamer while, at the same time, allowing for the free play of the imagination of the various group members as they work with the dream as their own. This serves to open up possibilities for

the dreamer. Even though a dreamer may have referred to many concerns and feelings around the time of the dream, a systematic exploration of the recent emotional context often helps the dreamer go beyond what he or she spontaneously offered. Reading a dream aloud to the dreamer results in a qualitatively different feeling than if the dreamer were simply asked to think about it. Hearing it read by someone else it is not subject to any biased oversight or emphasis by the dreamer. The soil for the further exploration of the dream has been prepared by the enriched associative context now available to the dreamer as a consequence of the preceding strategies. The playback offers the opportunity to examine images in depth that have not yet been developed by the dreamer. Orchestrating projections offer a final touch.

In this process the dreamer is, in effect, relying on the group to provide the instruments he needs as he explores the dream's metaphorical references to his life.

Notes

1. When the first person is used in any of the introductory remarks, it refers to M.U.

2. Functioning both as leader and participant it was difficult to get down on paper all that transpired. From here on my notes are my best approximation.

3. At this stage the group can continue to share feelings as they develop the metaphors.

4. I had given a lecture to the group the Friday night before the workshop.

5. "Cow pie," Hal explained, was dried cow dung.

6. His reference to the little ones he'll be leaving behind.

References

Bonime, W. *The Clinical Use of Dreams*. New York: Basic Books, 1962.

Fosshage, J. L., and Loew, C. A. *Dream Interpretation: A Comparative Study.* New York: PMA Publishing, 1987.

Greenberg R., and Pearlman, C. "Cutting the REM Nerve: An Approach to the Adaptive Role of REM Sleep." *Perspectives in Biology and Medicine,* 17, 4 (1974): 513–21.

Moffitt, A., Kramer, M., and Hoffmann, R. *The Function of Dreaming.* Albany: State University of New York Press, 1993.

Palumbo, S. R. *Dreaming and Memory.* New York: Basic Books,1978.

Shafton, A. *Dream Reader: Contemporary Approaches to the Understanding of Dreams.* Albany: State University of New York Press, 1995.

Snyder, F. "Toward an Evolutionary Theory of Dreaming." *American Journal of Psychiatry,* 123, 2 (1966): 121–36.

Ullman, M. "Hypotheses on Biological Roots of the Dream." *Journal of Clinical and Experimental Psychopathology and Quarterly Review of Psychiatry and Neurology,* 19, 2 (1958): 128–33.

Ullman, M. *Appreciating Dreams.* Thousand Oaks, Calif.: Sage, 1996.

Ullman, M., and Zimmerman, N. *Working with Dreams.* New York:Tarcher/Putnam, 1979.

CHAPTER TWO

After the Dream Is Over

NAN ZIMMERMAN

Nan Zimmerman is the co-author of our book, *Working with Dreams*. Poet, writer of children's stories, music teacher, homemaker, and mother, she has an unerring sense of metaphor. Her natural feel for the essence of the dream allows her access to its unique perspective. A dream presents us with an opportunity to realign our lives so that we can become more of what it is in our nature to be and less of what we are made to feel we have to be.

Since our early work together Nan has continued to be involved in the world of dreams, leading dream groups and workshops. In this chapter she is looking beyond the actual dream work experience and raises an important question concerning the nature of follow-up to dream work. What resources might be helpful to the dreamer once an emotionally vulnerable area has been exposed? In this instance, in addition to the issue of death and the feelings of loss that ensue, Nan shares a very poignant dream of her own and the steps it led her to take to resolve a painful and longstanding issue in her life.

In dream appreciation we seek to identify the current stress points in our lives. This clarity leads to an intricate question: How do we deal creatively with these dilemmas?

Dreams have been called "metaphors in motion" (Ullman and Zimmerman 1979); that is, they are animated expressions of our true emotions. We may run into difficulty, however, when we attempt to use the emotions we have named to revise assumptions, take definitive action, and become more at peace with ourselves. If we explore our dreams alone, we may correctly identify an emotion but incorrectly interpret how it relates to our life as it is being lived. We may use it to further entrench destructive ways of seeing ourselves. This is one reason why working with others is of value. Fellow dreamers give us a broader perspective.

The primary purpose of a dream appreciation group is educational—learning skills to unearth the vast deposit of understanding that our dreams provide. This context of safety and trust nurtures healing as we are touched and inspired by other members. We become sensitive to each other's pain, more desirous of finding ways of helping each other move through the crises with courage and hope. In ongoing groups our sense of interconnectedness increases. We could no more disregard our concern for a member's pain than we could ignore searching for the passageway through the emotions made evident in our own dreams.

A natural outgrowth of this depth of caring for each other among my friends and codreamers has been the sharing of books and other resources—newsletters, websites, community services. We pass on help we have gleaned from individual and group therapy, self-help groups, retreats and conferences sponsored by those familiar with the conflicts pictured in our dreams. All have the potential for extending encouragement as we travel down paths strewn with resistance, ambivalence, uncertain consequences—the gamut of our human dilemmas.

This exchange of information is not incorporated into the actual dream work format, but is distinctly separate and informal. The caveat essential to sharing material outside the dream is, however, identical to all dream work—the dreamer is in control. At no time is there pressure to assume that the data and readings contributed are anything other than exclusively individual responses to the dream's theme as experienced by either the dreamer or other members of the group.

My personal exploration for authenticity has given me an expanded appreciation for the diversity of theoretical frameworks and spiritual expressions. I consider the world to be bound together by a consistent reality so immense that viewing it at different times from different positions gives it the appearance of staggering complexity. I am a wave rising and falling among many waves. And I am water—within the unmeasurable sea.

In our work with dreams we come to appreciate all dream content as purposeful, and all comments on our dreams helpful in sorting out the dream's meaning. In literature, also, we look through many eyes at the reality that binds various views together. For some of us a biotic alliance transpires as we take dreams, writings, and other resources and come upon our own view, our own action, our own healing.

The greatest value of a dream metaphor is its pointing beyond itself to the emotional tone of our waking lives, pointing not to emotions as disembodied spirits: Guilt, Panic, Frustration, and so on, but emotions embodied in the immediate events of our days. So, too, the symbols of words often stimulate us to pass beyond the words themselves to inner direction. The words gesture toward truth that we have dimly known, but may not have been ready to trust or act upon. Words, if they are to have any genuine effect, are never accepted as static statements; rather, they lubricate the flow of our thoughts, and we sense the result as original and freeing.

The combined symbolism of the dream—guiding us to our honest emotions—and words, both spoken and written—guiding us toward an honest response to our emotions—releases within us certain excitement. We move from resignation to acceptance, to recognition of our own power to generate change. After the dream is over, the living of the dream begins again, with opportunities for transforming decisions.

As dreamers we are making an effort to understand the emotional forces that affect the way we experience life. We are urged on to a higher effort—to appreciate the resources available to us that support innovative action. Sharing what we read is a way of releasing dormant potential. I have come to believe that the artist within that created our dreams is reaching out to the artists beyond ourselves, the great writers, thinkers, engagers in life, who can urge us through the pain, into the freedom and grandeur surrounding us.

Our goal is not to master rising above suffering or to develop maneuvers averting danger. We are on a pilgrimage toward inner safety—the affirmation of ourselves as unique from all others, and the participation of our individuality in an underlying whole. When energy is no longer poured into attempts at escaping from loss and death we are released to stand in the soft light of compassionate appreciation of ourselves and others.

To be specific about how dream work may support our coping with life crises, let us look at several dreams that have metaphors relating to the themes of death or of loss through sexual abuse. We will see how the dreamer identifies the emotions in each dream, integrating them with waking consciousness. The result is emancipation from forces that had previously appeared as roadblocks to choice.

The dreams will be followed by a short bibliography including supportive organizations and websites. Perhaps you can retrieve words that fit your experience, that touch your dreams, that lead you beyond your conscious understanding, setting in motion the stirring of liberating alternatives.

Of the great mysteries, the one to which we are all ultimately heir is death. In some fashion we learn to live with its inevitability and survive the loss of those we love. How we absorb the reality of death and the weight of grief has much to do with the quality of all our days.

In our dreams death wears many faces and looks on life from many angles. Most typically "death dreams" deal not with the loss of life but the loss of a way of life or change not yet fully absorbed. A young man dreams he is flying in a powerful 747 to a foreign country. There is a bomb threat aboard the plane. Before it can be checked out by the flight attendant the plane explodes, and the young man is plunging to the ground. He awakens in a sweat, knowing death is imminent. The dreamer wonders if this is a precognitive dream. Should he cancel a planned trip? Possibly, but first the dream is talked over with a friend. She associates the bomb with sexual frustration and fear. Although the dreamer considers this logical, it clashes with his feelings, and does not touch his fear that the dream is a proclaimer of an actual impending disaster. Then he mentions that recently he has been selected for a significant promotion. Outwardly he expresses delight. Inwardly he wonders if this will shift him into a job so high powered that he will "bomb out." Is he capable of handling the escalation of responsibility? Does he want the pressure or is he being propelled by the assumption that "upward mobility" is the obvious vocational choice of direction?

As the emotions in the dream are identified with his waking circumstance, the fear of physical death fades, and the impending death of his familiar life-style is recognized.

The death of a child is a crushing reminder that death is to be part of all our lives. But death of a child by suicide is perhaps of all loss the most devastating. Sylvia was a member of some of my earliest workshops. She brought great perception to her dreams and offered projections to others that often led them into a more precise meaning of their dreams.

The Journey to the Dream

I had taught piano to her son, Paul, when he was in high school, and knew him as an attractive, shy young man, gracious and gifted. Sylvia and her husband, Bill, were well aware of Paul's struggle with depression. They had given him loving support. Paul was under the care of a psychiatrist but dropped out when he was moved from individual to group therapy. The psychiatrist had advised Bill and Sylvia to leave him alone and let him work out his own dependency needs. Six months later, at age twenty-five, Paul shot himself.

The year after Paul's death Sylvia and one of her daughters, Margaret, drove across the United States. In Sylvia's words, "One of the goals of this trip for me was to visit the relatives along the way and really sort of wrap up Paul's suicide." Sylvia felt some relatives had been too shocked by the suicide to react openly on the phone. Their trip released much talk about other tragedies in the family. Some had been unknown to Sylvia before their visit. One night after an intense conversation with her relatives she had the following dream.

The Dream

Bill and I were dragging a coffin into our living room. I looked in. There was Sammy [their dog, now dead], his dog form known to me. I was a bit shocked because I was sure it would be Paul. I ran my eyes over him—the ears, the spots, the flank, the tail, the paws. Dear Sammy. I turned away, and when I looked again, the body was no longer Sammy, but Paul as we found him. It was the whole suicide scene, just exactly as he was lying there, except he was in the coffin. Black blood caked on his face. As before, I ran my eyes over the beloved body. The body was clothed, and I paused at the hips, wondering if the lipoma from his childhood was still there. I looked for a while at the body as though from a distance of time. And it wasn't nightmare horrible, as at the time of death. When I awoke I immediately knew the meaning of the dream. We have brought the death into the living room. And we can live with it. I awoke satisfied that the dream reflected the truth.

The Search for Connectedness

When Sylvia returned home from her trip she told her husband her dream. They talked about how, for so long, it seemed Paul's death would never be put to rest. Now they had shared openly with their relatives and had faced the horrible loss. Paul was dead. Memories and desires remained, but their son was dead. The distance Sylvia felt as she looked at the blood-caked face and beloved body was not one of avoidance; it was distance from the immediacy of grief and an awareness that Paul must be released—a natural distance, a moving on. Sylvia was saying: I am here. I am alive, but Paul is dead. However I rage, or yearn, his death remains a death.

Sylvia's family knew before Paul's death that their dog, Sammy, had cancer and would soon die. But the cancer went into remission, and the dog lived on a year after the suicide. Sammy sensed the family's grief and would go from bedroom to bedroom after Paul's death. Sylvia called him "a minister to us." In the dream it was as if Sammy's death enabled Sylvia to get closer to Paul's death. In waking reality the visit to her relatives was the agent for laying her son's death out in the open, and by so doing, aided Sylvia in accepting her horrible loss.

The day Sylvia shared this dream with me she said, "Someone once asked me if I had known I would have a child who would die of suicide, would I have wanted to have the child? And I said, 'Yes, I really think I would.' Because those times, all those good experiences of having him and living with him and growing up with him, they were pretty terrific. Some people have none of that. If he had lived, we would have had other times. But what we've had, we've had. I remember sometimes at night Bill and I would talk and put the kids to bed. We'd say what a good day this was for them, and then we'd say, 'Well, it's one day under the belt,' in a contented voice, and think of all the good it will do, this one day. It was a good feeling. I have asked now: What about those days? Where are they? But I guess they are complete in themselves."

Later that day Sylvia read from James Hillman's *Suicide and the Soul*: "To put an end to oneself means to come to one's end, to find the end or limit of what one is, in order to arrive at what one is not—yet. Suicide is the attempt to move from one realm to another by force through death. . . .

There is an attempt at transformation." This book, she said, had helped her through times of deepest grief.

Gram Shriver was ninety-four when she died, leaving sadly empty the corner seat, second row, in the Episcopal Church she had attended longer than other members could remember. She had lived for years with her daughter, Lil, a widow of remarkable versatility. Lil loved her mother deeply.

Some months before her death Gram remembered two dreams that she shared with me and with Karen Anderson. Karen is the mother in "The Family That Dreams Together," whose story is told in *Working With Dreams* (Ullman and Zimmerman, chapter 9, 1979).

The Dreams

Dream 1: I saw two feet. They were surrounded in light. I knew they were the feet of Jesus. I tried to look up and see his face, but I couldn't. I wanted so much to see Jesus, but it wasn't possible. I was sad. I felt I had more to do.

Dream 2: I was in a plane. Then I was outside the plane. It was glorious. I was flying through the sky, up and down. Oh, I felt so free! Then Lil said I must come down immediately. She was very upset and certain it was not right for me to be flying outside the plane like that. I didn't want to come down, but I thought I should do what she wanted. She was so worried. I began to fall and landed in a hay stack. I was surprised I wasn't injured at all by the fall. Lil took me to the hospital, but I had no injuries.

The Journey to the Dream

Gram's physical condition was deteriorating, but otherwise she remained an alert, spirited lady. Her visitors invariably came away blessed by her insight and faith in the God she had worshiped and loved all her life. Gram was ready to die. She was not frightened. Death seemed practical and welcome. More than that, she believed she would be united with God in a way not possible while in her physical body. At first she felt that she continued to live because there was spiritual work remaining for her to accomplish. This was her understanding of her first dream when she couldn't raise her eyes to see Jesus. Several weeks later, when she had the second dream, this hindrance seemed to be resolved. Now Gram anticipated with exhilaration the freedom of physical death in her metaphor of flying outside the physical plane. Then, remembering her daughter's love and concern for her welfare, she was brought "down to earth." Gram was saying in her dream that she heard her daughter's earnest desire that she live. The "no injuries" of her dream was perhaps the recognition that despite her yearning to be free, no actual harm would come from staying a while longer within the confines of her body.

The Search for Connectedness

Lil talked to Karen and others about the great loss she would feel when her mother died. Slowly she began to accept the inevitable transition it would be for them both. As day followed day, Gram's physical condition continued to decline, while at the same time she planned her own funeral and burial. Gram got in touch with the Saint Francis Center, an organization in Washington, D.C. that provides support to people facing personal and practical difficulties associated with illness, death, and dying. She asked friends to make her pine coffin. It was assembled in the home of the Anderson family. Lil came to believe it was right for her mother to die. The coffin was finished, with a small cross carved in the lid of the simple box.

The next day Gram Shriver died.

For many years I struggled to accept a hidden part of myself. The following dream guided me to an encounter I had avoided a long time.

The Dream

I am walking alone in the city and come upon a large brownstone home. I remember trick or treating here several years ago, and meeting an interesting young woman. I knock on the door to say Hi to her. Her mother answers. She is fiercely defensive and refuses to let me in. I am amazed and slightly amused thinking she is like a witch doorkeeper. After assuring her I'll stay only a minute she reneges, reluctantly letting me pass into the house. The townhouse is one room wide, but spacious. I walk through many rooms, admiring the elegant originality of the art and furnishings. The dim lighting makes it hard to see, and I don't find the young woman.

I leave through the last room, the kitchen, and enter a small village. Groups of two and three sit in outdoor cafes. Other people stroll, some carrying small packages. Trees line the narrow street, and no cars are visible. I think, How inviting, a storybook place, *and hope that some day I can return.*

Now I am on a country road leading out of the village. Suddenly I think that I am very far from home. I have no money and have no idea where I am. Down the road on the left two old women sit on a bench. Some distance beyond them is a telephone booth. Relieved, I walk to them, explain my predicament and ask them for two quarters to call my husband, Howard. They give me disdainful looks and say nothing.

I am now quite anxious but decide to keep walking to the phone. It is then I see a man beyond the phone booth but moving toward me. I walk faster, trying to reach the phone before we meet, and trying not to run, embarrassed to display fear. The man's strides are long. As he approaches I see he is black. A deadly strength surrounds him. I feel an evil coming toward me and know that if he reaches me I will be murdered. I am crying out inside, filled with horror, but make no sound.

I wake up, terrified.

The Power of Metaphor

When I began working with others on this dream one person said the man in the last scene was the stereotypical reaction of a white woman to a black stranger on an empty street. That projection was amazingly powerful because I knew immediately it was wrong, and then recalled more details about the man. He was not Afro-American; rather, he was covered in black. There was no outward evidence of his true identity. He reminded me of Darth Vader in "Star Wars." I began thinking about this fantasy character who after being in mortal combat with Luke Skywalker reveals that he is Luke's father. Then it began to unfold why, years after I began the struggle to fathom his impact on my life, I had dreamed of this man draped in darkness.

The Journey to My Dream

My college years appeared adjusted and successful—a respectably high grade point average; a leader in the organizations and activities that reflected my interests and ambitions. What no one knew was that in the eighth grade I began experiencing phobic attacks. At college the isolating and exhausting fear of agoraphobia accelerated. Finally a failed romance plunged me even deeper into unbearable dread, and I left school believing suicide was the only escape.

My mother suggested I talk to a minister who was a friend of our family. I had been in awe of his gentle authority since I was a little girl. He was the sort of man who dared to break denominational presumptions. He risked new ways of expressing and sharing his Christian faith. And so in desperation I reached out to him. With his counsel, encouragement and help I returned to school. The man's lifestyle and ministry gave me the feeling of being home at last.

On a fall afternoon, the year I was graduated from college, the minister and I were sitting in my mother's living room. He had his arm around me protectively, and then, quite subtly, his touch changed from comforting to sexual. I was stunned, but continued trusting him. How could I question the man who brought me from hopelessness to a place of safety? He assured me he was my father, that the other members of our church completed my family, that I could put my weight down on God for he would not "break the bruised reed or quench the smoldering fire." Tragically I was not able to distinguish between him and God.

During the following years the secrecy of our complex, sexual relationship mutely concealed a profound portion of my being. Then came the time when his sexual interest in me lessened. With that change began his repeated question, asked with searing incredulity—why, after all the love he had given me was I now unable to go forward in life and give this love to others?

Years after I had married and left the church, the sound of those words haunted my soul. I believed I had failed hideously—I was unable to pass on to others all the unconditional love he had given to me. Ironically, the blindness of a multiple sclerosis episode forced me to access that darkness inside my heart, and I began the journey through many rooms, searching for the young woman I had once known. I entered therapy, finding a psychologist with patience, no easy answers, and a clear understanding of boundaries. I told more of my story to Howard and later, one by one, to four close friends.

But what of the minister? What was his version of the story and how would he react to mine? I asked him to meet me at my home. I was determined to describe to this man whom I had held in my heart as my father, the years of misery that were wrapped around the secrets we had kept. Until the silence was broken I knew it was impossible to join my voice, in a straightforward credulous way, with others who had been abused by people in power. I could not move from victim to survivor to free participator in life.

I did not believe that condemning held healing for either of us. Nor did I believe in the redemptive value of what Dietrich Bonhoeffer termed "cheap grace." Terrible pain had accompanied my struggle to exhume and examine the buried past. His position as minister was no protection against his arduous labor of truth finding.

When we met I told him why I had asked him to come. I then recalled explicitly the details of our sexual relationship. He denied nothing, simply repeated over and over, that he was sorry if I saw it as sex—he was simply trying to do everything possible to keep me from having to be hospitalized.

I was astounded. How could he reconstruct what we had experienced as unsuccessful therapy? What could that "therapy" possibly have been teaching? What had become of our covenant to be father and daughter? I still believed he had meant that relationship to be genuine, which led me to the most twisted, wrenching question of all: What would a father have been teaching a daughter through exploring the depths of her sexuality?

In a bizarre turn-around he was implying through his interpretation that it was all right to tell my story because what I knew as sex, he saw as therapy. Anyone can make a mistake in therapy. And he was sorry.

Now I was certain that secrecy was a destroyer, and I wrestled for the ways to break open my heart and tell the truth without further destruction. How could this be done and not hurt many people who trusted him as spiritual leader and benefited from his charismatic gifts? What harm would come to his family, and mine? The questions seemed to spin endlessly into further misery.

The Search for Connectedness

I searched in literature for words that would speak to the darkness within, and break open the isolation. I read *Sex in the Forbidden Zone* (Rutter 1989) and learned what motivates professional men to relinquish their nurturing and protective roles for erotic behavior. And why women who are seeking safety and spiritual guidance allow themselves to be lead into accepting a relationship with a minister on his terms.

I subscribed to *The ISTI Sun* (The Interfaith Sexual Trauma Institute's newsletter). I discovered that sexual misconduct is widespread, that what I had experienced existed in many variations, always with devastating consequences. I learned that there is a network of interfaith professionals and lay persons who care and are working to heal and curb sexual misconduct.

I drank in the wisdom of *Peace Is Every Step* (Nhat Hanh 1991). Into my dark secrets I carried his poem "Please Call Me By My True Names."

I was reminded in Henri Nouwen's *Life of the Beloved* (1993) that we must befriend the pain that paralyses us emotionally. Whether I am the one that goes for counsel or the one who counsels, I must live through the reality of my anguish and find ways of connecting with others. Nouwen says that our brokenness is often so profound that we are terrified by the possible consequences of having it known to others; and so we "live under the curse," that is, although we endlessly search for an explanation for what takes place in us, we reject ourselves at the very point of brokenness. If we share ourselves—through dreams, conversation with friends, therapy—what "seems intolerable becomes a challenge."

The night before attending an ISTI regional workshop at Saint Luke Institute in Washington, D.C., I had my dream.

The dream was saying to me that my secret of sexual abuse and the secrets of the minister with whom I had hidden sexual relations were deadly. This insidious brand of secrecy kills the spirit. In my dream secrecy is the death of freedom, of being able to walk unthreatened down a lonely road or move toward the phone booth for the help I need or the contacts I desire. It covers true identity in a veil of darkness. The dream also reveals that secrecy can transform a man who was like a father, and a discerning counselor into an analogue of death.

Dream Sequences as Metaphor

One of the many clues Monte Ullman has given me in understanding dreams is to look at the sequences within a REM period not as disparate tales, but as a metaphor for the overarching theme of the dream.

The theme of this dream is the journey I have taken to meet secrecy face to face. It brought me to the place where options end and confronting the darkness is unavoidable. My dream describes, sequence by sequence how, while searching for a hidden part of my past, I attempted to avoid meeting this darkness on the lonely country road, far away from help outside myself.

The dream begins in a carefree spirit, coming to a place with the memory of childhood adventure—trick or treating. As a young girl I did not take the phrase "trick or treat" literally. There was anticipation of being greeted with feigned surprise—"Oh, and who are you!"—and given candy. At worst, no one was home. Wouldn't I like to have that innocence and imagine that trying to reach the imprisoned past would be met with generous acceptance and no enigmatic consequences.

This possibility is short lived, and I am greeted by the witch doorkeeper mother. She is both a playful and quite serious reenactment of my own mother. Mother reveled in Halloween, often dressing up as a witch for parties. Balancing her fun-loving self was her vigilant protectiveness, fearful that something harmful would come near those she loved. In my dream I talk my way past this magical safeguard and enter the house. I am now actively in search of the young woman who disappeared into the dimness of the building. In waking life I recall the intellectual challenge, culture, and beauty experienced during those years with the minister and his church. I see this elegance reflected in the dream rooms.

Sadly, the young woman is not found. I remember, as I go back through the dream, that I felt certain she was somewhere in the house but was constrained from meeting me. I think of myself, at the beginning of my independent life after college. I was trying to leave the early fear that had become so crippling and find my place. But I was incapable of passing beyond the first rush of newness. I became trapped—living in a faith community that valued confession but unable to disclose my deepest conflicts because I was sexually bound to our minister. He created for me a private existence and blocked me from an authentic encounter with life. Now, more confident, I intensify my search for a lost part of myself.

Finally I reach the last room, the kitchen. Recalling this sequence I remember how appealing it would be to join the folks who were cooking and chatting in the warm room, and thinking that perhaps the young woman would appear. In waking life I would like to be nourished by the memories from that era. I yearn for relaxed comradery with the people I knew, and most of all I want the young woman that I was then not to be excluded. But in my dream I sense she is powerless to join me.

My journey continues, and I come upon an idyllic village. Here there is no conflict, no danger. Small groups of people sit, talking as in an outdoor coffee house. Folks walk at a leisurely pace. Children play without fear, and no cars pollute or threaten the landscape. I ache with sadness, recalling this idealized version of my past—a community where there is protection from outside dangers. Perhaps there exists a safe and walled off haven where no one is harmed. I travel on aware that this is not true, but without totally rejecting the illusion.

Now I am on a country road leading away from everything that has seemed safe and familiar and I have a high anxiety attack. My dream reaction is a typical phobic maneuver: I look for a way out, thinking Howard, my husband, might come and pick me up. He has indeed helped me many times. The problem intensifies in the dream when I realize I can not contact him.

Although I notice a phone booth at a great distance, I am without money, a metaphor for assuming a lack of personal resources when I experience rising fear. What of the two old women sitting on the bench? Surely they will help me. But I've gone too far. I am on a path where my plight is not considered worthy of consideration. Who will come to my aid? An old problem, an outdated answer: no one.

Finally, I see the man of darkness. My journey has guided me to this desolate place. I have tried to stop short of a solitary encounter, but none of the old coping devices have stayed my arrival. Here is my dilemma—to continue on course I risk the possibility of being murdered, the senseless destruction of my present life. Trapped in the darkness is the young woman for whom I search. Enclosed in the darkness hides the truth of who we are. Within the secrets is buried authentic relationship. (Darth Vader sealed off his fatherhood from his son, creating the symbol of evil.) Will I survive if I move toward the darkness, rather than avoid it? The encounter seems inevitable. Directly engaging with the evil of secrecy is overwhelming. In utter panic, and alone, I do the only thing I know to do to save myself, I abandon the dream state of consciousness, and awaken.

I *am* alone in determining what to do with my story. The strength of secrecy is deadly. Breaking the back of silence also seems to have ramifications beyond endurance. It is sometimes said that sin or evil is what hurts another, yourself, or your relationship with God. If sin is the opposite of connectedness, it is no wonder that on that lonely road, with the relationship of secrecy coming closer and closer, I see the man in black as evil. And filled with horror, I believe I cannot survive.How I will survive is yet to be lived out. But now I know I must open the door to my past and give others access to my story.

My dream of why the man of darkness came to meet me on the road that night is the journey through the process of choices that did not work well for me, and the actions that led me to the heart of my conflict: exposing the reality within the black secret.

My journey before the dream tells why on the night my dream occurred I was still unable to let this tangle of experiences be known publicly. I was so fearful that I ran away from the concealed truth, out of my dream and smack into the waking experience of this dilemma with pounding heart and dread. The dream, my journey to the dream and working with it, interlaced with therapy, friends, my husband's support, and many books, encouraged my writing the truth.

Several days after completing this account Howard and I met with two couples from the church I have described. I read a portion of my journey. Shocked and sad they asked us many questions, but by evening's end the four spoke with one voice: continue telling your story. Truth for them, no matter how painful, carries with it the opportunity to heal and re-form our lives.

After the dream is over, the work on the dream remains.

Dreams are seedpods in which the seeds of the past and the plantings of the future are encased. When we crack them open, reseeding of life can begin again. But where, how?

At best, recovery from the pain of life crises is jagged. The gritty demands of ongoing responsibilities need to become coherent with new levels of reality, often dimly perceived, and with sorrow not soothed by pat explanations. A number of national groups extend specialized support to people suffering from death experiences, and victims of sexual abuse. I include a partial listing.

The written word may be experienced as a pathway to our inner light. A word, a phrase, a paragraph brought into the silence of our own being may stimulate the self-healing process. It is for this purpose, as you work with your own dreams and reactions to loss through death and sexual abuse, that the following bibliography is offered. Some of these books have been a source of guidance and comfort to the dreamers whose dreams you have just read.

Life need not be a slow march toward degeneration and hopelessness. We can look for connectedness within and without. Within, our dreams sharpen the images of our stress until our emotions become defined. Dreams are a trustworthy support to our waking intuition and reason. They gather together old and new responses to our problems.

Some responses, outdated and inhibiting change, need to be discarded; others may, with refinement or repetition generate change.

We look without to a host of people who have moved through searing pain, disregarding easy answers, refusing defeat, to emerge with inner strength and compassion. They have helped us appreciate and release our resources as we have shared together in dream workshops and support groups, therapy, and as friends. And theirs also are the voices of the writers who, reaching deep within themselves, have spread out their discoveries so we might "drink from wells we did not dig."

Our dream theaters are never dark. Against the backdrop of these nightly revelations are the voices of the day, waiting for us to unite with them in courage and hope.

Self-Help Aids, Support Groups, and Organizations Available to People Suffering from Grief, Loss and Trauma

Candlelighters
7910 Woodmont Ave., Suite 460
Bethesda, MD 20814-33015
800-366-2223
301-657-8401 Fax:301-2686
Email: info@candlelighters.org

Candlelighters is part of a worldwide network of parents who have children with cancer, and parents whose children have died. They have an informative web site on the internet: http://www.candlelighters.org

The Compassionate Friends
P.O. Box 3696
Oak Brook, IL 60522-3696
630-990-0010 Fax:630-990-0246
Website: www.jjt.com/~tcf_national/

A nondenominational self-help organization for parents who have experienced the death of a child. Provides an excellent web page and extensive internet links to other organizations providing help for those experiencing the grief of loss and death.

New Harbinger Publication
5674 Shattuck Avenue
Oakland, CA 94609-1662
800-748-6273 510-652-0215
FAX: 510-652-5472
Email: nhhelp@newharbinger.com
Website: www.rivendell.org

A nonprofit group that sponsors Griefnet, a collection of resources for those experiencing loss or grief. Includes a variety of self-help publications such as *Beyond Grief*, available via internet orders or mail order.

Saint Francis Center
4880-A MacArthur Boulevard NW
Washington, D.C. 20007
202-333-4880
FAX: 202-333-4540
Email: sfcgrief@erols.com

A nonsectarian, nonprofit organization providing support and counsel to persons living with illness, loss, and bereavement. They are also active in the community, offering guidance and training to schools, agencies, religious institutions, and workplaces, responding compassionately to those affected by loss. Quarterly journal: *Centering*.

Interfaith Sexual Trauma Institute (ISTI)
Saint John's Abbey and University
Collegeville, MN 56321-2000
320-363-3931 Fax:320-363-2115
Website: www.osb.org/isti/
Email: isti@csbsju.edu

ISTI facilitates the building of healthy, safe, and trustworthy communities of faith. It addresses systemic causes of clergy sexual misconduct across traditions of religion and denominations through research, education, and training programs. Quarterly newsletter: *The ISTI Sun*.

Local Support

Suicide and sexual trauma support groups are a part of most local support organizations, such as community mental health centers. Check your phone directory for the one nearest you.

Internet Resources

In today's computer world, the variety of resources available via the internet is impressive and extensive. For those with access to the internet, help from a vast number of resources worldwide is only a local phone call away. A simple way to begin is to access either Yahoo or Alta Vista and type in one of the following search words: *grief, sexual trauma, suicide,* or *bereavement.*

References

Brener, Anne. *Mourning and Mitzvah.* Woodstock: Jewish Lights Publishing, 1993.

Grollman, Earl A., ed. *What Helped Me When My Loved One Died.* Boston: Beacon Press, 1981.

Hillman, James. *Suicide and the Soul.* Dallas: Spring Publications, 1983.

Hopkins, Nancy Myer, and Laaser, Mark, ed. *Restoring the Soul of a Church.* Collegeville: Liturgical Press, 1995.

Muller, Wayne. *How, Then, Shall We Live?* New York: Bantam Books, 1996.

Nhat Hanh, Thich. *Peace Is Every Step.* New York: Bantam Books, 1991.

Nouwen, Henri J. M. *Life of the Beloved.* New York: Crossroad, 1993.

Simpkinson, Anne A. "Soul Betrayal." *Common Boundary* 14, 6 (1996): 24–37.

Rutter, Peter. *Sex in the Forbidden Zone.* New York: St. Martin's, 1989.

Ullman, Montague. *Appreciating Dreams.* Thousand Oaks, Calif.: Sage, 1996.

Ullman, Montague, and Zimmerman, Nan. *Working with Dreams.* Los Angeles: Jeremy P. Tarcher, 1979.

Vail, Elaine. *A Personal Guide to Living with Loss.* New York: John Wiley, 1982.

Yalom, Irvin D. *Love's Executioner.* New York: Basic Books, 1989.

CHAPTER THREE

A Mothers' Dream Group

JENNY DODD

For dream work to move into the public domain in an effective way it will require people like Jenny Dodd, possessed of a passionate enough interest to learn the basics about dreams, to undertake the training that sharpens their skills in group dream work, and then to organize and develop their own groups.

Jenny Dodd came to the task with a unique endowment. She is the youngest of three generations of dream workers. Her grandmother, Dr. Winnifred Rushforth, one of the earliest physicians in Britain to turn to psychoanalysis, began to develop dream groups after her retirement from practice. When I saw her last in Edinburgh she was ninety-six, had just written a book, and was leading seven dream groups a week. Her daughter and Jenny's mother, Dr. Diana Bates, also leads dream groups.

Soon after her arrival in this country, Jenny sought out instruction and training with me.

The group described in this chapter was unique in a number of ways. The members were all women, adapting to life in this country, coming from abroad, most with young children. With the exception of Jenny they were all new to dream work. I had the pleasure of working with them on two occasions a year apart. The skill and sophistication they had developed was impressive. The dream group continued until December 1988 when Jenny moved to Geneva with her family.

Experiences like those described in this chapter have convinced me of the feasibility of extending dream work beyond the confines of the therapeutic consulting room and entrusting dreams to the care of those who dream them.

Our Friday morning dream group was started in January 1981 and has continued to meet every week without interruption. Originally it numbered seven women with ten children in tow, all under five years of age; now, four years later, we are nine women with only one or two children remaining, the rest now in school. A factor of some significance to our long survival, but by no means the only one, may have been our similar backgrounds; we were from England, South Africa, and Canada. There was only one American among us. Whether this was by accident or design is a matter of conjecture, but the fact remains that rather quickly we formed a cohesive group. We rotated meetings at one another's houses. Those with swimming pools or access to beaches were favored in the summer, those with warm basements, in the winter, for we soon found it necessary to organize child care efficiently. Each week one of us would take on the responsibility of providing snacks and entertainment for the children during the two hours or so of the meeting.

The Friday morning dream group is indeed a very special event in each of our lives. It is time to which we voluntarily commit ourselves to the search for deeper understanding of both ourselves and others. We believe that at the very least a dream is some sort of communication. None of us is a professional, but each of us brings an intelligent mind, a wealth of life experience, and a warm sensitivity to the world of feelings and intuition—all of which have served to deepen our sharing and helped to form quite a special dream group. We hesitate to make any great claims for ourselves as dream experts, but there is no doubt in any of our minds that being a member of this group and sharing dreams is now quite central to our lives.

One member begins to notice a significant effect on her writing, saying that sharing a dream can sometimes release greater creativity and freedom; another member, aware of conflicts in her professional artistic life is finding that sharing her dreams and isolating particular areas of conflict is helping her make the right decisions for her future development; a third woman values most the sharing of feelings at a more meaningful level than she finds in her daily life; yet another, older woman, feels enriched by meeting regularly with people who are engaged in a similar task of searching for a deeper significance in life and relationship, and by the sense of shared experience and struggle. As for myself, I value the continuously renewed experience of perceiving someone close to me grappling with issues honestly and bravely, coming away with a sense of having touched or reowned a part of herself for which she is now the richer.

This dream was shared:

I am at a summer school. I am sitting in a group. Two of my children, covered in mud, rush in and roll on the floor. I watch dismayed but unresponsive. They run out laughing. As my anger rises, I rush out after them, determined to punish them for their behavior.

I run down to the bottom of the garden and find them hidden in the showers. Their clothes are scattered everywhere. A German au pair girl appears to give me a hand. I find a large white towel with which to dry them, and as I wrap it around L. we notice a large worm has become enfolded in the towel. I am repulsed but L. is intrigued and tries to unwrap it. The worm turns out to have nipping claws and L. withdraws.

We go back to the house. I feel as if I still have to punish the children and have difficulty in finding clothes for them.

Then a woman appears displaying two beautiful dresses she has made. One is finished; she is wearing the second. It is gray and white, a beautifully tailored dress with a panier-type underskirt. I am impressed by the detailed work she has done, particularly the panniers. I watch her walking away with the underskirt showing but unfinished. I feel challenged by her, invited to do the same.

After the dream was presented, the following feelings were expressed as each member made the dream her own. There is a peaceful feeling at the beginning, which is disturbed by the children; things are happening too fast, there is confusion; I feel annoyed that I have to leave the group; I am resentful of the demands the children make on me; it's hard to reconcile these demands with my own needs and interests; I feel frustrated and impatient; there's a feeling of conflict; there is a feeling that I need help with the children; I am not being treated with consideration.

Working with the dream imagery, the group offered the following ideas: the group is the dream group, the work I do; the gardens are ordered and beautiful but also a place for mud; the showers are cleansing; the children are natural, free, and admirable; the worm seems to be part of that naturalness, the way things are, but it's a part of me snapping; the beautiful dresses are also a part of me, what I can and want to be. There is a contradiction between the freedom of the children and the discipline of dressmaking.

The dreamer then responded. She had a sure sense of where this dream had come from. The day before, her two children had gone out to play just as the family was leaving for an ice-skating expedition. In a matter of minutes they had become muddy, too muddy in fact for the dreamer to contemplate putting them into the car. Both she and her husband responded with anger, sending them upstairs, and the family expedition was cancelled. Secondly, the dreamer had hoped that over the weekend she would find time to start making her sister-in-law an exciting new outfit, but she had not been able to do anything at all. The main feeling for the dreamer was the anger she felt toward her children and the frustration she felt at not being able to start her dressmaking. The dream put her closely in touch with the anger felt toward the children the day before and her need to discipline them, reactions that created some conflict. The dried-up worm in the towel seemed to suggest the conflict. The snakelike creature was harmless, representing instinctual life, but also something repulsive, even dangerous. Perhaps this part of the dream was expressing the dilemma she experienced in having to discipline her children. It was necessary, but what harm might it do to a young child's naturalness? The intensity of the dreamer's anger and the frustration she felt had made her feel guilty. The woman in the dream who appeared with the beautiful dresses felt like the dreamer's self a few years earlier when she had no children and spent blissful uninterrupted hours creating handsome outfits for herself and others. There was a taunting quality about this dream figure, which the dreamer felt strongly. In reality the fabric she was hoping to sew into an outfit was lying in a bag; it beckoned and challenged her, and she was frustrated not to have been able to work on it.

As a mother, one is continually interrupted in thought, conversation, and work. I can remember clearly, as we started meeting on Friday mornings, how many of us appreciated the luxury of having two hours every week to work with dreams. We were not seeking advice or solutions, but just the opportunity to air our worries or joys and accept the conflicts and apparent contradictions in our lives. I am convinced that by now, after four years, most other voluntary peer groups would have petered out. It impresses me deeply that we are still functioning and growing, committed to the task of sharing our dreams in the knowledge that they do contain some valuable information for us. Not only is this information helpful to the dreamer, but we find it is frequently relevant to each of us. There is universality in most dreams.

An example springs to mind:

I can see a pyramid of fine, beautiful, shiny red apples on a table top. I am lying on my side looking at these apples. Shafts of light are coming down and around me from several different directions. These shafts of light are perpendicular, clear, almost like sheets of glass.

As I am watching, the hand of a child stretches out to take the top apple. I say to myself, "She's going to bite it, and it's rotten."

In her feedback the dreamer shared much that touched us all deeply. She felt that the apples were magical and "core things"; in fact, the whole dream had a magical, enlightening quality for her. It felt like a core experience. The light was layered, and the dream's message came through to her in layers. Her eldest daughter, the top of her pyramid of five children, had given up the magic that she, the mother, had tried to maintain and give her. She had in fact "turned rotten," left home, leaving no address, and remaining out of touch for many months at a time. All her life the dreamer had been affected by light; she could lie and look at it for hours. She had wondered as a child who was delivering the light, the sun or herself? She had been reading an article that evening about light and the connection between lack of sunlight and depression in certain people. She had said that her daughter experienced depression most often in the winter. She repeated that apples were, for her, "core" things and that, approaching middle age, she now felt she was discarding the frills, discarding doing what she'd always been told to do, was coming to the core of herself. The dream was speaking of something creative emerging, to do with light. She concluded poignantly by saying that she'd had to get rid of the most beautiful part of her family, her oldest daughter, in order to preserve the whole.

The striking simplicity and beauty of the dream image, the subtle weaving together of incidents from the dreamer's childhood and motherhood, the dispassionate observation of the removal of the top apple (as paralleling the painful experience of relinquishing any mother/daughter relationship with her eldest for the time being at least), and the sense of something creative emerging for herself were all shared simply, yet sincerely, without self-consciousness or shame or pride. The dream work drew us closer together as human beings, leaving us all enriched.

Another dream is offered for the way in which it produced a sense of healing in the dreamer:

I am visiting a man who was once very dear to me. He was living in a beautiful apartment. The rooms were huge, and his paintings were hung on every wall. He was dressed in a dressing gown, and I had the feeling that the woman who lived there with him was not there.

His son was calling him from down a long hall, but he was quite involved with discussing his paintings with me. The ones that I was most impressed with were of horses. He had done a lot of paintings with horses, in fine detail, almost living/breathing horses. Then his son came into the room, and he too seemed very proud of his father's paintings. I did feel that the paintings lacked spontaneity or originality.

It was night, and the lights were very bright.

The dream took the dreamer back to a period of her life thirty years ago. It was triggered by coming across, earlier in the day, a silver coin which the man in the dream had given her, and also by a violent political row with her husband the evening before the dream (it was the time of the recent political election). The argument took her back to the McCarthy era and the time when she had been romantically involved with another man and was on the verge of divorce. The dream was revealing the relationship to this man in its true light. In the thinly disguised sexual overtones (the dressing gown and the horses), in the theatrical air, in the distant relationship between the man and his son, the dreamer saw and understood why she had decided to stay with her husband rather than go with her lover. She had sensed then the nature of her husband's loyalty and could now perceive the shallowness and superficiality of her relationship with the other man despite the lure of his wealth and extravagant tastes. The dream was confirming of her actions, reassuring her that her instincts at the time had been right.

The dreamer proceeded to talk about the impossibility of achieving the fulfillment we seek in any one relationship, the desire to escape the conflicts of daily living, the questions of loyalties and making choices, the woman's drive for maternity, and her acute awareness of her children's needs. In the dream the man had ignored his son's calling, which distressed her. She was reminded of how distressed she had been many years ago when her lover stated that her children could visit "from time to time" after the divorce. As she viewed current issues against the background of her dream, the dreamer gained a sense of peace and reconciliation and a greater understanding of herself and her past. We were all touched by her candid sharing and evident triumph.

Not all of us have the kind of glowing, healing experience this dreamer experienced in the dream work. Indeed, for some it can be a painful, if ultimately rewarding, experience. For those of us with unhappy childhood memories a dream can often touch so directly on our pain and suffering that it takes some courage to face it honestly, to accept it as having been, and with the distance of maturity, perhaps to forgive.

In this dream:

I was sitting in a bar/restaurant, weeping quietly. A rather ghostly-type man sitting at the bar said to me, "You used to have class, but you don't anymore." Whereupon I looked around at him and at everybody in the bar. They were all wearing Pacific Northwest Coast Indian motifs on them. When I saw that I wept and wept.

The dream followed a particularly tense Thanksgiving celebration in which for the first time the dreamer had managed to prepare herself a vegetarian dinner while providing the traditional fare for the rest of the family. This had taken some not inconsiderable resolve. The dream was also directly triggered by the dreamer having viewed "Kramer vs. Kramer." She had been struck by the character portrayed by Meryl Streep, who seemed natural with her feeling and suffering; she had strength yet could also show feeling. The weeping in the dream was directly related to the movie. The dream brought the dreamer in touch with how much of her life she had spent doing and being what she was told to do and be. Her mother, described as "the perfect mother," had been extremely rigid. Everything had been done to absolute perfection, which denied her any fulfillment of the artistic potential with which she was endowed. The dreamer perceived her mother as being false, and of living up to false ideals. In the dream, triggered by the anxiety the dreamer had felt at following her own dictates, not those of her family or society, the dreamer was confronted with her true, sad feelings. The man in the dream would have admired the old role as she played it. He rejects her now as she is visibly weeping, being herself. The Indian sweaters bring back unhappy memories from childhood, of being regimented, unsympathetically handled, and overdressed by a rigid nanny. In the dream the dreamer is discarding parental images and contacting the childhood pain. "Something is changing and it's painful," she was able to say. A week later the dreamer reported that she had experienced a freeing-up from a lot of stuff, especially related to her mother.

Dream work can be just as meaningful if positive or happy childhood memories are recalled. What seems to happen is that the dreamer discovers hidden strengths and resources within herself which, when consciously mobilized by dream work, can serve her in whatever predicament she may currently be facing. The following dream did such a thing for one of our members.

I'm with R., and the countryside seems wild, dusty, and lovely. I'm on a road, near her house, standing in front of a lovely big tree. All the other dream group people have gone on ahead in their cars. It feels frivolous, lighthearted, and carefree. I see the dust in the air in front of us. I feel as if we're on top of a cliff. . . .

They're heading toward the water straight ahead. R. tells me how to follow. I'm on foot, barefooted. I feel excited; something is happening.

I chase after them; I reach a point after fifty yards where the road goes straight ahead down to the beach, over a cliff. A middle road curves along the cliff top. A third road goes off to the right beside a solid stone cottage with beautiful roses all over it. I know that the cars have not gone down to the beach, and I think, What a pity, *because I know it is the perfect place to be at the moment.*

There is another big tree where I'm standing. Resting against it are three rectangular boxes with three different types of citrus fruit. The fruit is dusty but beautiful, larger than life. The right-hand box had only one orange left; the others are full.

I take the orange, but as I take it something gets triggered, and I think, No, how could you take the last one? *and I drop it quickly. It rolls away. Eventually I take a beautiful tangerine from the left-hand box and go on to the cottage.*

A woman comes out, speaking German; she tells me that the wonderful fruit is from South Africa. She gets out a very old book with German prose set in the middle with a border around it on each page. I'm understanding it, and it does tell about South Africa. She tells me that the cars have gone down the road past the cottage.

This was a long, rich dream, and the dreamer's feedback was very personal, full of feeling yet increasingly tranquil. The dream was full of sensual experiences—barefoot, heat, space, luscious fruit, heavenly scented roses, quantities of them—all of which reminded the dreamer of her childhood spent in South Africa. That afternoon she had spoken to her mother in South Africa who had just returned there after a two-week visit to the States. The dream also appeared to stem from a viewing of *Alice in Wonderland*, which played into the feeling of things being bigger than life, unreal and slightly puzzling. But the overriding feeling for the dreamer was of standing in one spot. Her outer personal life was in such turmoil, full of uncertainty and conflict.

This dreamer's feedback was so eloquent, I've quoted it verbatim:

> I feel as if I am at a standstill with no directions, but this dream gives me something I can draw on, something out of my life—in particular my free, sensual childhood. The only thing I can pull out now is being in touch with my different senses; there is no other growth or movement right now. I'm staying in one spot. I really wasn't able to show my mother how much I had enjoyed her stay, what a good time we had had together. It was rather like not being able to catch up with the dream group (which is a very positive thing for me). Seeing the fruit takes me back to a time when I was young and things did seem bigger and better, nothing could mar it, a quality only a child can see. It's showing me that I don't really experience these feelings anymore, but they are there. In my upbringing I was taught to care for the other person first and myself last, but it hasn't worked out for me now to care for someone else above my own feelings; it hasn't proved to be healthy. I want something very sensuous in my life, the part that was nourished in me as a child, which now feels so denied. I feel that the dream is showing me that I have a rich place to stand still in and take my own time and find my own direction guided by the wealth and wisdom of my background.

In dream work we are learning to be guided by our feelings. It is not always possible to arrive at an "interpretation"; what we are guided by is how the dreamer feels about her own dream. In the above case, the peaceful way in which the dreamer could conclude a long and thorough response was sufficient for all of us to feel satisfied that we had served our purpose as a group and helped the dreamer to get in touch with her own inner strength, which she needed at that time in her life.

Our own mothers and our own aging have appeared as themes running through our dreams. Two of our members had recently lost their mothers. Here a third dreamer shares her dream:

I was walking in a rocky place, almost mountainous. Out of the blue I met a girl from school (she had never been a close friend) called L.L. (very slim, bony prominent nose, attractive, dark-eyed, thin hair). She was carrying a body under her arm. She had a machine round her neck, like a box on her chest, and tubes went into the body, connected in, like a life-support system.

I asked, "Why are you carrying this person?" She replied "Oh, it's my mother, I must keep her going." I said, "If you go on the rocks, the mountains will support her." The body was naked, but there was no hair; it was a clothlike body, but I knew it was alive and female.

The dreamer was anticipating the arrival of her aging parents for their annual holiday. She was wondering how she would be affected by the frailty in her mother who had been unwell, someone who had always been "such a strong person." She had been looking at photographs of the mountains and had been watching *The Return of the Jedi*; she had been thinking about space where a portable life-support system was essential. She had been impressed by how other dream-group members had coped with the death of a mother. The dreamer had always felt how important she was to her mother's survival after an earlier family tragedy. She felt a responsibility for her parents which was frustrated by the distance that usually separated them. The mountains gave her a feeling of support and solidity. The appearance of L.L. from her early school years put her in touch with the miracle of a sensitive person who had survived the tortuous atmosphere of boarding school, cut off from all family support. She was reassured by this and, in the dream, by L.L.'s strength and loyalty. In sharing anxious feelings, the dreamer was able to come to terms with the unease she was feeling with her parents' imminent arrival. In the dream image of L.L. she would identify with those aspects of herself that were resourceful and strong.

Some of us are artists working in the community. Dream work has proved valuable in helping us understand more clearly the nature of interpersonal relationships and in making decisions vital to the future of our careers. Here is a recent example:

I'm at Hawnes (boarding school in England), but the time is now, and I am me, now. The school is being run by D.W. (current head of a department where I work). It is being run totally differently. There are computers everywhere. At one point I am invited to join a class. At the end of each row there is a Rainbow System by Digital. The kids in school are able to wear their own clothes, with no restrictions.

Something has changed about the layout of the school. The long drive is the same, and the fields and woods are all there, and the front facade is the same, but at the back it opens out onto a street in an old town, with narrow, winding streets.

A lot of people from where I work are in the school. I stop to talk to D.W. as an equal, as a visiting colleague. We walk around the school together, talking. I'm telling him about what it was like when I was there, and how much I hated the headmistress, Miss Twist (an archetypal English headmistress; graduate in English from Cambridge, unmarried with a little dog called Ricky and very heavy on discipline).

As the dreamer worked on the dream a crucial feeling link was made between Miss Twist and her present boss, H., a link which the dreamer experienced as releasing. The dreamer had been having conflict in her work situation for some time, and the dream was triggered by a four-hour harangue from her boss in which the dreamer had been humiliated and embarrassed to the point of breaking down. The resentful feelings caused by this event were linked in the dream to a time of similar emotions at boarding school. It was an environment from which she had begged to leave every week in letters to her father for the two years she had spent there. The feelings of powerlessness, helplessness, and revenge were paralleled. The links thus made freed the dreamer from responding on an infantile level. They enabled her to remain clear and levelheaded in the present situation and not to allow herself to be further manipulated or humiliated. But perhaps more importantly, the dream also helped to confirm her growing ambition to set up her own studio, having at last found supportive and influential people in her own field (as represented by D.W. in the dream).

The last dream is an illustration of one of the times when the dreamer felt a creative outburst as a result of sharing the dream. It runs as follows:

I am in Oxford with my husband. I said, "Let's go and see A." (an old flame). So we went to Balliol College.

On the tower, inside the door, was a big, gaudy notice, a wooden plaque with red and green writing. It said, "In Memoriam Prof. G.S." (the same A.) I said, "It shouldn't say that; it should say A.H." and I realized that A. was dead.

Inside the college there was an exhibit about A. We were ushered in; a secretary was sitting behind the desk. Above the desk was a portrait of A., as a king or chief, dressed in Peruvian/Aztec costume with feathers and bright colors. I kept looking at the portrait to try to see his face clearly, but I couldn't. Also in the exhibit were photograph albums of A. as a child, with his sisters, in a Greek play.

I said, "What happened to him?" She said, "Oh, they made him a king and then they murdered him."

So then I said to my husband something about A. "Oh, you're one of the people who called him A.," said the secretary, and everyone started being very deferential toward me. I decided to go to A.'s room, which is now a cross between an office and a museum. There's a reception desk at the front, and I see on it, in A.'s handwriting, pieces of paper asking for money for lectures/work he had done—sort of like IOU's.

I think it is sad that they did not pay for the ordinary things he did. I say, "I want to see D." They say, "Oh yes, D.'s a junior professor and is doing some of A.'s teaching for him."

The dream was triggered by having spent some time the day before looking for a letter from A., distinctly remembering his handwriting but failing to find the letter. It was placed in the general context of writing a story about this period in her life, as well as having recently been home, having looked up A.'s address without contacting him. The main thing that emerged for the dreamer was that the dream highlighted two conflicting images of the same person: one, the mythic godlike figure; the other, the overly ordinary, day-to-day person. In reality A. was a manic-depressive personality, a powerful, wonderful person who was fatally flawed. The figure of A. was a prominent person in the dreamer's imagination and in her writing about him.

What the group helped the dreamer to see clearly reflected in the dream was what she was trying to do with A. in her short story. A week later the dreamer described the release she felt that affected her writing positively. In a strange way, she stated, as a result of the dream story she no longer felt quite so obsessed by the memory of A. How marvelous that a death in the psyche can be experienced as a release into a new stage of life!

And thus, with these examples from our dream work over the years I hope that some of the benefits can be felt. There is much that comes up that cannot be shared and much that is separate from specifically mothering experiences. I have offered a sampling with deep indebtedness to the members of the group for giving this material freely and so movingly.

It never ceases to amaze me that despite sick children, vacations, business trips, and difficult family times, we have always met. Whatever the weather, whatever the problems, at least three of us are there, though the number is usually seven or eight. On only one occasion do I remember there being no dream to share. I think that dream work of this kind is a unifying experience that satisfies in a unique way both social and personal needs. We have built up an arena in which we all feel safe, where there is an atmosphere of trust and sharing that all of us supremely value.

We all want to know more about ourselves and believe that the dream is an important phenomenon, serving this end precisely if we are given an effective tool with which to work. We are all discovering lost and forgotten things about ourselves, maybe even unlikeable things sometimes. We must surely be growing in tolerance if nothing else.

There is a deep feeling of satisfaction at the end of working with a dream, whether it be one's own or someone else's. We have been in touch with something meaningful, truthful, revelatory, creative, or painful, and all of us are enriched. The undivided attention and concentration we give are refreshing in themselves in the context of our often harried and fragmented lives with young children. We are touched and healed by the process of sharing a dream, fearing no censure or criticism or unwanted advice. We are not so isolated after all. To share our feelings and use our intuitive imagination is both consoling and stimulating. We are all equals whatever the perceived differences. Our dreams show us this truth. We each have a lot to give and to share, and we have quite unique gifts valued by everyone. Dream work assists us in the difficult task of facing ourselves honestly and coping with the troubled society in which we find ourselves. It is unifying and personally enriching. Dream work will continue to play a vital part in all our lives for as long as we wish and dream.

PART II

The Spread to Other Disciplines

CHAPTER FOUR

Dream Work and Field Work

Linking Cultural Anthropology and the Current Dream Work Movement

DEBORAH JAY HILLMAN

Deborah Hillman is a young anthropologist, a prolific dreamer, and a talented dream worker. She has been close to the dream scene as it has emerged in the United States in recent years, a fact that shaped her doctoral studies and her plans for the future. With fresh vision she assesses current developments in dream work and reassesses the role anthropologists might play as they take cognizance of a new sociocultural happening; namely the increasing interest and activity around dreams in the community at large. Paradoxically, it is an easier task for the cultural anthropologist to become immersed in dreams of vastly different cultures than it is to study dreams in the context of his or her own social milieu. A start has to be made, and here we have just such an effort.

Anthropological Fieldwork

Anthropologists are concerned with the cultural context that shapes and defines our human experiences.[1] They seek to understand the cultural frame of reference that gives meaning to particular beliefs, customs, attitudes, and ways of life. Anthropological fieldwork, whether carried out in a small, tribal culture, an urban environment, or an organizational setting, is a method in which the researcher (alone or as part of a team) plays a direct, personal role. Through the technique known as participant observation, she or he studies the patterns of a group by taking part in their world and attempting to see it from their point of view.

Ethnography describes a cultural setting in terms of the concepts and values of its members, and in terms of the perspective derived from the anthropologist's own background, experience, and training. In ethnography, analytical insights are combined with detailed description, and the overall viewpoint is holistic. It takes into account the cognitive, emotional, and social patterns found to exist in the setting, and it recognizes the varied perspectives of people who occupy different roles. All cultural domains contain some ambiguities and inconsistencies, as well as unusual or anomalous situations. Ethnography helps to illuminate these subtle aspects of social reality, which elude a purely quantitative method.

Anthropologists have traditionally traveled by some combination of boat, plane, jeep, donkey, foot, to arrive in another culture, their fieldwork destination. They have, in the vernacular, "gone to the field." Once there, the boundaries between personal and professional life are lost. The ethnographer is immersed in the culture, and in an effort to grasp what is "going on" there, every experience is revealing. It is increasingly common, however, for American anthropology to be concerned with cultural and social issues at home on its own turf. The traditional model of participant observation in a small foraging or horticultural society is adapted to various kinds of settings within the United States. Melinda Bollar Wagner (1983), for example, has studied the Spiritual Frontiers Fellowship, a "nonmainstream" religious movement that arose in the 1950s. In her ethnography, *Metaphysics* in *Midwestern America*, she writes: "One purpose of anthropology is to make the concepts that make up one culture understandable to readers in another. As anthropology 'moves into' the American scene, perhaps this function can be extended to promoting understanding among the various factions of our diverse culture" (p. ix).

My exploration of the dream work movement was in keeping with established trends toward an ethnographic focus on American culture. At the same time, it brought together anthropology and dreams in a new and unorthodox setting. Since I belonged to the same larger society as my informants, and shared an experience-centered knowledge of dreams, I occupied an "insider" position.[2] Yet an anthropologist is never wholly inside, even as an insider, since the researcher's role inherently sets her apart. Such ambiguity is the stuff of dreams, and fieldwork, itself, is a fertile ground for anthropological dreaming.

Dreams and Anthropology: An Overview

Since anthropologists must "attend to those things which have meaning for the people [they study]," and since "many of the peoples encountered by anthropologists have attributed significance to their dreams" (O'Nell 1976, p. 38), it is not surprising that dreams have always found a place in anthropology. Yet, despite evidence of an interest in dreams throughout anthropological history (for reviews of the literature, see Kennedy and Langness 1981, and Tedlock 1987) "dreams remain relatively neglected in the ethnographic descriptions of non-Western peoples" (Gregor 1981, p. 353). Furthermore, the subject of dreams in Western culture, including American society, was (until recent years) virtually ignored (Collins 1984).

The limited scope of traditional anthropological research on dreams reflects cultural assumptions that influence the way anthropologists view dreams. Except in those cultures where dreams play a prominent social role and are given some overt significance (see, for example, J. S. Lincoln's classic study first published in 1935), informants are seldom asked questions about their dream lives. So, although the outwardly visible realms, such as kinship, subsistence, and ritual, are routinely examined in the literature, dream experiences and dream beliefs are not.

Dorothy Eggan's (1949; 1952) midcentury challenge to social science (and to anthropology in particular) to pay more attention to dreams, had little impact on the discipline. She called for studies of the manifest content of dreams as a means of understanding the interplay between personality and culture. She imagined that the difficulties of psychoanalytic theory, as a framework for cross-cultural investigation, stood most firmly in the way of anthropological research on dreams. Yet I think that the problem was (and is) situated in the fact that "[a]ll anthropologists wear the blinders of their own civilization in approaching other cultures; our eyes are as conditioned as those of the people we study" (Reiter 1975, p. 13). Among the many factors that shape anthropological fieldwork are the methods and theories chosen as a means of gathering and analyzing data. In turn, these choices, along with the very selection of a research topic (and decisions regarding what to look for in the field), are affected by a host of unarticulated and assumed ideas about what is relevant, interesting, and valid. Only when these attitudes and assumptions are examined can fresh perspectives be admitted.

The dream work movement sets the stage for a new view of dreams within anthropology, and for the development of a multifaceted "anthropology of dreams." Just as the feminist movement inspired the growth of an anthropology of women, examining omissions and distortions in the discipline's view of women's lives, so can the dream work movement provide the necessary stimulus for anthropologists to take a look at their biases regarding dreams. At the same time, anthropologists, by attending to dreams in both Western and non-Western cultures, can contribute more fully to our understanding of the nature and importance of dreaming.

Signs of Change

Since the 1980s, new interest in dreams has begun to take root in the discipline, and anthropology's role in dream research is growing. Several modern anthropological approaches to the study of dreams are presented in two collections: the winter 1981 issue of *Ethos* (a special issue on dreams), published by the Society for Psychological Anthropology, and *Dreaming: Anthropological and Psychological Interpretations*, edited by Barbara Tedlock (1987). Both collections extend our cross-cultural knowledge of dreams and afford a look at the ways anthropologists think about dreaming. The writings continue to focus on dreams in non-Western cultures, but with implications for the broader study of dreams and imaginal experience.

Tedlock (1987) points out that "[t]he question of the nature of reality is a central philosophical issue that affects the way in which dreaming is valued in a particular culture" (p. 2). She describes both the philosophical underpinnings of Western culture's attitude toward dreams, and the "dream problem" found in North American society. She also calls attention (as does Herdt, same volume) to the narrative shaping of dreams, and highlights the particular communicative dilemma faced by American dreamers:

> [A]lthough most Americans publicly profess the cultural belief, or stereotype, that dreams are meaningless fantasies or confused mental imaginings with no true or lasting reality dimensions, a dream occasionally carries such a strong emotional impact that it is remembered and returns later to consciousness. When this happens, cultural belief wavers slightly, causing the dreamer to wonder if dreams, or at least this one dream, might mean something after all. But if the dreamer tries to tell this dream it may prove difficult. The first problems concern the choice of audience and discourse frame. Since dream telling is not an ordinary public communication in American society, the potential dream sharer faces a difficulty in finding the proper context for the speech event. For example, should it be told at the university to a group of colleagues over lunch? Or is this too public a discourse frame? (pp. 8–9)

Mary-T. Dombeck (1991), who is both an anthropologist and a psychotherapist, explores this question of when and how Americans tell their dreams. Her ethnography, *Dreams* and *Professional Personhood*, concerns the discussion of dreams among staff at two community mental health centers. She explains that, in these local settings, "most of the clinical theories and research in dream psychology have become a part of the constellation of ideas and beliefs about dreams and dream telling" (pp. 21–22). This makes sense in light of the fact that, although dreams lack "public importance," psychotherapy is "one of the private settings in which dream telling is designated to customarily occur" (p. 22).

With the advent of the dream work movement the situation is gradually changing, and dream groups are increasingly visible public contexts for sharing dreams (see Hillman 1990). Iain Edgar, an anthropologist in the United Kingdom, explores the significance of dream groups for anthropology and the mental health professions. Based on his experiences (as a leader and ethnographer) with groups in the United Kingdom, he develops, in *Dreamwork, Anthropology and the Caring Professions* (1995), a perspective on the social and political nature of dreams and dream sharing. He concludes:

> Dream interpretation is . . . a contested site for the contemporary generation of meaning. . . . In this sense I would argue against an absolute set of meanings being defined within a culture[,] with which to understand dream imagery. Rather, dreamwork is a culturally spe-

> cific process that changes over time and is a social, political, personal and professional resource of intriguing, and usually neglected potential. (p. 124)

Edgar builds a bridge not only between the cultural and personal dimensions of dreaming, but also between ethnography and the actual practice of dream work.

A Note on My Fieldwork

Initially, I intended to limit my attention to a single experiential dream group and to study the way in which gender issues—cultural concepts of femaleness and maleness—were reflected in both dream content and the interactions of the group. Then, as I began to explore the recent popular dream literature (including the [no longer published] *Sundance Community Dream Journal*, edited by Henry Reed), I discovered that my dream group was part of a developing social trend: an emphasis on the value of dream sharing and on the creative and practical uses of dreams. I decided to make this "movement" my focus, since it seemed like a good base for reenvisioning an anthropology of dreams in the United States.

Most of my participant observation in dream groups and workshops occurred in or near New York City. It was supplemented by several open-ended interviews, primarily with people who did not belong to dream groups, about the significance of dreams in their personal lives. In addition, I talked and corresponded with people who are professionally involved in dream work, and I spoke with many others about their personal experiences with dreams. The material that I gathered during that early period in the dream work movement's history (1979–1982), combined with my own experiences as a dreamer (both during and since that time), have formed the basis of my thinking about anthropology and dreams.

Fieldwork is by nature an activity that is both interpersonal and introspective. It brings to light many of the anthropologist's own beliefs and assumptions about the world. For me, this process of self-examination was intensified by the level of personal revelation inherent in doing dream work. It has been suggested that paying attention to dreams in the field setting, both one's own dreams and those of one's informants, can illuminate subtle and hidden aspects of the research relationship that influence the process of fieldwork (LeVine 1981). Since I was involved with my own and others' dreams not as an adjunct to fieldwork, but rather as one of its main facets, I experienced a "built-in" sense of these underlying issues. On several occasions, informants reported that they had dreamed about me, and I often dreamed not only of my informants, but also of the topics we discussed during our meetings. It was through the merging of my roles as anthropologist and dream worker that the process of fieldwork unfolded.

The Dream Work Movement

Background: The Cultural Bias Surrounding Dreams

One of the reasons I chose to study anthropology was to learn how cultural influences help to shape our *inner worlds*. In the spring of 1978, as a result of a talk given by Montague Ullman at The New School for Social Research in New York City, I began to consider the impact of Western culture's attitude toward dreams. In his lecture, Ullman spoke of the way in which our society both mystifies and devalues dreams, honoring their role in psychoanalysis, where they are considered the province of "experts," and denying them a place of importance outside this specialized arena. Since anthropologists (like others) learn to think in light of the biases of their own culture, it struck me that these insights into the nature of Western dream ideology were describing the very situation that had influenced anthropology's approach to dreams. That evening, Ullman also discussed the group process he had developed to help people become more familiar with the metaphorical language of dreams. This experiential approach to dream appreciation, in a nonclinical setting, sounded like an excellent way to start altering the personal and social effects of the biases surrounding dreams in our culture.

A member of the dream group observed, during my fieldwork, that "nobody *talks* about dreams, really." Although the discussion of dreams is becoming more common (at least in some circles), we are generally not encouraged, in the course of our everyday lives, to remember our dreams and share them with others. In my own life, telling people about my fieldwork often meant that I served as a catalyst, turning conversations to the subject of dreaming. This usually evoked curiosity and lively discussion (and became the occasion for some spontaneous fieldwork). I found that my willingness to talk about my own dream life helped to gain the trust of informants. Conversations about dreams often led to other topics, such as out-of-body experiences (see, for example, Gabbard and Twemlow 1984) and waking déjà vu. The fear that such experiences might be seen as weird, or dismissed as an emotional disturbance, increases the vulnerability that many people feel about sharing their private worlds. "One of the things that frustrates me about the culture," said one of my informants (a member of the dream group), "is that I can't talk about the things that interest me, in social situations, without being thought of as eccentric." She added that the dream group gave her "energy to go into those other situations."

Despite a social climate inhospitable to dreams and "altered" states of consciousness, many people privately nurture an interest in these realms. Tedlock (1987) makes the important observation that "[e]nthusiasm for the imaginal . . . surfaces again and again in Western culture within literary and artistic circles" (p. 4). One informant, a thirty-year-old man who grew up in a rural New England town, felt that paying attention to dreams was a "natural outgrowth" of the artistic encouragement he received from his parents. "I often tell people my dreams because they *excite* me," he said, "but I also hesitate because, while they have power for *me*, they often don't for others." He explained that when his dreams are "particularly intense," it is as though "everything is pregnant with possibilities. . . . There's life. . . . You feel in rapport with things. . . . It's what you call being 'high.'" Another informant, a thirty-eight-year-old woman who came to the United States from Latvia at the age of three, had begun, several years earlier, to keep a journal that included dreams. For her, dreams are "like going to a movie at night. You just never know what's going to happen." She finds that they "set a tone for the day" and "often work like a catalyst," leading to "new thoughts" of the people about whom she has dreamed. Neither of these informants felt inclined to join a dream group, yet both were keenly appreciative of the ways that dreaming touches their lives.

In a self-help resource guide on dreams, published in 1976, Dick McLeester reported that "scattered individuals" were "starting to listen to their dreams to see what they might offer" (p. 7). He regarded this trend as an early sign of a changing cultural attitude toward dreams. He wrote:

> People are looking to other times and cultures to see what different attitudes they had towards their dreams and what value [they] got from them. Dreams are being used as inspiration for art, theater and poetry. People are gathering in groups with the specific intention of sharing and working on their dreams, and exploring ways of integrating them into all areas of their lives. (p. 7)

These were the first visible stirrings of the current dream work movement.

History and Description of the Movement

Since the early 1970s, a growing number of people in the United States have become involved with dreams, and a popular dream literature, guiding and encouraging this activity, has been steadily increasing (see, for example, Bosnak 1988; Delaney 1979; Garfield 1974, 1984; McLeester 1976; Moss 1996; Reed 1985; Taylor 1983, 1992; and Ullman and Zimmerman 1979). In January 1982, Bill Stimson, of New York City, published the first issue of the grassroots newsletter known as the *Dream Network Bulletin.* The *Bulletin* gave ideas and information about dreams, made suggestions for starting dream groups, and enabled dream workers with similar interests to "find" one another. At the same time, a loosely structured organization, called the Dream Community of New York, began to offer free dream workshops on one or two evenings each month. For people in the New York City area who were interested in dreams, these evenings were a chance to meet and learn from one another.

Thus New York City, and other parts of the country, drew attention to the practice of "dream work" through a variety of dream-oriented events offered locally. For two years, publications affiliated with the parent newsletter in New York City were issued from other geographical areas. *Lucidity and Beyond* began in New Jersey and later moved to California, *Fusion* came out of Washington State, and *Dream Craft* originated in Virginia. During this period, the network of subscribers extended to other countries, and the *Dream Network Bulletin* became a lively forum for the developing grassroots dream movement.

In 1984, Chris Hudson assumed the editorship of the *Bulletin.* He unified the publication and started producing it on a bimonthly basis from his home in Brooklyn, New York. By May/June 1985 (which marked another editorial shift) about seven hundred people were regularly receiving the newsletter (Chris Hudson, personal communication). At that time, the *Bulletin* entered the hands of two well-known dream workers in Virginia, Robert Van de Castle and Henry Reed. They continued, for nearly two years, to provide a heterogeneous dream community with a vehicle for sharing diverse perspectives on dreams.

Another editorial transition occurred in March/April 1987. From that issue, through the special triple issue of July–December 1989, Linda Magallón, of California, was at the helm. Then, with the winter 1990 issue, a new name and editor appeared: the *Dream Network Journal,* produced by Roberta Ossana of Utah. Now (in 1997) the journal is simply called *Dream Network,* and Roberta Ossana remains its devoted editor. She expanded the overall theme to include both dreams and myth and has sought a greater cross-cultural focus. In the spring of 1997, the number of readers (as distinct from subscribers) was estimated to be about five thousand (Roberta Ossana, personal communication).

There have been many paths of entry into the dream work movement. One of the earliest routes was involvement in the human potential movement that was active during the 1960s (see Domhoff 1985, pp. 3, 4). Some of its members, advocating attention to "personal growth," saw dreams as a source of insight into themselves and our human condition. Other people have encountered dream work in the context of a metaphysical or spiritual organization, such as the Association for Research and Enlightenment (dedicated to the work of the American psychic, Edgar Cayce) or the Spiritual Frontiers Fellowship. Still others have been inspired to pursue dreams further as a result of their experiences in therapy. For many women, the feminist movement has become an avenue to dream work, prompting them to look toward dreams for a deeper understanding of their identities as women. Now, with the expansion of dream work itself, more people are "discovering" dreams as a result of direct exposure to the dream work movement. This occurs through workshops, classes, lectures, publications, and dream groups, as well as simple word of mouth concerning approaches to dream work.

So far, there has not been a sociocultural analysis of the dream work movement, showing how factors such as sex, age, ethnic background, and social class influence one's relationship to dreams. It is clear, for example, that although the ratio of women to men is becoming more balanced, the majority of dream workers are, and have been, women. In the early 1980s, they outnumbered men seven to one in Montague Ullman's experiential dream groups (Montague Ullman, personal communication). This is not surprising, since women's traditional role, in our society, calls for sensitivity to emotional issues and a concern for the quality of relationships—themes that figure prominently in dream work. On the other hand, more men are beginning to cultivate these traits, and some see dream work as a chance to explore their own "feminine" side.

People of many ages engage in dream work, and there has been some attention to the benefits of doing dream work with children (see, for example, Garfield 1984; Ullman and Zimmerman 1979, ch. 9). The potential value of dreams in the lives of the elderly, however, is a topic that still needs to be pursued (for a review of research on dreams and aging, see Van de Castle 1985).

Though white, middle-class dreamers are predominant in the movement, its appeal may be broadening with time. Diversity will be encouraged as more people of color assume leadership positions in conferences and groups, and as the dialogue on dreams and racism continues to grow (see Taylor 1992, ch. 5). It is important to remember that some people privately pay attention to dreams, without attending dream groups, conferences, and workshops. One of my informants, an African American woman in her late twenties, said it was taken for granted in her family that dreams enrich conversation. She had the impression that, among African Americans as a whole, dreams are "talked about and accepted" more readily than they are among white Americans. We need to explore the many variations in people's relationships to dreams within our complex, multiethnic culture.

The term *dream work movement* became popular during 1982 and 1983 to designate the growing trend toward awareness of dreams. As more and more people got together to share an interest in dreams, they extended their insights and enthusiasm to others. At the heart of this social movement is a belief in the intrinsic value of the dream as a source of knowledge about ourselves and the world we inhabit. Though a basic sense of the communicative power of dreams underlies the diverse approaches to dream work, the specific goals of this activity are expressed in a variety of ways. In my own group, Montague Ullman spoke of emotional repair and healing; another leader stated that dream work is the "safest, quickest way to develop the psychic faculty." And a third teacher of dream work techniques viewed dreams as a "direct line to the soul," enabling us to contact a deep source of inner wisdom. Most nonclinical approaches to dream work reflect an underlying belief that dreams can be understood by the lay person, without recourse to a professional analyst. Montague Ullman (1982) has referred to this principle as "deprofessionalizing the dream."

The dream work movement emphasizes experiential methods, rather than didactic and theoretical approaches. In the broadest sense, experiential dream work encompasses all the activities that are involved in maintaining an active relationship with dreams. These include learning to recall dreams, keeping a dream journal, and sharing dreams with others. Special emphasis, however, is placed on techniques that encourage the dreamer to reenter the dream and to experience it again from a waking perspective. Insight is thought to arise from this felt sense of the dream, combined with a careful unpacking of the images to discover which possible meanings ring true. Montague Ullman, in particular, stresses that dream appreciation "requires work and takes energy" (personal communication). His structured groups are designed to create a safe emotional environment for accomplishing the necessary work. At the same time, the dream work movement encourages creativity and play, through a variety of expressive techniques for engaging with dreams (see Reed 1985).

Collectively, the various styles of nonclinical dream work share a greater affinity with Jung's view of the dream than with Freud's. They assume, like Jung, that dreams are constructed to reveal, rather than hide, their messages, and they concur with his emphasis on the healthy dimensions of the self embodied in dreams (see Ullman and Zimmerman 1979, ch. 3). The Jungian technique of "amplification," which one workshop leader described as a "process of enrichment of the [dream] symbol" (by means of exploring its various facets), is among the popular dream work methods borrowed from particular schools of therapy.

Many dream workers are also attracted to Jung's theory of archetypes. It refers to the "*tendency* to form representations and motifs, *not* [to] 'inherited representations' themselves" (Krippner 1997, p. 24). By exploring cross-cultural ritual and myth

> Jung began to suspect that there were a number of universally recurrent themes. It was this speculation that produced his theory of archetypes, attributing the recurrence of various images and activities to mental structures that have characterized human beings throughout history. . . . Jung compares the process to the tendency or impulse of birds to build nests and of ants to form colonies. (Krippner 1997, p. 24)

The propensity for recurrent themes and patterns, toward which Jung's theory points, is often equated with the notion of fixed images. Efforts have been made by various writers to alter Jung's formulation and to reemphasize the contextual nature of imagery. Some feminist dream workers, for example, have addressed the restrictive gender stereotypes found in Jungian theory (see Lauter and Rupprecht 1985). They encourage modern women to participate in the creation of new archetypal images that speak to their changing situations as women. Similarly, Kelly Bulkeley (1994), in exploring the religious dimension of dreams, stresses the cultural context of metaphor. His concept of "root metaphor dreams" parallels Jung's "archetypal dreams," but explicitly rejects the idea of universal imagery (see pp. 169–171).[4]

The Gestalt techniques of Fritz Perls have also captured the attention of dream workers. Based on the theory that all dream elements represent parts of the self, these methods invite dreamers to identify with, and to act out, the various characters and objects that appear in their dreams. One exercise derived from the Gestalt approach involves "dialoguing" with a dream character in order to experience what it's like to "be" that character.

In addition to creating new contexts for sharing dreams outside the realm of therapy, and teaching new ways of attuning to the language of dreams, the dream work movement encourages investigation of the full range of consciousness associated with dreams and sleep. The conventional view holds not only that dreams are unintelligible to the lay person and that their importance lies solely in their usefulness for therapy, but also that they constitute a "unitary phenomenon" (Tart 1969, p. 171), lacking qualitative distinctions. Yet, as cognitive psychologist Harry Hunt shows in *The Multiplicity of Dreams*, our dreaming mind has rich and varied expressions.

Experimental research confirms that it is possible to experience a wakinglike consciousness while dreaming (La Berge 1985), a phenomenon with which many of my informants (and I) were familiar. Since the academic world both reflects and perpetuates culturally accepted biases, its initial doubts about "lucid dreaming" (knowing, in a dream, that one dreams) pointed to a more pervasive belief about the nature of consciousness (and dreaming). There is a strong current of interest, within the dream work movement, in the phenomenon of lucid dreaming and its relationship to several other altered states. Jayne Gackenbach edited *Lucidity Letter* (later known as *Lucidity*), which dealt with lucid dreaming and related topics. *Lucidity and Beyond* (edited by Sally Shute) was a quarterly of the *Dream Network Bulletin*, and it also focused exclusively on lucid dreaming. This particular branch of the dream work movement, perhaps more than any other, inspired an interest in the philosophical and spiritual aspects of our dream lives. It has pursued the links among lucidity, out-of-body consciousness, and near-death experience (on the subject of near-death experience see Ring 1980).

Experiential dream work can increase not only one's emotional openness and sensitivity to dreams, but also one's level of "sophistication" as a dreamer. Anthropologist Roy d'Andrade (1961) observed that "[c]ultural beliefs and theories about dreams . . . appear to affect [both] the content of dreams and emotional reactions to [them]" (pp. 314–15). We can witness this malleability of dream content in the well-known tendency for a client in therapy to dream in a style that matches the interpretive framework of the therapist. Likewise, it appears that the type of consciousness experienced during dreaming is amenable to our particular expectations. Several of my informants reported an increased amount of lucid dreaming simply as a result of their desire for the experience and their belief that it was possible. (This was coupled, no doubt, with the added power of suggestion stemming from regularly reading and talking about lucidity.) By learning to value our dreams, and by exploring realms of consciousness previously unknown to us, we challenge the cultural demand to limit attention to ordinary waking.

The Social Dimension of Dream Work

Many dream workers feel that engaging with dreams is a means toward community healing; that dream work has far-reaching implications for change. In his handbook on dreams, Dick McLeester (1976) speaks of consciousness raising and social change, reminding us that "[o]ur dreams reflect the world around us as well as within us" (p. 21). Attending to the cultural as well as the personal messages in dreams helps to shed light on the intimate connections between these two "realities." Furthermore, as Montague Ullman and Nan Zimmerman (1979) point out, "[t]he rigorously honest reflections of personal and social truths that appear in our dreams present us with the opportunity to reexamine both personal and social myths and to begin the process of dismantling them and moving forward" (p. 200). Despite a wealth of cultural information inherent in the dream, this dimension is seldom made explicit in dream work settings. An exception can be found in the group work of Iain Edgar, whose concern is to show "how the human capacity for meaning-making is embedded within the cultural context" (1995, p. 40).

Jeremy Taylor devotes a chapter of his book, *Dream Work*, to the question of "dream work and social responsibility," highlighting some of the concrete ways for putting this theme into practice. In summary, he states that dream work can help to effect social change by "breaking down our prematurely closed prejudices, opinions, ideologies, and world views. Group dream work can also create a community of support and understanding which can sustain us in the efforts to remake global society in a wiser, more humane and just form, as well as [offer] specific creative insights and ideas to accomplish this vitally important task" (p. 19).

The Academic Realm

The dream work movement, like the feminist movement, has academic and grassroots segments, and these represent complementary ways of addressing the same broad goal (Hillman 1984a). Both are concerned with making dreams more important, culturally: the academic by developing new avenues of research and practical application and creating a multidisciplinary perspective; the grassroots by encouraging group dream work, informal sharing of dreams, and various kinds of networking among dreamers. As the movement grows, an increasing number of people find themselves in both camps.

The Association for the Study of Dreams (ASD) was founded in 1983 by a small group of dream workers seeking to support professional interest in dreams. Its first annual conference was held in San Francisco during the summer of 1984, and it has since acquired an international membership. The creation of this organization elicited concern among some grassroots dream workers that it would undermine the egalitarian spirit of dream work. Thus it is noteworthy that Robert Van de Castle, a former president of ASD, has also served as editor of the grassroots journal, Dream Network. That one individual publicly represented both aspects of the dream work movement is perhaps symbolic of the trend toward unity that followed.[5]

Creating an Anthropology of Dreams

By increasing our awareness of the ways in which dreams have been devalued, the movement encourages a closer link between anthropology and dreaming. The presence of the dream work movement, and of new ways to integrate dreams into daily life, makes dreams more accessible to everyday reflection. The increasing social awareness of dreams is significant for anthropology because it means that, as part of a social milieu whose attitude toward dreams is changing, many anthropologists will become more interested in, and attuned to, dreams.

The Importance of Experiential Dream Work

The overall "consciousness" of dreams that results from exposure to the movement is brought home by an intimate, firsthand knowledge of dreaming. I think that a subjective knowledge of the dream world is as important as fieldwork skills for ethnographers who question others about their dream lives. Anthropologists must ultimately rely on themselves to make sense of events in the field, and their own perceptions serve as a primary tool. These will be more finely tuned to the many nuances of dreaming if they are rooted in a personal exploration of dreams.

Since I brought to the field a personal experience of many of the things I encountered, it was easier for me to ask questions and interpret responses. This meant using my experience as a means of awakening imagination and guiding me to alternative possibilities. The vocabulary used to talk about dreams is subject to wide variation in meaning, and expressions like "good dream," "bad dream," "strange dream," mean different things to different people. Furthermore, categories of dream experience, like "flying dream" and "lucid dream," do not have single, standard definitions (Tart 1984, discusses this problem in regard to lucid dreaming). It is important for anthropologists and informants, both, to clarify their use of terms, even when their native language is the same.

An experiential background is also beneficial for enhancing rapport with informants. Dream telling is a personal, and often sensitive, form of communication, and empathy on the part of the listener is necessary in order to establish trust. Being an "experienced dreamer" and a skilled dream worker, in the context of one's own culture, is helpful for studying dreams in any setting. The anthropologist familiar with the contours of his or her own dream landscape is more likely to respond with "felt" understanding to the dream experiences of others.

Cognicentrism and Ethnocentrism

The union of experiential and academic perspectives helps to minimize cognicentrism: ignorance, and prejudice stemming from the "narrowness of someone's *conscious* [inner world] experience" (Harner 1980, p. xiv). Though the problem of cognicentrism often arises in the context of one's own group, it can also appear as a form of ethnocentrism (i.e., *cultural* bias). This is because "reality itself [is] culturally defined" (Tedlock 1987, p. 2), though we usually take our world view for granted.

It is important, in approaching dreams, that we not impose our realities on others, and that attachments to our own point of view be carefully examined. In an ethnically diverse society such as the United States, our inner worlds are as varied as our outward customs and habits. This was illustrated in my relationship with a Puerto Rican informant who shared with me her gift for mediumship. To her, dreams were a means of receiving guidance from the spirits, and as she gave me advice on how to contact my own spirit guides, I learned about the terrain of both our dream worlds.

Anthropologists need to question whether the concepts and categories they adopt are adequate containers for what they find in the field (Hillman 1884b, p. 2). Thus it is appropriate to ask whether constructs such as "lucid dream" are useful tools for cross-cultural research. We may find, for example, that members of another culture experience what we call "lucid dreams," yet we may fail to learn what, if anything, those experiences mean to them. By offering rich descriptions of the role of dreaming in various settings, anthropologists can increase our appreciation of the cultural context of dreaming. "Moreover," writes Iain Edgar (1995), "social anthropology has provided us with a wide array of dreamwork uses in different, largely third-world, societies which make a powerful contribution to a broadening of our awareness of the potential social use of dream imagery" (p. 40).

Ethnography of Dreaming in America

Calling for anthropological studies of dreaming in "contemporary middle-class America," Kathleen Collins (1984) points out that "as is true cross-culturally, dream telling in America has a variety of purposes and patterns" (p. 3). Mary-T. Dombeck's pioneering study of dreaming in the United States was mentioned in an earlier section of this chapter. Another interesting contribution is an article by Larry Peters (1983) called "The Role of Dreams in the Life of a Mentally Retarded Individual." Based on ethnographic research in a California workshop for the mentally retarded, it offers an account of the significance of dreams in a young man's religious life. Since many people give dreams a special function in their lives (whether or not this meaning is actually stated), Peters's approach could be more widely used, by anthropologists, to study individuals' unique relationships with dreams.

Some of my informants, for example, had deliberately done, in waking life, things that corresponded to the contents of their dreams. They had telephoned people they dreamed of calling, and, in one case, visited the town where a "dream" vacation took place. Several said that they turned to dreams for guidance in personal relationships, and one used dreams to initiate difficult topics in conversation.

There are many aspects of dream life within the United States for cultural anthropologists to consider: What do dreamers "think" about dreams? What are their dream worlds like? How are their world views influenced by dreams? How do dreams shape daily life? For those involved in the area known as the anthropology of consciousness, the changing awareness of dreams is especially exciting. It has brought about a greater recognition of the psychic and spiritual dimensions of dreams, and of sleep as a pathway to several altered states. How these issues are actually experienced by contemporary dreamers merits ethnographic attention.

Furthermore, dreams need not be confined to studies that focus on them; much can be gained by including them in fieldwork, generally. (This is true of fieldwork in any cultural setting, in or outside the United States.) Since dreams can mirror and affect our cultural, social, and spiritual condition, their images lend perspective to many problems. An urban ethnographer told me that dreams come up in his drug research, and that some of the images shared by informants enhance his knowledge of drug use.

For informants, sharing dreams is akin to telling a life story, and it frequently has a strong emotional impact. In a culture that equates the formal dream-telling interview with therapy, anthropologists must be mindful of their position. Without acting as therapists, they must give the kind of support that allows the dreams to do their own healing. One of my informants looked forward to his second dream-sharing interview, when he would have an opportunity to continue "going through a lot of hard stuff."

Dream Work and "Practicing Anthropology"

Many anthropologists are employed in settings outside academia, doing what is known as "practicing anthropology." They work in the public and private sectors, in institutions and programs, often as part of an interdisciplinary team. Practicing anthropologists who are interested in dreams can explore the dream's role in the workplace, and even introduce the idea of regular dream work sessions for staff. Iain Edgar (1995), for example, has "used dream and imagework as part of a team-building process" and "found that working with a mixed gender, multi-professional health sector staff . . . [can] be successful," as long as the staff group is committed (p. 49).

There is even a potential job description directly linked to dreams, for anthropologists who would like to further the spread of dream work. They can serve as consultants to schools, hospitals, senior centers, prisons, and so on—places that want to develop programs on dreams. Such a role would combine the skills of dream worker and ethnographer, since successful programs must be tailored to their settings.

Anthropological Imagery in Dreams and Dream Work

The emotional intensity of fieldwork makes it a rich impetus for dreams. Iain Edgar (1989) has suggested that ethnographers' dreams are a "relevant source of data," contributing knowledge and insight in the field. He describes how his study of a therapeutic community for disturbed adolescents in Britain was enriched by attending to the imagery of his dreams.

I, too, remained close to my dreams in the field and found them to be good guides. When, as a beginning anthropologist, I questioned the validity of my work, my dreams were quick to offer a bit of humor. My true ethnographic purpose, they said, was to go to the countryside, immersing myself in research on the nature of farm life. In my pastoral image, I harbored a wish for a simpler task, and setting, than to live in the city and be in graduate school. And "country" is a playful reference to a common theme for anthropologists: fieldwork "in" or "out" of the country. Moreover, the idea of fieldwork on a farm suggests another pun: "fieldwork" is something that farmers do, too! Metaphorically, I was a farmer learning to cultivate a field, and thus to develop the central skill of my trade.

As I continued to explore the dream work movement, I found myself dreaming not only about fieldwork, but also about the nature of anthropology and the significance of working with dreams. In a dream that occurred at the time I was writing the original version of this chapter (in 1985), a sculptural image captured the essence of experiential dream work, compared with traditional dream interpretation. In the dream, I attended a conference where an exhibit had been set up to represent these two approaches to dreams. It consisted of two square boxes in which identical dream scenes were fashioned (the same dream, but dealt with in different ways). One of the sculptures—the one representing experiential dream work—was mechanical. When a button was pressed, the box lit up, and the parts began to move. This lively display was in contrast to a dull, motionless companion—the sculpture that symbolized orthodox dream analysis.

The message of this dream can be summarized by a passage I came across several months later: "*Working with* dreams is a dynamic and constructive response to the whole potential of the dream, whereas *interpreting* dreams may become a static or passive response to a limited portion of that with which the dream deals" (Puryear 1982, p. 137). My image captures the dynamic quality of experience-centered dream work, as well as the sense of surprise and play that so often accompanies the process. In addition, the public setting of the dream suggests that, beyond my personal view, I perceive a similar "meaning" afloat in the dream work movement generally.

The dream's ability to reflect the complex feelings that accompany fieldwork, and to help illuminate ethnographic concerns, is only one of the ways in which a felt connection arises between anthropology and dreams. Just as *dreams* can contribute to anthropologists' self-understanding, and to their grasp of events that occur in the field, so can *anthropology* offer metaphorical images that are capable of enriching our understanding of dreams. One of my dreams, for example, posed an analogy between dream work and fieldwork. The dream included a conversation about dreams, described in this excerpt from my journal:

> I explain that meaning is inherent in the making of a dream, and that, although the images and symbols may lend themselves to metaphorical description of a particular circumstance in the dreamer's life, that does not necessarily mean that the dream mind *intended* such a connection. To get at the dream's own meaning, the dreamer has to suspend waking judgment and learn to "think" with the "dream mind." I am saying that the dream world constitutes its own reality, and one has to be an ethnographer of that realm in order to understand it.

For me, the most interesting aspect of having an individual "dream partner"[6] was the mutual exploration of two very different dream worlds. Just as a single dream embodies one's individuality, so does the dream world—manifested in a body of dreams that occur over time—bear the stamp of one's uniqueness. Along with an ability to appreciate the meaning and creativity of a single dream, dream work can foster sensitivity to the character of the dream world as a whole. In dream groups, the more familiar the dreamer's inner landscape is to the rest of the group (as a result of frequent dream sharing), the more often will the projected meanings supplied by the group flow from their intuitive sense of the dreamer's "style." The kind of awareness involved in this process resembles ethnographic understanding—the ability to imagine thinking and seeing with the mind and eyes of an "insider."

Conclusion

Anthropologists can make an important contribution to the field of dream research and to the grassroots effort to change our Western cultural attitude toward dreams. Besides expanding the scope of cross-cultural research on dreams and increasing our knowledge of the cultural context of dreaming, anthropologists can offer practical support for the changes that are occurring in the settings and methods of dream sharing.

To accomplish these goals, anthropologists need to start lifting the cultural blinders that have conditioned their perspective on dreams in the past. They need to strengthen their interest in the role of dreams in human experience, including their role in cultures where they have previously been ignored. Since several anthropologists have joined the Association for the Study of Dreams, and published innovative studies on dreaming, there is evidence that an interweaving is already under way between anthropology and dream work.

An experience-centered knowledge of dreams is a valuable adjunct to fieldwork skills for anthropologists who do dream research. Familiarity with the image-based language of dreams, and with the multidimensional dream world, increases sensitivity to the emotional and cognitive subtleties of dream sharing. This, in turn, helps to build rapport with informants and enhances the ability to elicit and clarify information about dreams.

Dream work offers the anthropologist an added perspective on fieldwork, in its ethnographic and personal dimensions, and fieldwork offers the dream worker a useful metaphorical image for guiding waking journeys into the dream world. The combined roles of dream worker and fieldworker can bring about a finer awareness of the "objectivity" practiced by observers. Inherent in looking at the world "out there" is the play of our own images; we are, as biologist Rupert Sheldrake notes, "projecting out images as well as taking them in" (Fox and Sheldrake 1996, p. 90). Our dreams can help us to understand the intricacies of this process, and the personal and social lenses through which we have grown accustomed to see.

Notes

1. I wrote the original version of this chapter more than a decade ago, while still in graduate school. My view of the anthropology of dreams had been shaped by recent fieldwork, which brought me in touch with the burgeoning dream work movement. Since then, the movement has grown considerably, becoming international in scope, and several anthropologists have played a part in its unfolding. Not only does this show a revitalized interest in dreams within anthropology, but it brings to the dream work movement, with its multidisciplinary focus, a strong anthropological presence.

Though my own fieldwork, in recent years, has not focused on dreams, dreaming is still a vital part of my world. It enriches my anthropological imagination, as well as my everyday life, and it remains a theme in my reading, letter-writing, conversation, and reflection.

2. This chapter refers to cultural anthropology and cultural anthropologists. Anthropology, as a whole, embraces four separate but closely related subfields: archeology, linguistics, physical anthropology, and cultural anthropology.

3. So that the reader is aware of my cultural background in the context of studying dreams: I am a middle-class white American who grew up in the United States (in Midwestern and Eastern parts of the country).

4. For a stunning example of dreams that exhibit a collective theme, see Michael Ortiz Hill (1994), *Dreaming the End of the World: Apocalypse as a Rite of Passage.*

5. The ASD publishes its own newsletter, as well as a scholarly journal called *Dreaming.*

6. A "dream partner" is a person with whom one regularly works on dreams in a one-to-one, rather than group, format.

References

Bosnak, R. *A Little Course in Dreams.* Boston: Shambhala, 1988.

Bulkeley, K. *The Wilderness of Dreams.* Albany: State University of New York Press, 1994.

Collins, K. "Anthropology of Dreaming in America." *ASD Newsletter,* 1, 4 (1984): 1, 3.

D'Andrade, R.G. "Anthropological Studies of Dreams." In Francis L. K. Hsu, ed. *Psychological Anthropology.* Homewood, Ill.: Dorsey Press, 1961.

Delaney, G. *Living Your Dreams.* San Francisco: Harper & Row, 1979.

Dombeck, M.-T.B. *Dreams and Professional Personhood.* Albany: State University of New York Press, 1991.

Domhoff, G. W. *The Mystique of Dreams.* Berkeley: University of California Press, 1985.

Edgar, I. R. "Dreaming as Ethnography." Paper presented at the annual conference of the U.K. Association of Social Anthropology, 1989.

———. *Dreamwork, Anthropology and the Caring Professions.* Aldershot, U.K.: Avebury, 1995.

Eggan, D. "The Significance of Dreams for Anthropological Research." *American Anthropologist,* 51, 12 (1949): 177–98.

———. "The Manifest Content of Dreams: A Challenge to Social Science." *American Anthropologist,* 54, 4 (1952): 469–85.

Fox, M., and Sheldrake, R. *Natural Grace.* New York: Doubleday, 1996.

Gabbard, G. O., and Twemlow, S. W. *With the Eyes of the Mind.* New York: Praeger, 1984.

Garfield, P. *Creative Dreaming.* New York: Ballantine, 1974.

———. *Your Child's Dreams.* New York: Ballantine, 1984.

Gregor, T. "A Content Analysis of Mehinaku Dreams." *Ethos,* 9, 4 (1981): 353–90.

Harner, M. *The Way of the Shaman.* New York: Harper & Row, 1980.

Herdt, G. "Selfhood and Discourse in Sambia Dream Sharing." In B. Tedlock, ed. *Dreaming: Anthropological and Psychological Interpretations.* Cambridge: Cambridge University Press, 1987.

Hill, M. O. *Dreaming the End of the World.* Dallas: Spring Publications, 1994.

Hillman, D. J. "Making Room: A Perspective on the Existence of a Professional Dream Association." *Dream Network Bulletin,* 3, 4 (1984a): 10–13.

———. "Lucid Dream Consciousness: A Subjective Account." *Dream Network Bulletin,* 3, 5 (1984b): 1–5.

———. "The Emergence of the Grassroots Dreamwork Movement." In S. Krippner, ed. *Dreamtime and Dreamwork.* Los Angeles: Jeremy P. Tarcher, 1990.

Hunt, H. T. *The Multiplicity of Dreams.* New Haven, Conn.: Yale University Press, 1989.

Kennedy, J. G., and Langness, L. L. "Introduction." *Ethos,* 9, 4 (1981): 249–57.

Krippner, S. "The Role Played by Mandalas in Navajo and Tibetan Rituals." *Anthropology of Consciousness,* 8, 1 (1997): 22–31.

LaBerge, S. *Lucid Dreaming.* Los Angeles: Jeremy P. Tarcher, 1985.

Lauter, E., and Rupprecht, C. S., eds. *Feminist Archetypal Theory.* Knoxville: University of Tennessee Press, 1985.

LeVine, S. “Dreams of the Informant about the Researcher: Some Difficulties Inherent in the Research Relationships.” *Ethos,* 9, 4 (1981): 276–93.

Lincoln, J. S. *The Dream in Primitive Cultures.* New York: Johnson Reprint Corporation, 1970 [originally published 1935].

McLeester, D. *Welcome to the Magic Theater.* Amherst, Mass.: Food for Thought Publications [self-published], 1976.

Moss, R. *Conscious Dreaming.* New York: Crown Trade Paperbacks, 1996.

O'Nell, C. W. *Dreams, Culture, and the Individual.* San Francisco: Chandler and Sharp, 1976.

Peters, L. G. “The Role of Dreams in the Life of a Mentally Retarded Individual.” *Ethos,* 11, 1/2 (1983): 49–65.

Puryear, H. B. *The Edgar Cayce Primer.* New York: Bantam Books, 1982.

Reed, H. *Getting Help from Your Dreams.* Virginia Beach, Va.: Inner Vision Publishing, 1985.

Reiter, R. R. “Introduction.” In R. R. Reiter, ed. *Toward an Anthropology of Women.* New York: Monthly Review Press, 1975.

Ring, K. *Life at Death.* New York: Coward, McCann, and Geohegan, 1980.

Tart, C. T. “The ‘High’ Dream: A New State of Consciousness.” In C. T. Tart, ed. *Altered States of Consciousness.* New York: Anchor Books, 1969.

———. “Terminology in Lucid Dream Research.” *Lucidity Letter,* 3, 1 (1984): 4–6.

Taylor, J. *Dream Work.* Ramsey, N.J.: Paulist Press, 1983.

———. *Where People Fly and Water Runs Uphill.* New York: Warner Books, 1992.

Tedlock, B., ed. *Dreaming: Anthropological and Psychological Interpretations.* Cambridge: Cambridge University Press, 1987.

———. “Dreaming and Dream Research.” In B. Tedlock, ed. *Dreaming: Anthropological and Psychological Interpretations.* Cambridge: Cambridge University Press, 1987.

Ullman, M. “On Relearning the Forgotten Language: Deprofessionalizing the Dream.” *Contemporary Psychoanalysis,* 18, 1 (1982): 153–59.

Ullman, M., and Zimmerman, N. *Working with Dreams.* Los Angeles: Jeremy P. Tarcher, 1979.

Van de Castle, B. "Dreams and the Aging Process." *Dream Network Bulletin,* 4, 4 (1985): 1, 3, 4.

Wagner, M. B. *Metaphysics in Midwestern America.* Columbus: Ohio State University Press, 1983.

CHAPTER FIVE

Dream Reflection and Creative Writing

RICHARD M. JONES

Several decades ago Richard Jones chose as the setting for his interest in dreams a small experimental college on the West Coast, the Evergreen State College in Olympia, Washington. At that time he had already published his first book on dreams, *Ego Synthesis in Dreams.* Two more books were to follow. In *The New Psychology of Dreaming* Jones developed his own theoretical ideas against the background of the new experimental work on sleep and dreams. *The Dream Poet,* a most original contribution, was based on a college course Jones developed that combined what he referred to as dream reflection and literature. His goal, a successful one, was to help students tap into the creativity that goes into the fashioning of meaningful dream images, to use dream work both as a way of deepening their appreciation of literature and to strengthen writings of their own creation.

Jones's studies have led him into a deeper pursuit of the connection between the metaphorical potential of dream imagery and the origin of language. In a book he was working on at the time of his death, he further developed his ideas on the relationship of literature, dreams, and the nature of metaphor.

The program he initiated at Evergreen, introducing dream reflection into a literature course, is unique and one that could profitably be emulated at all institutions of higher learning.

Creative writing requires transcendence, or at least subordination of self. This truism is the foundation of creative writing.

Dreams, we are told by Freudian psychologists, seek to hide us from ourselves; and, we are told by some post-Freudian psychologists, dreams seek to reveal us to ourselves. Neither view can illuminate the relation of dreams to creativity, because both raise the self to the focus of their attention. This was inevitable in view of the fact that dreams were rediscovered in modern times by the first psychoanalyst, and the study of dreams has since continued almost exclusively in psychotherapeutic settings. People go to psychotherapists for help in getting more satisfyingly into themselves—not for help in getting more creatively out of themselves—although this sometimes does also occur as a result of successful psychotherapy.

What if dreams had been discovered for our time not by a psychiatrist but by, say, an epistemologist? An epistemologist would not feel obliged to pursue his interest in dreams by reference to ego defense or ego synthesis or ego anything else. He need not even feel obliged to begin his study of dreams by asking what they might mean, or be made to mean, to their hosts. He could simply start by recognizing dreams for what they are. I believe such a basic epistemological view is that a dream is an effortlessly and unself-consciously produced series of potential metaphors connected by a story line.

In dreams we kiss ourselves good-by. *Of* us dreams are; for us they are not. They are neither more honest than we are (Fromm) nor more dishonest than we are (Freud). Dreams can be made to respond to our selfish wakeful interests in the insightful ways with which psychotherapists and their patients are familiar, because dreams are *not responsible*. They are not irresponsible either; dreams are simply and sublimely indifferent to the only locus of responsibility that makes any sense in the modern world: ourselves. Dreams are metaphorical visions of being alive cleared of the shades of being alive inside a self.

This might now be obvious had dreams not been rediscovered for our time as a part of the invention of psychoanalysis. For example, Erich Fromm (1951): "In dreams we need not look at the outside world; we look at our inner world, are concerned exclusively with ourselves." . . . "In sleep the realm of necessity has given way to the realm of freedom in which 'I am' is the only system to which thoughts and feelings refer" (p. 27). Freedom?! If freedom to think and feel nothing but my "I am" system were truly what my dreams did for me, I should here and now resolve to perform the very easy task of forgetting them forevermore.

To have to think and feel the unending noontime of self is the necessity placed on my wakeful life by the society into which I was born that I most regret. I don't go sulking round about this ever-pressing injunction to hold the treasures of being alive fast on the spindle of my little view of life, but I do mean to avoid the necessity whenever possible. My dreams, I find, provide ingenious guidance in pursuit of this avoidance. Whenever I find myself having traversed the morning distance from the bed to the bathroom with naught but thoughts of relieving my bladder and shaving my whiskers; whenever I notice my lady and I to have repeated the same sequence of love moves; whenever a whole day passes in which I have not recalled a line from Shakespeare; whenever my reading of the daily newspaper begins to seem an activity of some durable significance; whenever, that is, the burdens of being nothing but myself become noticeable—I try to remember a dream. Wherein I may discover something akin to the illuminating confusions of Bottom, whom Shakespeare[1] had say: "I have had a most rare vision. I have had a dream past the wit of man to say what dream it was. Man is but an ass if he go about to expound this dream. Methought I was —there is no man can tell what. Methought I was—and methought I had—but man is but a patched fool if he will offer to say what methought I had. The eye of man hath not heard, the ear of man hath not seen, man's hand is not able to taste, his tongue to conceive, nor his heart to report, what my dream was."

It is not our "I am" systems to which our dreams refer; it is our "I am *not*" systems to which our dreams refer. Fromm is exquisitely wrong in this matter of what it is that dreams free us from. Dreams take us not into ourselves but *out* of ourselves. Therein lies their potential value in preparing us for creative thought.

I share this perspective with Montague Ullman (1981), who has expressed it as follows:

> While awake, our view of ourselves is one in which we see and stress our autonomy, our individuality, our discreteness. . . . (Our dreams are) organized by a different principle. Our dreams are more concerned with the nature of our connections with *all* others. . . . The history of the human race, while awake, is a history of fragmentation, of separating people and communities of people . . . nationally, reli-

> giously, politically. Our dreams are connected with the basic truth that we are all members of a single species.
>
> While awake we move through our lives in a sequential, linear moment-by-moment fashion with a point representing birth and another point the present moment. But when we go to sleep and begin to dream we create pictures of what's going on in our psyche from points in space and time which are outside of our waking organizations. (p. 1)

There's the truth: In dreams our sentence to the individual view of life is suspended, as our perceptions of living are reconnected with those of our species, by way of a transcendent mental function which has united the human race over all human space and over all human time. No wonder that even some "bad" dreams leave us feeling more whole, more human.

I may now refine my thesis: In dreams, where ego was shall species-feeling be. Our dreams are authored from within our individual lives merely to the extent that our self-interests provide their materials, their stuff, exactly the extent to which Shakespeare's plays were authored by the stuff of old histories and legends. Indeed, it was Shakespeare from whom I learned what I am trying to say here: "We *are* such stuff as dreams are made on. And our little lives *are* rounded with a sleep."[2] ("Rounded," in Elizabethan time, meant rounded *out*, not rounded *in*.)

It is also true, though, as Fromm and others are right to emphasize, that in this modern time of psychological, I-am systemmed man, we can use the selfless creations of our dreams to amplify the intricacies of pressingly self-centered problems. For example, I recently went to sleep after a vexing (over how long television could be watched) evening with my two sons, resolving, as I dozed off, that I really did love them anyway, and would always love them, come what may. In an ensuing dream, there was a newspaper article which said that the United States Congress had passed a law declaring a turkey farmer's turkeys worthless, and also requiring that he continue to feed his turkeys for the rest of his life. A few minutes of reflection on the dream enabled me to sharpen the implications of my mixed feelings toward my sons: Yes, I love them, and I shall always love them, but I need not, therefore, overlook that they are, at times, a couple of turkeys. And so, at times with them, am I a turkey. As a consequence of that brief dream reflection I shall now enjoy a more honest relationship with myself. And with my sons. But I will not so demean the poetic license of my dreams as to assign the intention of bringing that element of honesty into my life to the dream. That intention was mine, first in remembering the dream and then in projecting my personal life into it. The dream could not care less.

Do I split a superfluous hair, here, in dwelling on this distinction between dreaming and reflecting on dreams? It is admittedly a sad thing that our society belittles dreams; and, if we can counter that bias by perceiving dreams as intending us more honest lives, what can be the harm? The harm could be, as Hamlet foresaw, that in taking up arms against one ill we might invite another ill that we know not sufficiently of. What then could be the harm in assuming that, because we can extract more honest living from our dreams, our dreams must mean for us to do so? It is the harm in continuing to deny Herman Melville's Dionysian insight that we are, as a species, alone in this vastly uninterested universe. Because we are the species that experiences life in words, that is, which connects its experiences by way of disconnecting and reassembling than—through the making of metaphor.

This tendency not to distinguish the purposelessness of dreaming from the purpose of reflecting on dreams parallels one to which Morse Peckham brings our attention in the fields of art and aesthetics. The popular assumption of aestheticians has for centuries been that art reveals the essential quest for order of the unconscious human mind. Peckham (1967) refutes the assumption as follows:

> That order is a defining character of art is so utterly untrue that it is downright absurd. . . . Not art but perception is ordered. . . . Since we value—and often madly overvalue—whatever is ordered, we tend to impute order to whatever we value. . . . Man desires above all a predictable and ordered world. . . . But because man desires such a world so passionately, he is very much inclined to ignore anything that intimates that he does not have it. . . . It is clear that art is useless, that perceiver and artist are arrogant and indifferent. . . . Art tells us nothing about the world that we cannot find elsewhere and more reliably. Art does not make us better citizens, or more moral, or more honest. . . . Clearly the perception of art and the affective response to its signs and its discontinuities prepare us for no mode of behavior, no role, no pattern, no style. But it is preparation. . . . We rehearse for various roles all our lives. We rehearse our national, our local and our personal styles. These things we rehearse so that we may participate in a predictable world of social and environmental interaction. But we also must rehearse the power to perceive the failure, the necessary failure, of all those patterns of behavior. . . . Art is the reinforcement

> of the capacity to endure disorientation which makes innovation possible. (pp. 313–14)

The same may be said of dreams—almost verbatim: Remembering and reflecting on dreams reinforces our capacity to endure selflessness, which makes creative processes possible. Or *can*, of which more below.

Another example of our tendency to attribute to nature what we choose to find in nature is at the heart of no less than the scientific method, the Null hypothesis, which arbitrarily defines knowledge as that which cannot happen by chance. Enter Jacques Monod (1971), the Nobel-Prize-winning biologist, who has shown that the Null hypothesis will lead us to knowledge of organic life only if we restrict our interests in organic life to those of its forms that are presently, as the biologists say, "selected in"—a kind of Baba Ram Dass, be-here-now biology. It is true that the processes that govern the developments, the behaviors, and the perpetuations of these established life forms, while exceedingly complex, are unambiguously lawful and not influenced by chance. However, as scientific knowledge moves into questions of how new forms of organic life are introduced onto the planet—occurrences more frequent in evolution than are the occurrences which perpetuate the established forms—the Null hypothesis must lead us astray of knowledge. Because the introduction of new forms of organic life onto the planet is entirely and exclusively governed by chance. The complete view of organic life consists, then, of the macromolecular realm of established life forms *feeding into which for at least the last four billion years* have been vastly more frequent micromolecular changes occurring by chance alone.

> We call these events accidental; we say that they are random occurrences. And since they constitute the only possible source of modifications in the genetic text, itself the *sole* repository of the organism's hereditary structure, it necessarily follows that chance *alone is* at the source of every innovation of all creation in the biosphere. Pure chance, absolutely free but blind, at the very root of the stupendous edifice of evolution. (Monod 1971, p. 112)

"Absolutely free but blind." The same is true of dreams. And correspondingly, dreams may be at the root of the stupendous edifice of human language—of which more below.

In summary: we can and do so perceive art that life feels more unified, but it does not follow from that that art intends to unify life. Similarly, we can and do order our relations with nature by applying the scientific method to our observations of nature, but it does not follow from that that all of nature is ordered. Likewise, returning to our subject, reflection on dreams can help us to live more honest personal lives, but it does not follow from that that dreams intend for us to live more honest personal lives.

"In dreams we kiss ourselves good-by" wants a systematic statement in psychological language. Jean Piaget's will serve. According to Piaget (1951), dreams are composed almost exclusively of "ludic (Greek for playful) imagery." Other mental functions, such as those that support artistic perception and the play of children, are composed *predominantly* of ludic imagery; dreams are composed almost *exclusively* of ludic imagery. What is ludic imagery? It is, writes Piaget, "that form of symbolization which originates in conditions of suppression of consciousness of the ego by absorption in, and identification with the external world" (p. 209). *Suppression of consciousness of the ego by absorption in, and identification with the external world.* I interpret that to mean that dreams show us our *external* worlds *un*self-consciously imbued with the desires, the beliefs, the interests, and the values of the self. Thus, dreams are of the self, but they cannot be either by or for the self because they originate in conditions in which there is a complete lack of differentiation between the self and the external world, and consequently, a state of nonconsciousness of the self as differentiated from the external world in waking life. The comparison between the turkey farmer's strange relationship with his turkeys and my familiar relationship with my sons could be as refreshing to my waking life as it was, *because* the imagery of the turkey farmer's predicament was imagined in a mental state in which such a comparison is not possible. The infinite freedom of imagination characteristic of dreams is thus a consequence of their blindness to the self-interests of their makers. It is in the course of *reflecting* on dreams that we may accommodate their strangely interesting views to the familiar self-interests of our "real" lives.

Reflecting on dreams cannot, in our time, be unself-conscious, as may once have been so in Homer's time. (Read *The Odyssey* as a series of dreams and see what you think.) Our post-Cartesian culture has made the importance of self-centeredness much too compelling for that to be possible. *But* reflecting on dreams can be *only* self-conscious, and almost always is so, for the reason that reflecting on dreams, as a culturally sanctioned activity, has been largely limited in modern time to psychotherapeutic settings. Thus, the literature on how dream reflection may set its sights *beyond* the pursuit of self-knowledge is just beginning.

I daresay the little knowledge I can share on the subject is primarily due to my having chosen to follow my professional interests in dreams within educational as well as within clinical settings. College students, I discovered, welcome discussions of their dreams in class, and they prize the liberating personal insights that grow from these discussions; but, over time, they come to suspect the motives of a professor who expects no more of them than this.

Bootlegged psychotherapy is not what they signed on for when they enrolled in my course, and the ambiguity surrounding our commitments as students and teacher would in time make "interpreting the resistance" inane. Consequently, I orient dream reflection seminars as much to a piece of good literature as to the dream. I also require that the seminar participants augment their sometimes startling insights into their own developing lives with a piece of interesting writing out in the world. The element of paradox introduced into the dream reflection process by these expectations is what most clearly distinguishes my approach to dream reflection from "sensitivity training," "encounter groups," "self-consciousness raising" and other forms of abetting our society's addiction to "I am" systems; they invite the seminar to begin with a private production completely lacking in self-consciousness and to end with public productions that extend self-consciousness beyond the self.

It seems to me only right that as dreams are given to us from outside ourselves we should express our gratitude to them outside ourselves. Writing to and from reflections on dreams can remind us of the power we have over our language, and of the responsibility that goes with that power. Responsibility for what? Responsibility for using language as an organ of perception as well as a tool of communication. Language enables us to see as well as to say; and, if we do not use language for both purposes, language suffers.

I need not explain what is meant by using language as a tool of communication. We have heard of nothing else from English teachers our whole lives. Thus the current "literacy crisis" in America, as generations of school children are given nothing but utilitarian reasons for wanting to cultivate literacy. How can language also serve as an organ of perception? By lending itself to the making of metaphors, that is, to the employment of the words for a familiar experience to express the perception of a novel experience. The life of every word in every language began as someone's metaphor. Every word, before it became useful for the communication of a common experience, was first someone's way of expressing the perception of a novel experience.

Do you catch my drift? I say, do you catch my drift? Probably, but wait a minute. Have you ever seen a "drift" "caught"? Has anyone ever seen anyone "catch" a "drift"? No, because it is not physically possible to catch a drift. But you know, when I use those words, that I mean: "Do you anticipate the direction in which my thoughts are moving?" And I knew that you would know that, and so I could use the phrase as a tool of communication—and save six words in the bargain. But first, someone had to perceive that image, which only words could be used to perceive it with, by way of making a metaphor. Someone, that is, had first to use language as an organ of perception so that I could later improve my use of language as a tool of communication. And this prior function of language must be exercised frequently. And we should all feel obliged to see that it is exercised frequently. Else our language will get tired. Species-feeling. Species-feeling. Where ego was shall species-feeling be.

My drift is that reflecting on dreams must instruct us in the use of language as an organ of perception. Because dreams make nothing but the stuff of metaphors. And they make them for nothing; and, according to recent scientific reports, they make them in extravagant supply. I have speculated from these scientific reports that dreaming may have played a generative part in the evolution of languages for probably millions of years (Jones 1980). If so, then the future that lies in our power, which Auden's exiles long for, might be the future of our language. I like to urge, therefore, that whenever we feel a debt of gratitude to a dream for helping us to live more honest personal lives, that we seek to pay that debt *in writing.*

For example, the following dream provided the metaphors for a dream reflection seminar:

I am driving a big old rounded car. I am also taking care of a friend's child. Suddenly the child is naked and multiplies into two babies. One of the babies crawls up my chest and puts arms around my neck, desperate like.

The babies disappear, and I am still in the car. A child's voice from the back seat says, "I want money." I park the car, get out and open the back door. The two babies have turned into white paper penguins, about the size of writing tablets, one of them wearing a top hat. I reply, "You always want something." It feels like I'm talking to my schoolwork.

For the next hour each seminar member tried to articulate the focal conflict in their own lives that the dream could have symbolized, and how it did so—as the author of the dream kept her silence. One man, the father of two adolescent boys, saw in the dream a metaphorical expression of his painful awareness that he enjoys a close relationship with one son and a distant relationship with the other; and that both sons, as they have grown older, have come to love him increasingly as a source of money. The dream reminded one of the women of a pregnancy scare she had recently lived through, and the acute conflict that this experience had brought into focus over whether she will ever want to have children. Other such projections into the dream centered on the making of irreversible decisions, the consequences that inevitably follow, and the equally inevitable doubts which must then respond to the question of "what if ?" What if I had not registered for the draft? What if I had not had the abortion? What if my wife *had* had the abortion? And so on.

We then turned to the dreamer to hear of the focal conflict for which the dream had in fact been a metaphor. She had dreamed the dream on the anniversary (sure enough) of her abortion. She thought she had resolved her mixed feelings, but the dream showed differently. With long pauses for tears and calmings of voice, she admitted to herself for the first time the love she had felt for the not-to-be-born child and the guilt she later felt for having "killed" it. She knew the decision had been right, and she would make it again in the same situation. After all, having the abortion enabled her to stay in school, which explained why she felt in the dream as if she were talking to her schoolwork. "But there was that baby crawling up my chest and wrapping its arms around my neck as though holding onto *me* for its *life*." As always happens, the dreamer received much empathy, support, and acceptance from her friends around the table. And, as also always happens, her understanding of the dream was deeply amplified by her friends' projections of their lives into it.

It had been a very therapeutic two hours for us all, and we could have counted the time very well spent had we left it at that. However, anticipating that we would need a piece of good literature through which to pay our debt to the dream, we had previously read and discussed Mark Twain's essay "Taming the Bicycle." So, after lunch, we each went off for two hours to compose something in writing that sought, as artfully as possible, to relate the morning's dream to Twain's essay. And then we came back and read to one another what we had written.

Here are a few lines from the essay, to give you its flavor:

> The bicycle had what is called the "wobbles," and had them very badly. In order to keep my position, a good many things were required of me, and in every instance the thing required was against nature.... There are those who imagine that the unlucky accidents of life—life's experiences—are in some way useful to us. I wish I could find out how. I never knew one of them to happen twice. They always change off and swap around and catch you on your inexperienced side.

And here is how one student sought to give something back to our language in return for the gifts of self-knowledge we had taken from the dream:

> I agree with Mark Twain's nihilistic assertion that the useful portions of life's experiences, or "accidents," are not readily available to the layman. My past has consistently done a very patchy job of preparing me for current events. For example, how do I stop my kid from abusing me? I could wear a sign: Please be gentle, you're dealing with an inexperienced good example. But he can't read yet, so the effect could be limited.
>
> It doesn't seem fair when most insignificant domestic considerations force me to become—Parentman. I really don't enjoy hurried changes in the cramped quarters of my patriarchal phone booth. Child rearing could be revolutionized by simply reversing the speed of life. We could start slow and finish fast. Slowly merging with life's energy at birth would have the immediate advantage of eliminating the bright roaring clash of postnatal shock. You could enter the world like a slug with a hangover; irritated by the obstreperous jolt of transition, but not moving fast enough to be affected. Physical activity would very gradually increase with age, while the rate of intellectual growth could maintain its present rate.
>
> The advantage of a late-blooming metabolism could recivilize civilization. The emotional intensity of childhood would seem like a day at the zoo. There could be some problems with late-middle-aged street gangs; or an occasional geriatric rock concert may take a rowdy turn—but a slower more deliberate youth would have to pick up and absorb a little more of life along the way. The despondence and infirmity of old age would vanish, as we would, with our bodies speeding toward a flaming and glorious demise, like meteors with a mission—Kamikaze comets.
>
> Don Mills

The writing will not stand comparison with Twain's essay as a work of literature, but that is beside the point. The author merely sought, in two hours, to extend the occasion of understanding a dream beyond his understanding of the dream—and to do so in writing. Along the way he had of necessity to use language to see as well as to say ("like a slug with a hangover"; "like a day at the zoo"; "like meteors with a mission—Kamikaze comets").

I have sought to combine dream reflection with the teaching of creative writing for the past ten years. This is the sequence of activities as it has evolved to date:

1. We read a work of great literature and discuss it in a seminar, from the points of view of the possible meanings intended by the author, the meanings suggested by the text, and our personal responses to the work.
2. On a subsequent morning, someone brings a dream to the seminar—typed and dittoed, so that everyone has a copy.
3. The dreamer reads the dream aloud.
4. As we close our eyes and try to visualize our own versions of the dream's imagery, the dreamer reads the dream again. This has the effect of calming inevitable personal jitters and getting into a studious frame of mind.
5. As the dreamer listens, volunteers (including the teacher) state the feelings the dream aroused in them and how the dream's various images might have functioned as metaphors for personal conflicts in their lives if the dream had been their own.
6. The dreamer then identifies the day residue and shares his or her understanding of the dream as this has been amplified by the various projections into it.
7. We then discuss the dream from two points of view: What it may be saying to us and what we may be prompted to say back to it. Thus, our objectives are to understand the dream and enjoy it. In this latter venture we learn to respond to the dream's play on words and images; its sound symbolisms and flourishes of synesthesia; its visually alliterative sequences; its deployments of the figurative and literal; its double entendres, stagings, artifices, puns, and jokes.

   The discussion is guided by the rule that we are free to advance any hunch, speculation, or intuition; ask any question; or offer any interpretation or outright guess that may help achieve the two objectives: understanding and enjoyment freedom is limited only by the common acknowledgment that the dreamer will be the judge of the correctness of the understanding and of the tastefulness of the enjoyment.

8. Then we go off individually and write for two hours — a poem, an essay, a letter—a story, some dialogue that links reflections on the dream to our understanding of the week's common reading assignment. This is the most challenging step in the sequence, and when successful, the most rewarding.
9. Then we reconvene as a seminar, and read to one another what we wrote. The writings tend to be of such startlingly liberated quality as to generate a mood of uncommon mutual respect — sometimes falling not far short of shock.

Here is an extended example of the complete sequence: We read and held a seminar on two of E. B. White's essays: "Ring of Time" and "A Report in January." Next, we reflected on the following dream:

I'm at a football stadium sitting in the grandstands with some of the players and the coach. We are the only ones there, but people will soon be coming and a game will be played. They explain to me that they like to come early to get the feel of the place, especially when not playing a home game. One of the players goes down on the field, and suddenly he is in a game from the past that we are watching. He is in an amazing play, and runs a long way down the field, where he is finally tackled and sustains a shoulder injury. He is then back in the grandstand, and I ask the players if they ever get cold while playing. They say that they are always trying to prevent frostbite, and sometimes when the coach puts his hand inside their jerseys to see if they are OK, he gets so hot that he begins to hyperventilate. I see him pale from this. Now people are arriving, and I go down to get some food. I walk by where one buys tickets and see a press agent buying one. I ask him why he's doing so, because I thought that the press gets in free. He says normally this is so, but here everyone knows each other, and they check. He puts a card into a machine (like he's done this before) and receives a ticket. I figure that I better buy a ticket or I might get caught, so I go to a window. The cashier is Walter Matthau. He asks me where I'm sitting, and when I point to the area, he tells me it costs four dollars. I look into my wallet and there is only a five-dollar bill, which I give to him. After fumbling, he gives me back sixteen dollars. I realize his mistake and start to walk away, and then upon seeing the five-dollar bill, he also realizes his error, and calls out my name, which I pretend not to hear, and keep walking. After a minute, I think better of what I've done and walk back to return the money. As I'm going in the door of the ticket office, he is walking out, apparently going out to find me. I tell him I've returned with the money, and he gives me a cynical look, but says nothing. I walk inside with him, and ask him how he would have found me. He looks at me with an air of confidence and replies, "I would have found you; I know people." He asks me if I want something to drink and I tell him soda water. He then puts dry ice in a large glass and fills it with water so that the mixture bubbles, and then transfers it to a smaller glass with regular ice. Before I drink it, I wake up.

As the dreamer listened, a sample of the feelings aroused in the group by the dream were as follows:

"I get a strong feeling of guilt."

"Secretiveness."

"A feeling of superiority, of being able to put things over on people."

"Trickiness treachery."

"I get a feeling of trying to be very macho, with just a hint of fear."

"Curiosity, mistrust, mystery."

"Vindictiveness and guilt."

As the dreamer continued to listen, here is a sample of personal conflicts projected into some of the dream's metaphors by other members of the class:

"The part about coming to the stadium before the game is to be played and then seeing a game from the past would be a metaphor for my trying to decide whether to take the GRE this year or next, whether I'm ready, whether I'll ever be ready, whether I even want to go to graduate school. Taking stock of myself, sizing myself up, so as to make the best plans."

"The players always trying to prevent frostbite, and the coach getting hot to the point of hyperventilation when he puts his hand into their jerseys is a perfect metaphor for my relationship with my boyfriend. Our passion times are out of this world. For both of us. Neither of us has ever experienced anything like it with anyone else—exhilarating, fulfilling, and confident. But much of the rest of the time we bore each other. We don't have much in common except the way we enjoy each other physically. The dry ice could tie into that metaphor, too. It looks like ice, feels like ice, but it really burns you."

"I sense some homosexual overtones in the image of the coach getting hot putting his hand inside the players' jerseys. A male friend of mine recently told me that he is gay. I would never have guessed, because he is such a fraternity jock. He said I was the only person he has ever told. Just wanted to share it with a woman he trusts. It put me on the spot, because I can't help him. He didn't ask for help, but even if he had, I wouldn't have known how. And now I've got this unwanted secret to keep. Which makes the press agent who has to buy a ticket the key metaphor for me, if it was my dream. Most things that friends tell you, you feel free to do something with. This one made me feel stuck, trapped, wary. No free pass. Now that I'm talking about it I'm getting angry. I'm angry because I feel guilty, and I didn't do anything to feel guilty for. I just listened. Jesus!"

"The press agent who has to buy a ticket because everyone knows each other, and they check, is a nice metaphor for a lifelong situation of mine that may be coming to a head soon. All my life I've had a free pass. My family is wealthy and I can have anything I want. I have friends like that who feel guilty about it, but I never have. For example, I know I got into Cornell because of my family, not because of my grades. But that's OK with me. I like it here and I'm getting a good education. Sometimes I've thought they might be buying me into their way of life, but, like in the dream, it usually turns out they know me very well. Like what they want for me I usually end up wanting for myself. (Hah!) They 'check.' The dream, if it were mine, gets pretty cute there. My father sure does 'check' me, i.e., write me checks!

"What may be coming to a head (Hey, I really like this, because I've been avoiding thinking about it) is this: My father and I have always just assumed that when I graduate I'll start working in his brokerage firm. I probably will, too. I've never questioned it— even looked forward to it. Why not? The money is good and the life is easy. My father's had a good life. But I have this friend who grew up in China who is going to get a Ph.D. in the School of Agriculture—water conservation. His heart and soul is in it. I'll have a good life on Wall Street. No, I'll make a good *living* on Wall Street, and have a good life doing something else. Like my father. But will my heart and soul be in anything? Like my friend? I don't know. I have another year of college. What if something really grabs me, like teaching or social work? How will my father react? I don't think he'll stop 'checking' me, but I do know I wouldn't feel so entitled to the free passes I've always taken for granted. Transferring the soda water from the large glass with dry ice to the smaller glass with regular ice also fits in."

"If this was my dream it would relate to my deciding to drink soda water instead of soda pop. It's cheaper and healthier. I also found five dollars on the road last week. But the whole dream would symbolize for me my efforts to regard my life as a game. It helps me to resolve a lot of conflicts when I succeed, but it isn't easy. Because the *game* of life is confusing. You can't be absolutely sure what skills you need, what the rules are, or what winning or losing means. I've been watching people lately to see who is doing well and why. Does doing well mean getting ahead? What does getting ahead mean? By whose standards—theirs or society's? I'm getting ahead in my own game, dance, but I'm doing it dishonestly. My parents were skeptical, but I convinced them I would someday dance professionally. I love dance and I'm getting very good, but I know I don't have the talent to dance professionally. What I really expect to do is *teach* dance. I'll be good at it, and I'll be happy doing it, but, as often as not, I allow myself to feel less than good because I'm following my private plan—not the public one. I should realize that that kind of dissembling is an important skill in playing the game of life, and give myself credit for it. I would prefer to judge myself from the inside only. In my best moments I do. But, if this were my dream, it would represent those times when the outside is doing the judging—getting a cynical look after returning the money, being checked up on, found out, known."

The above does not exhaust the various simulations of the dream, but it will suffice.

We took a short break and then turned to the dreamer to hear what he had made of the dream and of our various translations of it:

"I was only able to make a few connections after I wrote the dream down:

> The day before I quit my job in the lab. This, I'm sure was the dream's day residue.
>
> Sometimes, when no one is around in the lab, I sneak a piece of dry ice into a glass. I like to see the vapors rise up.

> My dad and I used to go to the N.Y. Jets football games a lot. Sometimes it was bitter, painful cold.
> The part about giving the money back reminds me of a time in Israel when my girlfriend paid an undercharged bill at the right amount. It pissed me off.

"That's all I had when I came to class. Now the whole dream is much more coherent. First, last year, while working in the lab, I cut my finger very badly when I broke a glass. A nerve was severed. Just by luck one of the top neurosurgeons in the country happened to be in the lab at the time. He had me rushed to the hospital and reconnected the nerve. If he hadn't been there on the spot I'd have had a permanently damaged finger, which would have ruled out a lot of possible medical specialties. Then my dad called a lawyer friend of his who got me sixteen hundred dollars in compensation. Hell, sixteen hundred dollars was more than I made at the lab in a whole school year! That memory of being lucky, mixed with guilt, put the whole dream in perspective. The dream is all about guilt. My dad had given me permission to quit the lab job, and that made me feel guilty. He's paying for everything here and I feel I should be contributing something. I also felt guilty about quitting because my boss had gone out on a limb to give me the job.

"But what Chris said about possibly not joining his father on Wall Street, and Kim's seeing the game as the game of life, really hit me where I live. The dream is a guilt dream, all right, but what it's really doing, metaphorically, is raising the question of whether I'll do what I *should* do with my life or what I *want* to do with it. That's a question I haven't even let myself ask, consciously. As far back as I can remember I've wanted to become a doctor. My dad is a doctor. I'm his only son. I've always been in love with the idea of being a doctor, too. I never thought of any other possibility. I'm taking the Med School exam next semester, and I know I'll score in one of the top percentiles. What my family expects me to do and what I *want* to do have always been mirror images of each other. What your projections into the dream have forced me to verbalize is that I quit the lab job so I'll have more time to read philosophy and to write. Those are two things I've discovered at Cornell that I do just because I *want* to do *them.* I'm good at them and I enjoy them. I don't seriously think I'd decide to become a philosopher or a writer instead of a doctor, but I shouldn't be following those interests on the sly. Hell, I can follow my philosophical and literary interests avocationally when I'm a doctor. But I'm less likely to actually do that if I start letting myself feel guilty about them before I even graduate from college. You're right, Kim, life is a game (or should be), so we ought to leave as much room for play in it as we can.

"Thank you all, very much."

Then followed about ten minutes of dialogue between the dreamer and the rest of us on some of the dream's niceties (for example, *hyperventilation* being as appropriate a term for what occurred in the dream reflection seminar as for what occurred in the dream; 16 + 5 equaling the dreamer's age; dry ice possibly playing on the sound of dry eyes, and so on).

Another round of thank you's between the dreamer and his classmates followed as they left class.

Here are two representative pieces of writing connecting the dream reflection seminar and the E. B. White essays, in the form of letters to the dreamer:

> Dear Barry,
>
> In trying to understand your dream as well as E. B. White's *The Ring of Time*, I think it necessary to do what you were attempting in class—to peel back the layers to get to the core underneath.
>
> White describes the circus as the world in microcosm, but he could also be describing the football game of your dream. "Its magic is universal and complex, out of its wild disorder comes order; from its rank smell arises the good aroma of courage and daring; out of its preliminary shabbiness comes the final splendor. . . . It is at its best at certain moments when it comes to a point, as through a burning glass, in the activity and destiny of a single performer out of so many." White watches the rehearsal and becomes painfully aware of the element of time; which itself began running in circles. You watch a pregame warmup but are suddenly seeing a game from the past. Perhaps you are the single performer who makes an amazing play, whose destiny is being observed in both the past and the future.
>
> But the complexities of living in the world intrude on that destiny, on the sense of timelessness. White describes the apparent idyllic South as contrasting sharply with the softness of its music; as also being cruel, hard, and prickly. The football players guard against frostbite but their skin is hot to touch. Dry ice looks hot but is cold and gaseous. Things are not what they seem—the familiar is unfamiliar. The Florida days are models of beauty, wonder, and comfort but the treatment of many of its citizens is appalling. White perhaps feels the guilt that you do from taking too much change as he lives in the

midst of a great social crisis and sees hardly a sign of it. He tries to discharge his duty to society by observing, commenting on, and recording it. You try to pursue your personal goals, to find your place in the world, to play in your own game but feel pulled by expectations of others. And all the while the world and time are spinning.

Or are they moving in a straight line down the playing field?

Dear Barry,

If I were an automobile, my motor oil would consist of guilt. I could operate adequately when it is low, but sooner or later I'll need a whopping dose of it to continue. Guilt is a funny emotion. It's right there like my shadow, following me, leading me, depending on the time of day.

Some people were born with original sin. I was born with guilt. It comes with the territory. From day one I was eating bagels and lox with a side order of guilt.

Grandma prepares a wonderful dish of guilt. A culinary masterpiece. She serves it at almost every meal, and if you don't eat it, she wails "What's the matter, don't you like my cooking?"

The anxiety you felt about quitting your job and your subsequent dream tell me that you must have eaten guilt soufflé in the near past. Parents make delicious guilt soufflé, carefully nurturing their creation, giving it the best in life, teaching it to be independent. Finally, father places the soufflé in the oven, and it begins to grow. It develops into a mature dish—self-supporting, high, beautiful. Then, it wants to make a decision for itself, and father slams the oven door. Good-bye soufflé.

I believe E. B. White's venison was seasoned with a bit of guilt. He is determined to remain a naturalist of sorts, "yet slips into the role of a murderer" and uses steer to feed a woodpecker (not to mention himself). He must feel that twinge of guilt. In his struggle to remain simple and unaffected, he also makes a large amount of money. Maybe this is why the wealthy woodcutter is in his essay; an easy way to absolve himself of his guilt by showing another victim of affluence as untouched.

So Barry, don't fret. Guilt will forever find its way into your kitchen and will ruthlessly contaminate your food. "OK," you think, "I won't eat." But what about those starving people in India, just dying for your food. Won't you feel guilty?

There is not space here to systematically compare the post-dream reflection writings of these students with their other school writings. My impressions are that the two examples are representative of the differences. They are not technically "better" pieces of writing; but they are less hurried, they have more voice, they are more personally particular without being egotistical. They seem to have been written with more pleasure than obligation. They take more risks. They amplify rather than merely reflect the views of E. B. White. Best of all, they are much, much more metaphorical. They use language to see and not just to say. So what, for now, that the metaphors threaten to become mixed and are in less than exquisite control? Students must first try to use metaphor before they can learn to use it well.

The tone of the seminar sequence tends to be one of scholarly good humor. Therapeutic gains in self-knowledge are expected and accepted, but the prevailing expectation is that personal insights will be extended to grace some aspect of our academic commitments with creative meaning. Here is the way one student, Lloyd Houston, described the experience:

> We come in alone and we go out alone, but in between we have each other; the tight throats, the full and empty days, the tears, the unions of minds and hearts, the laughter, the limbo of chaos—the magic. Feeling the moment as it breaks on the nerve of the heart, turns time timeless, as here and now cease to matter and we grope for the mysteries—the magic. Of sharing and knowing, and sharing the knowing and knowing the sharing.
>
> Hear a quiet woman talk of her life and feel the thread that binds her to me, as though we'd loved. Hear a tender man who turns his dreams—and mine—into wriggling, flashing poetry. To find a watch pocket we thought the world had taken from us, or a blue tin cup we thought our childhood had lost, or a new blue streetcar named desire, or a hidden hinge hitched to integrity, or the real thing in a coke bottle.
>
> The uncertainty is still there within each of us, every Friday. But rather than holding us back, spontaneity stifled, we become instead almost childlike in freedom and vitality of mind. And then the afternoon writing shows that we are anything but children.
>
> The quality of uncertainty characteristic of the dream reflection seminar seems to act as a catalyst freeing our thoughts from their usual musty pathways. The integrity and quality of "the play" becomes the prevailing concern. Everyone becomes more sensitive to everyone, more civil, more thoughtful, more human. And as is true of a good play, the sign of a good dream reflection seminar sequence is lots of hearty laughter.

Here are some excerpts from written statements by students who were asked to describe the effects of the dream reflection seminar sequence on their writing:

"What I like most is the intellectual fencing with the dream poet. I enjoy the free form parrying between seminar members. Colliding associations forming a fascinating kind of fusion."

"I love the mood—relaxing and exciting. After the dream seminar I feel creative."

"I enjoy the surprise connections that occur. When seemingly obscure images come to form a logical and relevant relationship."

"It's a good exercise for getting the brain loosened up."

"I had to let go of a lot of rigid ideas of what writing was due to seeing the credibility of confused and scrambled but creative dreams."

"I've always written a lot, but dream reflection has given my writing a richer backbone—made it more concrete, less flowery. Dreams are oblique to normal associations, as art tries to be—a good balancing."

"I attribute my success in writing this year to the dream poet. I was so amused by the metaphors utilized in the dreams that I was inspired to let go and give him a little competition."

"I can place the responsibility for what I write on the content of the dream. It provides proof that the subject is of interest (at least to the dreamer) and worth thinking and writing about."

"I guess one of the main causes for everybody's amazing creative output is tied in with the tremendous energy flow and excitement of the seminars. Bantering with key words from the dream; playing with phrases and images; reversing cliches."

"Dreams are very creative pieces of work that come from you. Never thought you could dream up something this original, did you? But you did! So you write."

"Having to force a connection between a dream and an essay seems so impossible, but it turns out to be so excitingly easy."

"Dreams are so intrinsically interesting. They make anything seem possible when you start writing."

"Connecting a product of the unconscious with a product of the conscious does what comparing two pieces of literature can never do."

"Language is usually used to describe concrete images in unconcrete ways. Writing after the dream seminar prevents that."

"It helps me write from the heart. Not just the mind."

"More personal, more reachable, less hurried, less tense."

"One feels free to push aside all of that English class stiffness."

"My writing becomes more colorful, more intense, and more salient to my life."

"It allows me to use metaphors in my own way—not in the way the author makes me feel I should use them."

"Getting inside the dream makes metaphorical thinking less foreboding."

"After toying with the metaphors of the dream, forgotten as well as new experience is generated."

"It gives me more confidence. There is no mock or menace in writing after overcoming the fear of the dream. After that, the fear of self-exposure in writing seems less."

"For once, if only for the moment, I can give patience to my words."

"I don't know if the dream reflection seminar is an operator or a catalyst in my writing. Some of both, I think."

"I feel more open to communicate in this class. I really know the audience. . . . Also the realization that I could have dreamed the dream and could not have experienced the essay."

"I had to write more honestly, because I felt so honored, so dignified, by the responses to my dream."

How, theoretically, may this approach to writing produce these effects? I think an adequate answer will not be forthcoming until a satisfying epistemology of dreams has been formulated. My presently incomplete answer is that the approach to writing by way of reflecting on dreams requires the employment of language as an organ of perception as well as a tool for communication. In this I have been instructed by Julian Jaynes (1976), who has amplified this observation as follows:

> The most fascinating property of language is its capacity to make metaphors. But what an understatement! For metaphor is not a mere extra trick of language, as it is so often slighted in the old schoolbooks on composition; it is the very constitutive ground of language. I am using metaphor here in its most general sense: the use of a term for one thing to describe another because of some kind of similarity between them or between their relations to other things. There are thus always two terms in a metaphor, the thing to be described, which I shall call the *metaphrand*, and the thing or relation used to elucidate it, which I shall call the *metaphier*. A metaphor is always a known metaphier operating on a less known metaphrand. I have

coined these hybrid terms simply to echo multiplication where a multiplier operates on a multiplicand.

It is by metaphor that language grows. The common reply to the question, "What is it?" is, when the reply is difficult or the experience unique, "Well, it is like. . . ." In laboratory studies, both children and adults describing nonsense objects (or metaphrands) to others who cannot see them use extended metaphiers that with repetition become contracted into labels. This is the major way in which the vocabulary of language is formed. The grand and vigorous function of metaphor is the generation of new language as it is needed, as human culture becomes more and more complex.

A random glance at the etymologies of common words in a dictionary will demonstrate this assertion. Or take the naming of various fauna and flora in their Latin indicants, or even in their wonderful common English names, such as stag beetle, lady's slipper, darning needle, Queen Anne's lace, or buttercup. The human body is a particularly generative metaphier, creating preciously unspeakable distinctions in a throng of areas. The *head* of an army, table, page, bed, ship, household, or nail, or of steam or water; the *face* of a clock, cliff, card, or crystal; the eyes of needles, winds, storms, targets, flowers, or potatoes; the *brow* of a hill; the *cheeks* of a vice, the *teeth* of cogs or combs; the *lips* of pitchers, craters, augers, the *tongues* of shoes, boardjoints, or railway switches; the *arm* of a chair and so on and on. Or the *foot* of this page. Or the *leaf* you will soon turn. All of these concrete metaphors increase enormously our powers of perception of the world about us and our understanding of it, and literally create new objects. *Indeed language is an organ of perception, not simply a means of communication.* (Italics mine—R.M.J.)

In early times, language and its referents climbed up from the concrete to the abstract on the steps of metaphors, even, we may say, created the abstract on the bases of metaphors.

It is not always obvious that metaphor has played this all important function. But this is because the concrete metaphiers become hidden in phonemic change, leaving the words to exist on their own. Even such an unmetaphorical sounding word as the verb "to be" was generated from a metaphor. It comes from the Sanskrit bhu "to grow, or make grow," while the English forms "*am*" and "*is*" have evolved from the same root as the Sanskrit asmi, "to breathe." It is something of a lovely surprise that the irregular conjugation of our most nondescript verb is thus a record of a time when man had no independent word for "*existence*" and could only say that something "grows" or that it "breathes." Of course we are not conscious that the

> concept of being is thus generated from a metaphor about growing and breathing. Abstract words are ancient coins whose concrete images in the busy give-and-take of talk have worn away with use. Because in our brief lives we catch so little of the vastnesses of history, we tend too much to think of language as being solid as a dictionary, with a granite-like permanence, rather than as the rampant restless sea of metaphor which it is. Indeed, if we consider the changes in vocabulary that have occurred over the last few millennia, and project them several millennia hence, an interesting paradox arises. For if we ever achieve a language that has the power of expressing everything, then metaphor will no longer be possible. I would not say, in that case, my love is like a red, red rose, for love would have exploded into terms for its thousands of nuances and applying the correct term would leave the rose metaphorically dead.
>
> The lexicon of language, then, is a finite set of terms that by metaphor is able to stretch out over an infinite set of circumstances, even to creating new circumstances thereby. (pp. 48–52)

What was the biologically evolved process that abetted this function of the use of words as an organ of perception? I have speculated elsewhere that it was rapid-eye-movement sleep, which served the development of certain singularly mammalian neurophysiological functions, which, in turn, and in time, became the psychophysiological foundations for the evolution of human dreaming (Jones 1970).

The possible merit of this speculation is unimportant for the purpose of understanding the influence that dream reflection has on writing. The important fact is the obvious one: Human dreaming produces the stuff of metaphors infinitely. A dream, I repeat, is nothing but an effortlessly and unself-consciously produced collection of metaphorical images connected by a story line. To pay attention to a dream (any dream), to reflect on and discuss it, to simulate it as your own, to try to understand and enjoy it and then to write to and from it is to be steeped in the use of language as an organ of perception—while incidentally also using language as a means of communication.

Indeed, the very act of remembering, much less recording, a dream requires the use of language as an organ of perception. Words do occasionally figure in the composition of a dream in sleep, but only infrequently. The fundamental aliment of dreams is that of emotion-charged images, largely, although not exclusively, visual images. The only way a dream can be remembered is to translate its images into words, that is, to employ language in its perceptual function. Whatever else is then done with the remembered dream in a social setting must seek to coordinate the use of language as an organ of perception *with* the use of language as a means of communication. Bear in mind, moreover, that this coordinating sequence of events must proceed along a gradient, and must resolve problems of communication, which are next to impossible to experience in modern civilized waking life. Thus, this approach to dream reflection puts a premium on the inherent selflessness of dreams by requiring that, having used them to project further into ourselves, we then also use them to get further out of ourselves.

There is one more observation to make, which I think may be the most important to understanding why the approach to writing described above works as excitingly as it does. Reflecting on dreams in a social setting requires not only that we engage metaphors in intimate proximity to the unconscious level of their production, but, by virtue of doing so, *we must cope with a metaphorical strategy that is the reverse of conscious metaphor production.* In conscious symbolization a metaphor is, as Jaynes (1976) says, "always a known metaphier operating on a less known metaphrand" (p. 48). The symbolization which produces dreams employs the reverse of this strategy. The metaphors that constitute dreams consist of *less*-known metaphiers operating on more known metaphrands. In the vocabulary of dream psychology the dream's metaphrands are its "day residues," those incomplete, or unresolved or problematic or new experiences from the preceding day which precipitated the dream and with which the dream is playing. (This is why the dreamer *must* be regarded as the ultimate authority in a dream reflection seminar. No one on God's earth can possibly know what a dream's day residues are, except the author of the dream, who almost always does. The dreamer is, therefore, the only person who has access to the information necessary to confirm or disconfirm the relevance and interest values of the various projections, simulations, and hypotheses to which the others may subject the dream.)

For example, what was the day residue, that is, the metaphrand of the dream of the two babies who turned into white paper penguins the size of writing tablets? It was the fleeting recollection of the day before that it was the anniversary of the dreamer's abortion. Nothing unknown or mysterious about this—as far as it went, but it obviously needed to be *more* known. So, now we have a metaphrand that is more, not less, known than the metaphiers that made up the manifest dream. It is these metaphiers that were mysterious, at least at first. In the process of reflecting on the dream, and with the help of her friends' projections, the dreamer came to see how these metaphiers amplified the metaphrand, making it even more known, more vivid, more conscious as she came to appreciate the relevance of the dream's visual metaphors to the choice she had had to make between her maternal desires and her responsibilities to her schoolwork.

This reverse strategy in the use of metaphor may be unique to the symbolization process characteristic of dreaming. And it is the invitation of the dream reflection seminar not only to embrace the metaphorical process but to embrace it, as it were, *from the inside out*, which, I believe, accounts for the excitement and enthusiasm with which the students turn to their writing assignments afterward. Thus: "Getting inside the dream makes metaphorical thinking less foreboding." "I enjoy the surprise connections that occur. When seemingly obscure images come to form a logical and relevant relationship." "I had to let go of a lot of rigid ideas of what writing was, due to seeing the credibility of confused and scrambled but creative dreams."

Notes

1. *A Midsummer Night's Dream.*
2. *The Tempest.*

References

Auden, W. H. *Collected Shorter Poems*, Faber and Faber, 1966.

Fromm, E. *The Forgotten Language*. New York: Rinehart, 1951.

Jaynes, J. *The Origin of Consciousness in the Breakdown of the Bicameral Mind.* Boston: Houghton Mifflin, 1976.

Jones, R. M. *The Dream Poet.* Cambridge, Mass: Schenkman, 1980.

———. *The New Psychology of Dreaming.* New York: Grune and Stratton, 1970.

Monod, J. *Chance and Necessity*. New York: Knopf, 1971.

Peckham, M. *Man's Rage for Chaos*. New York: Schocken Books, 1967.

Piaget, J. *Play, Dreams and Imitation in Childhood.* New York: Norton, 1951.

Ullman, M. "Psi Communication through Dream Sharing." *Parapsychology Review* 12, 2 (1981): 1–8.

CHAPTER SIX

Dreaming and Learning

The Dream in a College Classroom

EDWARD F. STORM

Edward Storm is a computer scientist who has taken to dream work. His special concern is the language of the dream and what this can tell us about the way the brain works.

This chapter, along with the chapter by Richard Jones, represents an effort to link dreams to creativity and learning, two issues central to the student experience. Both authors present cogent arguments for introducing the study of the dream into a college curriculum and for shifting dreams away from the trivial position they generally occupy in the mind of the student to the significance they can acquire once they are taken seriously. In Storm's case, what at first seems a most unlikely linkage, namely, the connection of the dreams to computer science, turns out in his hands to offer rich returns to both disciplines. An analogy is drawn between the content that has to be mastered in the computer work and in the dream work and the appropriate way of talking about that content, namely, its grammar. In seeking the grammar that shapes the manifest content of the dream Professor Storm is taking a step toward identifying the language base of the dream.

Professor Storm's concerns extend beyond the dream's relation to computer science to a broader consideration of the significance of dream work to learning in general. Let us hope that he is correct in seeing this linkage of dreaming and learning as a "newly forming tradition" that can bring "insight, encouragement, and perspective for the learning student."

For three years I taught an elective course in the School of Computer and Information Science at Syracuse University. This course might be called "The computer in the mind." As part of it the students read about and discuss the phenomenon of dreaming. In this chapter I will describe the course, indicate why dreaming constitutes a natural topic in a course about the mind's computer, and summarize some student responses.

The subject matter for this course and the student responses to it form the body of this chapter. But just as interesting, and perhaps just as important, are my reasons for continuing to offer such a course in a high-technology curriculum. As a result of giving these courses, I have concluded that dreaming and learning (as the latter occurs in many college classrooms) have much in common. This chapter may be understood then as standing in a newly forming tradition in which dreaming is an important source of insight, encouragement, and perspective for the learning student.

I first came to appreciate the significance of dream work in 1979. Since then I have been involved with experiential dream group work both as a group member and as a leader. I have guided a number of small student groups and two adult groups and have participated in three leadership workshops. In addition, I regularly discuss dreams with individuals, in person, by mail, and through interactive computer networks.

The most powerful motive for studying dreaming, of course, is that doing so may enhance our understanding of human nature and the human condition. Among other things, dreams sometimes point to sources of conflict and tension and do so in a way that underscores the significance of those sources for the dreamer. The dream helps us to approach the underpinnings of our suffering. In its role as a source of insight the dream is a powerful instrument for healing. From a more specifically scientific perspective, dreaming is of great importance in our efforts to understand the nature of the mind and its relation to brain and matter. The surprising originality that invests the dream reminds us again and again that spontaneous creativity is a central and universal capacity no matter what may be our beliefs about the biological or psychological function of dreaming. Dream images are novel and often unexpected, colorful, rich, and very personal. And their building blocks are often nearly universal to the human condition.

My efforts to identify a relationship between dreaming and the computer science curriculum in a high-technology setting were stimulated by Richard Jones's beautiful study on the use of dreams in a creative writing program. Although the opportunity for experiential dream work is limited in a computer science curriculum, the dream capacity can be observed and described by means similar to those used for language, music, reasoning, and other functions of the mind. If the grammar of one's native language is in important ways described as a computational mechanism, then perhaps so may be described the instrument that assembles dream sequences. And they are both managed by the mind. This is the scientific topic that brings the dream into the course I will describe.

Dreaming and Learning

The course offerings and the student responses have led to one observation that I find of considerable interest: Dreaming and learning are similar in a number of important ways. Before turning to a discussion of the course itself I will summarize these common points.

When I speak of learning, I am thinking of the situation where a student is confronted with a mass of symbolic, abstract, conceptual material. For example, the science student is expected to master his material in such a way that mathematical principles can, in new and novel situations, be correctly applied to obtain useful solutions to real problems. Or he may be required to understand the mathematics as a source of new combinatorial puzzles. A history student faces a similar task. He must deal with a mass of material that must be approached without prejudice—indeed, with little interpretation of any sort. And he must organize and summarize it so that something new can be obtained. The student in literary criticism confronts a mass of strange and unfamiliar symbols (metaphors). He must understand their references and how those references fit together into a piece of creative writing. In short, my notion of learning is the one appropriate for a college student in a conventional classroom situation.

In the first place, the individual occupies a place of primacy in both the dreaming experience and the learning experience. The dream may inform us about our relationships with others, but the dream (under ordinary circumstances) is addressed to exactly one individual, and it speaks to the dreamer in his own unique language. And as every thoughtful student knows, no one participates in the learning experience except the student. We have classrooms, blackboards, libraries, computers, professors, laboratories, and whatever. But the learning experience itself takes place in the privacy of one mind.

Indeed, the privacy of the experience is a second point of similarity. Even if we allow for the occurrence of dream telepathy, no one shares in the dream experience itself. Like the unrecognized beliefs, fears, and desires that subtly influence our actions and our conscious thoughts, the dream maker presents the scenario to the dreamer alone.

Perhaps we will one day have a device, a learning observer, that we will fasten to a student's head. It will indicate to us, through various quantitative readings, that the student has now grasped how to solve this or that kind of differential equation. Or that he now understands why light bends in its path near the sun. I suspect that if we ever get this device, we may be able to tinker with it enough to use it as a dream observer. Fastened to the dreamer's skull, it will indicate (as usual through the quantitative measures) that the dreamer is now dreaming of a seedy and tacky lunchroom that serves to remind the dreamer of the seedy and tacky aspects of his current and past life situations. We may have these devices someday, but we do not have them now. And it is not technological inadequacy that is keeping them from us. The significant part of the experience of dreaming, like the significant part of the experience of learning, is not only private, but there are no known means to observe it instrumentally. Although the dream state is accompanied by well-defined brain-wave patterns, these patterns are completely irrelevant to the images in the dream or to the affective content of these images.

In the third place, both experiences involve comprehending a complex system of unfamiliar ideas. When we come finally to understand exactly what we have dreamed about, it is often a surprise. The process of learning to speak and read mathematics is often a surprise, and the experiences of chemistry, physics, and biology are full of surprises. But dreams do not speak to us in the language of science or of mathematics, and what they say is rarely simple. Calling, as they do, on subtly intrusive elements from immediate experience, on habits of long standing, on forgotten experiences in the distant past, the dream can assemble a complex of factors into a meaningful whole. I think we don't need to review the complexity of what confronts the college student in many of his classes.

A fourth similarity is found in the fact that in both cases the important material is concealed in a highly structured and systematic code, where the code is unknown to the individual who is experiencing it. For the physicist the code is the language of mathematics, a language in which functions are applied to arguments, in which functions are added together to get other functions, in which functions are assumed to be well behaved and orderly in ways that are commonly taken for granted. For the dreamer, the code is just as complex and just as hidden as is the code of mathematics from the physics student. It does not make the dreamer's job any easier to tell him that he is dealing with elaborate and hidden metaphors. Most of us have only a superficial grasp of the art of expression in metaphor, just as most students have only a casual grasp of what it means to apply a function to its arguments.

Another similarity is found in the spark of recognition that accompanies the breakthrough in learning. Too many times to mention we have the experience of dealing intensively with a body of material, but without any genuine "insight." Fortunately, there is often a critical moment when separate factors come together and the whole begins to make sense. Just so with the dream. We may examine this or that detail, turn over one or another aspect of the dream, until finally just one incisive piece of insight seems to decipher a large part of the puzzle. This is of course a widespread phenomenon in learning. The little people are sometimes surprised at that magic moment when they learn to maintain balance on a bicycle, or when they learn to stay afloat in the water, or put the ball in the hoop.

In my own experience, both of learning and of dreaming, this spark of recognition is accompanied by an unanticipated affect. In the case of grasping a dream, this affect is more or less strong depending on the issue that the dream has addressed. It sometimes expresses a great sadness, that so much of the past brought so much unhappiness. Sometimes it expresses a great sense of relief—a hidden source of anxiety is brought to light. Sometimes this affect provokes laughter. In the Sunday newspaper there is a little game in which the letters in English words are scrambled. The goal is to identify the unscrambled word. This experience is in many respects like trying to understand a dream, or fathom a set of mathematical theorem, or recognize the metaphors in a poem, or recognize the phrase structure in a Beethoven piano sonata. The letter string "LEMPOC," for example, resisted a number of attacks throughout one whole afternoon. I wanted to shout for joy when the "proper" arrangement sprang out! The affect that accompanies the jolt of recognition is more intense, the longer we have had to wait for it.

Dream work, like learning, also benefits from a small group setting. Such an environment is itself supportive, at least for a dream group, and it certainly ought to be in a college classroom. Moreover, if the context is not too saturated with competition, students benefit from the direct intellectual experiences of other students. It is a commonplace that one student often helps another much more effectively than does the professor.

Finally, both dream work and the college classroom work are bound up very much with relationships with others, with judgmental issues, and with questions of self-worth. I have even known people who felt inadequate because they could not recall their dreams, and people whose dreams were "not as rich or exciting as everybody else's." Indeed, if we consider the subject matter of dreams, we find that issues of judging and being judged, of self-worth, and of the pain or pleasure associated with the dreamer's relations with others are almost universal categories for dreams. In a similar way, the classroom is often (improperly, I think) concerned with competition, with scoring points, with coming out on top, with demonstrating self-worth in terms of performance at a technological skill.

The Learning Experience

Now that we have considered the close relationship between dreaming and learning, we ask if the study of dreams can shed light on the learning experience. One of the most serious defects of the educational system is that despite earnest pronouncements to the contrary, very little respect is shown for the individual apart from his possible roles in social structures. One way to appreciate this defect is to contrast the perspective of the individual who learns with the perspectives of the institutions with which the individual is or may become involved. These include family, the school, its faculty, staff, and the administrators, possible employers, the communities of classmates, friends, companions, dormitory mates, and a variety of other social structures. In the primary grades, the focus is necessarily on the individual. The child is conditioned to cultivate reading and writing skills, the principles of simple quantification, "correct" reasoning, and even social and personal skills in hygiene and the management of the individual's affairs. As the student advances through the primary grades into secondary school and then into college, the focus shifts to the needs and values of the institutions that surround him. Almost nowhere in the formal learning experience, after the primary grades, is there a substantial commitment to the individual, unqualified by institutionally administered social and political influences. In many respects it seems that the purpose of modern education is to turn us all into one great Borg Collective, despite earnest protestations to the contrary from the leaders of educational institutions.

For many, the entire college experience is expressed as a set of "requirements." There must be so many credit hours, so much of this, and so much of that. This course must be taken ahead of that course, and such and such must be done sometime in the sophomore year. And there are those grade point average requirements! What is much worse, the content of these requirements is often determined by the condition that the graduate must be equipped to take his proper place in some institutional structure. "The employers expect them to know how to do that." It sometimes seems that the school is embarrassed by the possibility that the individual may have any independent value. Now there is a lot of value for the individual in acquiring a new skill or a new body of knowledge. At a minimum learning is learning how to see clearly, how to hear clearly, how to perceive. Each time one learns a new thing the opportunity is presented to refine and sharpen personal skill in attention, in analysis, in the inspection and appreciation of detail, in expressing what has been learned, and even explaining it to someone else. Unhappily, the leaning experience as I have known it ignores many of these issues and indeed pretends they have little or no validity. It's all a bit like the stiff-upper-lip approach: of course those issues are there, but it's in poor taste to acknowledge them. The predominant measure of value is in terms of "career preparation," a euphemism for the idea that we go to college in order to learn how to behave as we are instructed by society's institutions. Not until the student reaches graduate or professional school does his individual integrity play any important part, and even then only to the extent that his analytical and creative skills can be exploited to institutional advantage.

It may be important for the educational enterprise to develop practices to enhance the status of the individual, even if some restraint has to be exercised in teaching employable skills. When closely considered, the individual student is often experienced as a vague and confused personality, unmotivated, inarticulate, insecure, and unaware. The vagueness and inarticulateness manifest themselves in low test scores, reflecting an inability to use verbal and quantitative tools beyond a minimal level. Lack of motivation shows up in an attitude expressed in one prevalent inquiry: "Why do we have to know that? Will we need that to get a job?"

If academic institutions were to ignore the muscle structures of their athletes as diligently as they ignore the "mental muscles" of their students, athletic performance would be as appalling as is performance in the simple skills of reading, writing, and arithmetic. In general, of course, these and similar deficiencies are part of what it means to be a finite and fragile human being, acting out an undefined part in a sometimes ludicrous bit of theater. But in an institutional setting where the individual has no value except as a player in that physical drama, these characteristics lead to frustration, anxiety, and hostility. Learning can hardly be expected to flourish in such a setting.

Acknowledging a problem does not solve it. But learning deficits cannot be managed unless the learner is himself aware of the nature of the deficiencies and how they are manifested in performance. Careful and close self-inspection is an essential first step toward the development of insight, surely a critical ingredient of successful learning. Indeed this kind of insight is essential for quality experience and quality action in all aspects of human affairs. Now the study of one's dream is a paradigm for self-inspection. I have already described the marked similarities between the experience of dreaming and the experience of learning. In addition, like dream work, learning requires patience and diligence, and profits from skillful guidance. Each is an experience of discovery, and like all discoveries, the attainment of success is accompanied by a spark of recognition. In short, the strong and significant connection between dream work and learning may and ought to help us understand better how to introduce fundamental and badly needed improvement into the educational system.

The Computer in the Mind: Course Outline

The course itself begins with a discussion of the nature of computing. We are not concerned with any particular technological artifact, however commercially attractive (or unattractive) it might be. We look rather to understand the very nature of computing, much as a physicist looks to understand the nature of motion, or a literary critic the nature of metaphor. So we begin with a presentation of the simplest adequate computing machine we know about. This is a little device designed by Alan M. Turing and described to the world in 1936. His machine does all its "figuring" on a strip of tape marked off into squares, each square capable of holding either Zero or One. The individual acts that this little machine can commit include: inspect a square to determine whether it holds a Zero or a One, mark a square with a Zero, or with a One, shift its attention from the square it currently inspects to the square adjacent on the left or on the right. Finite sequences of these acts are then organized into "programs." Alternative paths through the program are chosen by distinguishing what occurs in the currently inspected square, and then choosing one of two alternate paths of instructions in the program on the basis of the outcome of the act of distinguishing. A computation takes place when one "activates" such a set of instructions on a machine that is looking at a suitably prepared tape. We note that there is no arithmetic involved in this machine's activities, and that there are no alphabetic characters available to it. The behavior of this machine and of all machines like it, for all possible programs, is simply described: to rearrange, copy, and erase sequences of Zeros and Ones solely by marking individual squares, by inspecting squares, and by shifting attention from one square to another. In the half century since Turing offered this machine as a paradigm of a digital computer no evidence has appeared to suggest that his model is not adequate. That is, all known computations can in principle be carried out by a suitably prepared (and sufficiently fast!) Turing machine. One may build a computer that can in fact "do" arithmetic. But Turing's description tells us that arithmetic is not a part of the essence of computing. It is merely a cultural fascination that we find it convenient to build in. It is also a fact that diskettes, tapes, keyboards, and yes, even windows, have nothing at all to do with computation. They have a great deal to do with how we interact with our technological devices but nothing at all to do with the micro processor chips. It's kind of a shame. The truly great idea about computation is that it is fully automatic. Indeed, the term *interactive computing* is nearly an oxymoron.

One reasonably asks how it is, that if we do not have arithmetic built into the machine we can still use the machine to "do" arithmetic, since numerical processing is surely something we want the computer to do. Just so. And in answering this question we explain how *anything* that is done on a computer is actually done. We adopt a *convention* whereby certain arrangements of Zeros and Ones are to be *interpreted* as numbers. These arrangements "represent" numbers. Suppose, for example, that we want to provide a facility for adding two numbers together. Keeping the convention in mind, we assemble a sequence of instructions that will manipulate and rearrange the Zeros and Ones that represent the two numbers in such a way that at the end of the program the sum of two numbers is what is represented by the resulting sequence of Zeros and Ones. Now it is a fact that all the arithmetic we will ever want to do can be encoded in this way on a Turing machine. Alphabetic characters are similarly "represented." In one current standard, for example, the capital letter "E" is represented by the sequence "1000110." Complex operations that search for things in alphabetical order, for example, need only know about the conventions for representation. The programs may be complex and tedious to write, but that, as they say, is the way things are.

In general, then, in order to compute something we first decide how to represent the relevant things as sequences of Zeros and Ones. Then we write the programs to manipulate these sequences, remembering all the time what these sequences are supposed to represent. When we are all finished, if we have done everything correctly, the representation of the correct result will be represented in a specified sequence of Zeros and Ones on the machine's tape. We can now see what is meant by the statement that computation is the manipulation of an uninterpreted symbolic structure. Whatever meaning there is in computation, that meaning resides in the minds of those who choose representations and what to do with them. It is worth noting that we cannot envision a computing system in which the representation convention is somehow incorporated into the program. For then the representation would vanish into the resulting enlarged meaningless manipulation of even more complex symbolic structures.

I have summarized the concept of representation here in somewhat loose and condensed form. In the course itself, a more complete treatment of this material is presented to the students, together with illustrative examples. Considerable emphasis is also placed on the central observation in the theory of computing. This is the observation, or definition, that in order to compute something we first decide how to represent it and then write programs to manipulate the representations. (The reader will find a rigorous treatment of the topic in Davis 1958.)

The second technical result presented in the course explains the relationship between formal deductive logic and computing. This relation is so intimate, in fact, that deducing (or inferring) and computing are but two sides of one and the same coin. This is a mathematical and theoretical result also expressed in Turing's original paper. If you can deduce something, that deduction can be constructed by a computer, and if you can compute something with a set of programs, that same thing can be deduced from a suitable set of hypotheses. It is easy to see that this is the case. A formal logical inference generates a new expression from ones that occur earlier in a proof. For example, consider the familiar inference that "Socrates is mortal" follows from the pair "All humans are mortal" and "Socrates is human." We put these expressions into a precise syntactic form and say that "Mortal (Socrates)" follows from "(For all x) (If Human (x) then Mortal (x))" and "Human (Socrates)." It is clear that if we adhere rigorously to syntactic rules of this kind the individual steps in any logical inference can be carried out by a suitable programmed computer. It is a bit more tedious to see that every computation can be described as a deduction, where the role of inference rules is taken over by the built-in basic operations that turn one state of computation into its successor state. But the principle is the same for both deductions and computations. This formal identity of logic and computing is exploited later in the course in specific applications.

Following these rigorous and technical topics, the focus shifts to selected readings. In the fall semester in 1983, four books were read in a specified order. First, the students read Erich Harth's (1982) treatment of the central nervous system from the point of view of the mind-brain problem. This book surveys the state of the art in neurophysiology, discusses what is known about sensory processes, and explores the relations between traditional views about the mind-brain puzzle and the current state of neurophysiology. Next, the students studied Chomsky (1972) on the relation between mind and language, and the assumption that there is a species-specific and species-universal element in the human mind that can acquire a generative (computational) grammatical capacity. The reading is successful if the student appreciates the importance of the questions of fact that Chomsky raises: What is the structure of the sound-meaning correspondence? How is it physically realized? What is common to all human languages—species specific but universal? How does a normal child acquire his native language? The third book concerned the experience of music (Sessions 1950) and constituted a shift from the physical to the mental, but without surrendering an interest in precisely specified structures. The last book was the treatment of dream work by Ullman and Zimmerman (1979). There is a natural progression in the reading selected from the objective to the subjective, from the experientially unfamiliar to the personally intimate. The chain begins with anatomy and physiology, moves to grammar, then to the structure of music, and finally to dreams.

For each topic the students were asked to consider what they read from the point of view that there is some kind of computing agent at work in the human mind. From the physiological perspective one asks how the computing agent is to be identified in the central nervous system. From the Chomskyan perspective one asks what it means to identify a generative (computational) organ in the mind. The treatment of music is challenging. There is well-defined structure of music, but we have to look very carefully to identify it. One way to appreciate this structure is to compare a piece of music with a piece of prose with attention to the structural details. Apart from the context, a sentence has a meaning that is determined by the meanings of the words that occur in it (in a definite order). It is undisputed that subsequences of the words form units—phrases—that have meaning germane to that of the sentence whole. But the individual letters that make up these words contribute next to nothing to meaning. Similarly, the individual notes in a musical score contribute almost nothing to the significance of the music. It is the orderly grouping of the notes into musical phrases, and these into more complex units, serially (melody) and in parallel (harmonic), that provides the significant elements in a piece of music. In the Western musical tradition there are "grammar rules" as well. The principle of voice leading (briefly—a requirement that one changes as little as possible to achieve as much effect as possible) is like a universal grammar rule governing not only chord progressions but contrapuntal elaboration too. Certain chord sequences (for example, cadences) occur in preferred positions. And the unfolding of rhythmic patterns is far from arbitrary, not only in traditional music but in more contemporary music forms as well. (For an interesting discussion of the foundation of musical forms, see Pierce, 1983). To the extent that these structures can be logically described, they can also be incorporated into computations, for we already know of the intimate connection between logic and computing.

When dreams are discussed in the course, I try to cover at least the following: The principal value of the dream is that it gives you insight into your self, and the prominent characteristic of the dream is that it is essentially a private experience. The dream state may have physiological accompaniments that can be observed, such as rapid eye movement, changes in pulse, oxygen consumption, and so on. The substance of a dream—the staging, the cast of characters, the plot, and the peculiar style in which the characters and the props express the plot—is directly perceived only by the dreamer. A dream, with its complex elaborated story line, intense affect, and sometimes richly decorated and significant texture, is a model of private experience.

These are encouraging times for the dreamer and for the study of dreams. Essential realities about the unconscious are once again allowed to affect the attitudes and life styles of intelligent and compassionate men and women (Ferguson 1980). The flourishing of underground movements in healing, meditation practice, dream sharing, and spiritual development in general all signal an awakening of interest in the not so material aspects of human affairs. At the same time, we are more fully aware that there is at present no general theory of dream structure that provides an adequate account for the biological function of dreaming, except for the proposal that the vigilance function in the brain takes over in the dream state and alerts us to emotional threats in a highly specific way. (See Ullman 1956 for an exposition of these ideas.) There have been proposals in recent years that the dream state occurs when the brain sifts through the day's events, determined to save only what is important. None of these proposals is worth considering, for lots of reasons. I'll mention two good reasons here. There are no coherent proposals for what makes an event "important" enough to be saved. Second, there are no proposals to explain how electrophysiological neural events could make such judgments about importance.

Nor do we have any real understanding of the precise means by which a dream is delivered to the sleeper's awareness. The physiological accompaniments of dreams have been investigated in some depth. The psychiatric aspect of dreaming has been appreciated at least since the discoveries of Sigmund Freud. If the psychological dimension of dreaming is not well understood, it is only because the psychology of human nature itself remains imprecisely characterized. Mystical and religious aspects of dreaming are receiving increasing attention, and the paranormal dream has been studied in the controlled setting of the experimental laboratory. (For a current summary of what we know about the dream see Wolman, 1979.)

It is important to appreciate that dreams do not instruct us with respect to what is right or wrong. The dream draws attention to conflicts, to sources of fear, anxiety, and tension. Or it may draw attention to sources of great joy, or to an available means of self-expression or personal development. In general, the dream points to significant and often intense issues in the dreamer's current life situation. In this respect, the dream is a means of clarifying our appreciation of ourselves. The dream shows us what the realities are and leaves aside any judgment of what is good or bad, and any direct suggestion of treatment or therapy. The dream is a powerful instrument for the experience of personal insight.

A dream also has a form, I think, that is distinct from its substance. Its substance is found in feelings and in emotions, in the linkage between the bits and pieces of experience that show up in the dream and the issues in the waking life of the dreamer. The substance is what is supplied by a cogent and compelling interpretation. If the dream is a sometimes elaborate complex of symbols, then an interpretation specifies what these symbols stand for. The form of a dream is that part that is subject to interpretation. It is the part that is constant as interpretations vary. If the same object or situation can mean different things to different dreamers at different times, then the form of a dream is that part that is the " same." We might look for this form in the verbal report of the dream, but the verbal report is not the dream itself. It seems more natural to take the "cognitive content" of the dream as an approximation to its form. We particularly mean, however, to exclude all subjective and affective aspects of the dream experience. The form is what may be organized by a syntactic mental capacity.

If we postulate a mental capacity for organizing this cognitive structure of dreams, and if we can describe the forms generated by this capacity, we will have gained new insight into the formal structural capacities of the mind. And we may further enlighten our understanding of the process of dreaming and of the way in which dream forms arise in sleeping. But we note that this understanding in no way accounts for the metaphorical aspect of dreams. The proper analogy is informative. A computation is itself a meaningless manipulation of symbolic structures, one that takes meaning only when some external agency assigns coherent interpretation to these structures and to the computing processes that act upon them. Similarly, the scenario for a dream may be expressed as the script for a theatrical performance. This script might be acted out by a collection of actors and "special effects" men. When shown to an audience of people acquainted with the dreamer, the event could be regarded simply as a piece of entertainment, or it might be interpreted by the people in the audience each according to his or her own disposition at the time. The important associations and the metaphorically expressed connections felt by the dreamer are in general not derivable from any doctrinal framework. It is this script, apart from the individual's interpretation, that makes up the formal structure of the dream. In short, this formal structure is what could be controlled and generated by a computing machine.

We separated out the form of a dream from its substance with reference to the notion of sameness—the idea that two different dreamers would interpret the "same" dream fragment in different ways. It is natural, then, to try to determine when two dream forms are alike or different. When are two dreams (or dream fragments) the same?

We are interested in the question whether two dreams are the same because this concept of identity or equality underlies all other discriminations we might want to make. Any respectable theory defines its basic objects and then specifies when two such objects are equal. I'll begin by supposing, with very little fanfare, that a traditional kind of phrase-structure grammar is available for our natural language (English). Such a grammar "parses" expressions into phrases, whose constituents may in turn be further parsed. For example, the sentence

Dogs bark so that they may get attention

might very reasonably be parsed as

(Dogs(bark((so that) (they((may get) attention))))).

We need this phrase-structure concept so that we can introduce a "denotation function" in an orderly way. The basic idea is that every phrase in a language denotes something, relative to the context in which the phrase occurs. The individual words in the language denote according to social convention, which is usually recorded in a dictionary, or lexicon. Then each composite phrase in the language has a denotation that is determined by what its constituent parts denote and by the context in which it occurs. Thus "dog," "face," and "dream," despite ambiguity in general, denote something when they occur in an utterance in a particular context. "Please don't dog my footsteps." "Face the music." " The dream theory is not right." In the first of these, "dog" denotes an ongoing action. In the second, "face" denotes a more abstract kind of action. In the third, "dream" denotes a qualifier which applies to whatever "theory" denotes. If "pretty" and "little" denote properties, or characteristics, and if "puppy" denotes a four-legged object, then "pretty little puppy" denotes one of those four-legged objects having the properties which "pretty" and "little" denote. In general the denotation of a complex phrase is determined in part by what the grammatical parts of the phrase denote. What the phrase "the tall, dark-haired woman who came to the café looking for her lover" denotes is determined by what the phrase "the tall dark-haired woman" denotes and by the qualifier which the relative clause denotes. And the denotation of "the tall, dark-haired woman" is in turn determined by whatever "the woman" denotes, and by what "tall" and "dark-haired" denote. It is exactly like the language of arithmetic: if "x" denotes 6, and "y" denotes 3, and "+" denotes the addition function, then "x +y" denotes the result adding 6 and 3.

In general a meaningful (significant and understandable) piece of discourse denotes a collection of things. It also contains certain qualifiers and properties which hold for particular things in the collection, and certain relationships that obtain among some of those qualified objects. All of this is part of the meaning of the discourse, the part that is directly determined by the grammar of the utterance.

Now consider the following fragment from a dream report:

I am riding a bicycle across a high wire in a circus tent. The wire seems to dip under my weight more than I would have expected, and I am puzzled, a little frightened. My mother is standing on the ground looking up at me, her arms folded across her chest. My brother is standing on the platform I'll reach when I cross the wire. He is smiling and holding out his hand.

The objects in this manifest dream content are: the dreamer, the dreamer's mother, the dreamer's brother, a circus tent, a high wire, a platform, and a bicycle. There is one action in progress involving the dreamer, the bicycle, and the high wire. There are three qualifiers—the mother's arms are folded, the brother is smiling, and the brother's hands are out. And there are two feelings—attitudes—the dreamer is frightened, and the dreamer is puzzled.

The relationships among these people and things are clear: mother-dreamer, brother-dreamer, bicycle-dreamer, bicycle-wire, wire-circus tent. This much analysis constitutes the grammar of the dream. One can easily represent all of this manifest content in a computer, as a situation and not as a verbal depiction. It is, of course, interesting that the phrase structure of the verbal depiction is so intimately related to the manifest dream content. On the other hand, we have no "direct" access to the dream. Only the dreamer had that, and had it exactly once, probably in the middle of the night, while asleep. We are fortunate that the structure of the manifest content (as described above) is so nicely reflected in the verbal depiction.

We may ask the dreamer what feelings were associated with the people, things, and events in the dream. In this example she might say, "I am apprehensive and afraid of failure, of failure in general. I resent the judgment of others that I might fail, and I appreciate the support of those who are there for me whether I fail or succeed." Such feelings tell us little, however, until the dreamer connects them with the people in the dream. "As usual, my mother is keeping out of my way. She will be there for me if I need her, but she isn't making any judgment. Everything is up to me. My brother got me into this mess in the first place. I'm no trapeze artist and he knows it. He's always playing amateur psychiatrist with me, encouraging me to try things I don't understand and don't even care about. He's up there on the platform which means he'll only be there for me if I succeed. My mother's down on the ground where it counts."

Technically, the dreamer's feeling response might be called an "interpretation" but it doesn't seem so much an interpretation as an enrichment, a filling in. The feeling response disambiguates the dream and breathes life into it. It is the flesh and blood that turns a grammatical skeleton into a hot piece of human experience.

This example has been given in terms of an analysis whereby objects, qualities, and relationships make up the grammatical structure of the dream, and in which these people, things, and events, and the relations among them, become carriers of the dreamer's feelings. The affective dimension of a dream is completely distinct from its grammatical structure.

We have, of course, by now lost interest in the question when two dreams are the same. They are grammatically the same if they have the same grammatical structure. Or perhaps then grammatical structures are just "similar." But you could write an affective content for the dream just cited which is quite distinct from what was given here. In fact, you can do that in more than one way.

Dreams can be alike, or very similar, in interesting ways, corresponding relatives or similar house pets appear in the cast. A forest is a forest in anybody's dream. Common familiar settings turn up in dreams—my seventh-grade classroom, the avenue in my hometown, the rented room, the snake, the faceless man. And of course, there are the common dreams—to dream of running breathlessly without going anywhere, to dream of weightlessness, to dream of public nakedness, to dream of someone whose face you cannot see and whose identity is not revealed in the dream.

There is no common inherent affect associated with teeth, rooms, streets, weightlessness, nakedness, or indeed with any object. If we set all emotions and feelings aside, then a cigar *is* just a cigar, a key is only a key, and a bridge is nothing more than a piece of infrastructure. At the same level of description there is a script for the manifest content of the dream, a precise objective specification of what would be perceived if someone could see someone else's dream. It is just this kind of structure that can be specified in an elaborate computational form. In fact, these forms are similar to the "frames," "scripts," or "scenarios" that are common in the efforts to make computers understand natural language. It is tedious but straightforward to represent such scripts as otherwise uninterpreted patterns of occurrences of signs. (The reader can explore these structures starting with Barr and Feigenbaum 1981.) It is reasonable to conclude that a dream has a well-defined form that is independent of its substantial significance to the dreamer.

The significance of denotation in human mental capacities may be clarified by considering very briefly the language of mathematics (and science) and the "language" of music. In the language of mathematics denoting is all there is. "x + y" denotes 9 and that is all. There is no variety, no affect, no attitudinal disposition. It does not vary from one individual to another. The significance of mathematical language is all in the denotation. The situation with the language of music is dramatically different. Individual notes denote nothing. As a consequence, complex musical phrases cannot in general denote anything in a way that is determined by what its parts denote. Music is completely void of denotation. On the other hand, music is always significant. Indeed, if it isn't significant it probably isn't music. And the significance of a piece of music may vary widely from one individual to another. We cannot help noticing that dream structure partakes essentially of both styles of significance. The objects in a dream are subject to a denotational significance, and at the same time are carriers of affect and attitude, both of which transfer through the whole structure of the dream, giving the dream coherent and definite significance.

Student Responses

Student participation is not easily arranged with such a body of material. Formally, the students are asked to write two or three papers throughout the course, and at the end a single paper that integrates the topics covered in the reading with the technical ideas presented at the start. In other years, some students elected to make class presentations on related topics, and a few asked to be permitted to carry out some kind of computer implementation, usually in the spirit of the "artificial intelligence" tradition.

A majority of the students felt that dreams are interesting, exciting, and important. The idea of examining dreams in a formal, highly structured curriculum seems novel, challenging, and possibly of personal value. Some of these students express an interest in dream work and ask if direct experience with dream groups is possible. In one class a few students organized an experiential dream group, but it yielded to "academic pressures" after the fourth meeting. In all three classes there were students who pursued dream sharing, to a limited extent, by the use of the electronic mail and message systems available on the university's computer system. One student explored a complex and obviously troublesome issue arising in a dream, using a dynamic message system in which the student's anonymity was assured. There were a few who thought that dreams had no significance, and a few who thought that one needed professional training in order to deal effectively with dreams. There were a few who were actually embarrassed by the discussion of dreams. One student told me that she had been working with her dreams for some years and that dream work is far too intimate a matter for classroom treatment.

But aside from these few exceptions most of the students were both interested and enthusiastic about our study of dreams. One girl told me that the course should have begun with the discussion of dreams, so that everyone could appreciate right away the personal dimension of the course material. In the papers submitted by the students there were a number of insights offered.

One paper explored the similarity between the capacity for dreaming and the capacity for language. In each case one uses forms in a completely different category—the experience of life itself. This paper observed that just as complex grammatical elements are made up of simpler ones, so the complex images in a dream are often composed of much simpler ones. And just as words are constructed from an arbitrary arrangement of letters (there is no reason that any particular arrangements of the letters *a, d, n,* and *s* should denote the stuff we find at beaches), so a dream image is constructed from simple sensations and complexes of sensations that are not essentially related to the issues dreamed about.

Another student called the dream maker a "communicator between the outer you and the inner you" and described its job as "the least well-understood of all the functions of the human mind." This student went on to describe his own dreams as a means for enriching his life, making available to him experiences and perspectives he would not otherwise have. Whether or not he connects his dreams with waking life, all his dreams are an "invitation to an open mind."

Another student speculated that the dream maker is at work all day long, collecting raw material for later dreams, sifting the novel from the banal, spotting the individual's unconscious emotional responses to scarcely noticeable intrusions. This fellow described the dream as articulating "the traumas lurking around in our highly adaptive minds" and considered the notion that dreaming is a principle instrument for adapting the organism to emotional realities.

Many of the students were taken by the contrast between the issues of concealment and revelation, and by the obvious fact that a cigar is not always just a cigar. (They also noted that a cigar is not always a lollipop, either!) One student tried to tie this contrast with memory. He observed that although one form of consciousness is held in abeyance during sleep and dreaming, access to the contents seems to be facilitated while dreaming. He saw this as evidence that memory is but one among a number of different "mental organs," one that is accessible by many of the others.

Another student asked why some dreams are so real, so authentic, whereas others are so exotic or fantastic. He speculated that personal difficulties of long standing can be classified by whether they are expressed in a realistic dream, a fantastic dream, or an exotic dream. He said that he had some "boring" dreams but that boredom itself was part of the dream's message.

Several students commented in depth on the creative capacity that the dream maker uses. Many reached even farther to get a technical notion of creative freedom—the idea that the shape, the physical texture, of the symbol is unrelated to what is represented. The complete freedom with which the dreamer establishes metaphorical relationships was widely noted, for poetry, for fiction, for music, and above all for the dream. Speaking of his dreams, one boy wrote, "The mind is free to act exactly as it pleases." He explained further that during sleep the mind is not preoccupied with the continuous processing of sensory inputs and does not have to organize motor responses. Thus the dream arises effortlessly and spontaneously.

Finally, one girl reported something special about the similarity between our ability to dream and our ability to make music:

> Creativity is the element that is common to both the artist and the dreamer. For example, the poet/composer and the dreamer are both

> concerned with using imagination to express a feeling or an emotion. These concepts can best be illustrated in quotes from authors. Ullman and Zimmerman (1979) speak of dreamers in general: " We have learned, then, to use images the same way a poet has learned to use language: to play with them and recombine them in new ways to express feelings, moods, and stirrings within us that cannot be adequately expressed in any other way."
>
> Sessions (1950) documents the role of the performer and composer in a strikingly similar manner: "All the elements of this movement-rhythm, tempo, pitch, accent, dynamic shading, tone quality, . . . are . . . kept under the most exquisite control, by performer and composer alike; . . . By these means a musical gesture gains what we sometimes call 'musical sense.' It achieves a meaning which can be conveyed in no other way."

My own response to the teaching experience is that I am now seeking ways to apply the experience of dreaming to the particular problems that confront a student in computing. These problems arise in the attempt to master unfamiliar and complex combinatorial structures and to connect them in coherent and fruitful ways. On the one hand, a problem for computational treatment may be specified in precise mathematical terms; on the other hand, algorithms for extracting meaningful results from these mathematical terms have their own peculiar combinatorial properties. The successful student must learn how to read, write, and "pair up" these two distinct kinds of structures—the well-defined problem and the correct algorithm.

More generally, the college experience is successful to the extent that it nurtures self-reliance. The teacher is pleased when the student emerges articulate, disciplined, and curious. We may use programming as an acquired skill that enhances these desirable effects. The complex and rigid character of computer programming offers special advantages in the development of patience and even compassion. But we know the signs of the onset of success in learning. The student begins to exhibit the rudiments of style, and even a little finesse. These issues arise in other classrooms, and the fact that they are germane throughout adult life suggests that it is appropriate to address them directly. What Richard Jones (1979) has done with creative writing students can be done and perhaps ought to be done with students in other disciplines. In working with a dream we invest the dreamer with a certain value not derived from measurable academic performance. What kind of result would we see if students moved from an experience of this kind of nonjudgmental awareness directly to a demanding combinatorial task? What is the larger-scale merit of valuing oneself enough to tend to one's relationship with others?

In his study of the recent history of intellectual measurement Stephen Jay Gould (1981) quotes Alfred Binet, speaking of small children with learning difficulties:

> What they should learn first is not the subjects ordinarily taught, however important they may be; they should be given lessons of will, of attention, of discipline; before exercises in grammar, they need to be exercised in mental orthopedics; in a word they must learn how to learn. (p. 154)

Binet in fact went on to develop a concrete program of "mental orthopedics," and to implement that program in the classroom. Gould quotes him again:

> It is in this practical sense, the only one accessible to us, that we say that the intelligence of these children has been increased. We have increased what constitutes the intelligence of a pupil: the capacity to learn and to assimilate instruction. (p. 154)

One envies Binet the opportunity to invest the student with such respect. One envies him the chance to exclude fear, authority, and excessive conformity as primary motivating forces in the learning situation. And one admires his appreciation for the fact that precision and clarity in immediate awareness are not only of transcendent importance in learning, but can actually be cultivated and enhanced. How much real distance can there be between Binet's mental orthopedics and the emotional orthopedics of honest, nonmanipulative dream work?

Summary

In this chapter I have reviewed my treatment of dreams in an undergraduate course where the perspective is the theory of computation. We saw that dreaming and learning are both concerned with attempting to understand material that is strange and sometimes threatening, and that they are most deeply involved with the intrinsic worth of the individual. We observed a variety of other similarities between the two experiences.

A number of other "intellectual" activities were reviewed and were seen to be consistent with the assumption that the mind manipulates structures that are specifiable in terms of computation. There was a search for a specific kind of structure—the form of the dream—that might be generated by a capacity that functions in an exact and explicit way, much as Chomsky's grammatical capacity to generate a syntactic structure.

The content of the reading for the course was summarized, and the responses of the students were reviewed. We surveyed some basic experimentally determined facts about the central nervous system, its structure and its function. We examined the well-defined structures that Chomsky has postulated to account for the grammar of natural human language, and we considered the existence of musical forms as mental constructs.

My own response to the teaching experience was described—an intuition that the college learning experience may profit from a redirection toward basic mental skills—self-awareness, the management of will, attention, and discipline, and a sense of compassion for and trust in one's own personality.

Note

This chapter is a modest revision of the chapter I wrote for the first edition of this book. I have changed some phrasing here and there and have added a handful of phrases. There is a major addition on the grammar of dreams that compares the structure of dreams with the structure of music and with the structure of the language of mathematics. None of these ideas is developed in a scientifically respectable way, but I have tried to sketch in enough of their genes so that you can speculate what the baby might look like. Although it is ten years later, I am keeping the tense appropriate for 1987.

References

Barr, A., and Feignbaum, E. A., eds. *The Handbook of Artificial Intelligence.* Los Altos: William Kaufmann, 1981.

Chomsky, N. *Language and Mind* (enlarged ed.). New York: Harcourt Brace Jovanovich, 1972.

Davis, M. *Computability and Unsolvability.* New York: McGraw-Hill, 1958.

Ferguson, M. *The Aquarian Conspiracy.* Los Angeles: Jeremy P. Tarcher, 1980.

Gould, S. J. *The Mismeasure of Man.* New York: W. W. Norton, 1981.

Harth, E. *Windows on the Mind.* New York: Quill, 1982.

Jones, R. M. *The Dream Poet.* Cambridge, Mass.: Schenkman, 1979.

Pierce, J. R. *The Science of Musical Sound.* New York: Scientific American Library, 1983.

Sessions, R. *The Musical Experience of Composer, Performer, Listener.* New York: Atheneum, 1950.

Turing, A. M. "On Computable Numbers, with an Application to the Entscheidungsproblem." *Proceedings of the London Mathematical Society, ser.* 2, 1936, 42, pp. 230–65, 431, 544–46.

Ullman, M., "Physiological Determinants of the Dream Process," *Journal of Nervous and Mental Disorders* 124, 1 (1956).

Ullman, M., and Zimmerman, N. *Working with Dreams.* Los Angeles: Jeremy P. Tarcher, 1979.

Wolman, B. B., ed. *Handbook of Dreams.* New York: Van Nostrand Reinhold, 1979.

CHAPTER SEVEN

Night Rule

Dreams as Social Intelligence

John R. Wikse

John Wikse is an unusual breed of political scientist. His career was shaped in part by the turmoil and unrest of the sixties. He found himself torn between a way of life linked to academia and an inner drive to seek out a setting more congenial to his scholarly and aesthetic aspirations.

Dr. Wikse takes seriously the often ignored reality that political arrangements have to be understood in terms of their harmful as well as their beneficial impact on human subjectivity. He has brought this view to his interest in and understanding of dreams. Endowed with a rich sense of metaphor, he has used the dream as an instrument to explore some of the critical connections between unsolved problems at the personal level and unresolved issues at the broader social level. In an innovative way he has introduced dream work into his courses in political science.

In the chapter that follows he has clearly illustrated, through the examples he provides, the way the dream can be viewed as social intelligence and can be used an an instrument to explore the way personal issues are critically connected to political, social, and economic issues.

Introduction

Here comes my messenger. How now, mad spirit?
What night-rule now about this haunted grove?

—Shakespeare, *A Midsummer Night's Dream*

Our dreams are our closest counselors. Near to us, like a mirror, they reflect our inmost dialogue with ourselves. Dreams provide our most expansive views of the horizons that are coming into being in us, coming to consciousness. These horizons are various and overlapping, interconnected contexts of significance. Through them, we can identify and recognize ourselves and others.

I once stood in a hallway speaking with a fellow faculty member between classes when a student joined us addressing my colleague: "I had a dream about our class. You were standing at the blackboard, looking over your shoulder at us while trying to hammer a nail into the blackboard. You kept hitting all around the nail, but not hitting it on the head!" We all laughed, recognizing the pun. The instructor responded that he knew he sometimes talked around a subject, not getting to the point.

This exchange points to one of the most healing aspects of dream sharing, dream humor, which enabled a student to communicate a perception to her teacher that might otherwise have been held back in frustration or expressed as criticism. Because the dream metaphor was so apt and apparent, clear and playful, the exchange of this perception was direct and friendly. It was facilitated by the humor that bridged the gap between teacher and student. As the young woman spoke the dream, we discovered the pun and its obvious significance simultaneously. We saw the meaning through the humor. Here is our social intelligence at work.

I place this dream at the introduction to this chapter in order to get to the point at the beginning, to exemplify the direct, powerful simplicity of dream communication as a source of social insight. I began studying dreams as social information when I came to understand how limited was my own ability to perceive unresolved tensions and blind spots in myself and others. As I learned to appreciate dream metaphors, I saw that I had come to rely upon and affirm partial self and social images that split me into parts, like jigsaw puzzles. I first became conscious of this schism when I came face to face with myself in a dream in which I stood pointing a rifle at myself. To see so vividly that I was at war with myself confronted me with a form of doubt, the intuition of a deep-lying ignorance. In our dreams we can become aware of the need to bridge the gaps and schisms separating us from ourselves and others.

I once dreamed that I was swimming in the bloodstream of a large organic body, moving from person to person among members of a research group to which I belonged. The feeling has remained with me as a guide. In this dream, it was as if each other with whom I was related was a unique organ functioning within the larger body that composed us. As I approached each member of the group, I was sometimes repelled backward through the arteries which connected us; at times I remained in peaceful equilibrium; at times there was the feeling of friction within a fluid medium. I realized that this dream had offered me a vantage point on the patterns of conflict in my exchanges with others in my "social body." This standpoint is accessible through dream appreciation.

In our dreams lie the memories and metaphors of our search for sanity. To learn from the dream work is to feel the metaphors, to appreciate the cultural symbols of the image-making social organism of which we are a part in our dreams. We are a part of this complex, interpersonal organism when we wake as well, though often we do not recognize ourselves. Through appreciating our dreams we can better see the whole of which we are an aspect, the limits that define our possibilities in relationship to particular, contextual, historical conditions. In our dreams we can perceive the interconnectedness of social, individual, and political reality—an insight basic to the development of our sociological imaginations.

The structure of the dream work is timeless. In our dreams we see from the standpoint of a moment that stretches past into future, projecting the history of our emotional associations toward the anticipated horizons of our experience. In the dream space, timebound assumptions are open to scrutiny.

To learn to appreciate this social scrutiny aspect of dreams we must face the contradictions through which we can "identify the collective aspects of individual problems as reflected in dreams" (Ullman, 1969 p. 3). Our dreams are pictograms, that is, linguistic and visual representations of our emotions, our social realities. They are composed of our deepest needs and aspirations, our values and interests. They depict the sources of discontent in the relationships we are living, point out possible patterns of adaptation to novel circumstances, provide perspective on our cherished self-images to broaden our understanding of who we are.

When I first started thinking about dreams as social information, I dreamed I was in a class studying English, my native tongue, as a foreign language, something familiar yet strange. My intent in this chapter is to demonstrate the value of appreciating this language. My aim is to help to formulate a psychology that is grounded in a description of the social unconscious, which develops out from the dream toward a fuller awareness of our social selves and which encourages people to learn from their dreams.

Dreams as Social Information

Several years ago I offered a seminar on the political theory of fraternity. Some of the graduate students had worked together and with me before. Toward the end of the term one of the students dreamed that we were all playing a game called "ultimate frisbee." Contrary to the usual practice of the game in which there is no referee, in his dream I was both the referee and a player on one of the competing sides.

This dream depicts a contradiction in the organizational structure of the seminar. While we were a group of people who saw ourselves as friends cooperatively studying the politics of fraternity, nonetheless there were competing sides. I was formally responsible, by virtue of my position, for evaluating the performance of others. I was both participant and referee.

This is an example of the social information that is present in our dreams. Dream imagery is the result of the personal rearrangement of social metaphors available to us to express aspects of ourselves coming into being and not yet articulated consciously. Dream images arise in dialectical fashion out of contradictory emotional tensions reflecting the gaps between the known and familiar on the one hand and the novel and unknown on the other.

The perspective of this dream is that of critical imagination. It asks us to wonder how our seminar compares to an imaginary game. It presents a metaphoric standard through which to view the dreamer's situation. It is focused along the critical edge of our experience, something familiar but out of kilter, odd. By learning to appreciate this tilted reality, an aspect of the organizational structure of the seminar emerges in sharp relief, juxtaposed with an image that leads us to explore something contradictory about our experience, a dilemma, an ambivalence in the situation.

A dream metaphor brings together at least two assumptions in tension with each other. In the "ultimate frisbee" dream, my student-friend expressed the awareness that he was part of a group that is like another social activity with which he was acquainted. This other activity is characterized by an ethic of equal participation, and the seminar resembles it in this respect. Yet it is also a group in which one individual is distinguished from all the rest by virtue of a position that is like being a referee in a game without a referee. The dream presents the seminar as both this and that, ambivalent, contradictory, novel.

Dreams speak the language of imagination. They do so through images that do not obey the laws of noncontradiction, through metaphors which bring together and focus our emotional ambivalences. Dreams reflect our affective connections with others and the world, placing us in an ever-changing field of exchanges and relationships. In our dream imaginations we see from the standpoint of the social animal, concerned about our connections, involved in an interpersonal experience, in an emotional, social agitation produced involuntarily within us. As such our dreams can be the source of significant information about the character and quality of our associations.

However, like many things of value, we have privatized our dreams. We tend to view dreams as occurring within the private, separate person, rather than as messages communicating social information. To the degree to which we are unable to recognize our dreams as tools for social insight and analysis, our capacity to act intelligently, our cooperative, communicative competency is impaired. Most of the social information in our dreams goes unacknowledged and unused, is not fed back to the relationships to which it refers, or is done so in certain prescribed ways via professional intermediaries, for example, in therapeutic transactions. We do not usually share our dreams with those with whom we work, though we dream about them. For the most part we are therefore not conscious of the intelligence that we possess about the connections between our feelings and emotions and the relationships, institutions, and issues they represent.

Where interaction takes place along a hierarchy of status, power, or wealth, where one is placed "one up" or "one down" with respect to others within a structure of privilege, communication tends not toward open dialogue but is distorted by the tacit necessity to preserve one's position. The relational antinomies of, for example, student-teacher, worker-manager, patient-healer may each involve power-knowledge imbalances in which we learn to say what we mean and need in ways compatible with our perception of danger present. Wherever there are age, class, race, gender, or other invidious divisions among people that correspond to actual power imbalances, there will be some distortion of perceptions that could call these assumptions to consciousness, and therefore potentially into question. It is in this sense that the dream referred to above reflects a kind of danger about the dreamer's situation. On the one hand, the situation seems open and playful, friendly. On the other it is competitive. There are sides and a referee in an ambiguous position, with the power to reward and punish. This sort of danger is the stuff from which the social metaphors of dreams are constructed. Thus our dreams contain potentially subversive information, opening a vantage point beneath assumptions that are coming-to-consciousness.

Our organism as a whole picks up more information than our consciousness can process. As sociocultural animals we adapt and survive by producing our environment. If our organizations are open to experimentation in terms of their basic organizing assumptions, then information that focuses the tensions and irritations of the social body, its problems and dilemmas, is of great value. But where association is fearful, coercive, and closed, social information will be factional, partial, and distorted. Wherever we are unable to examine and modify the assumptions of our relationships with others we are confronted with potential information that has no place to go except our dreams.

In Germany before World War II many people reported dreaming that the State had abolished dreams (Beradt 1972). This points to the invasion of our dream life by the totalistic State systems of our times. Many people do not remember their dreams. Some believe they do not dream at all. Wherever people are not free to speak and act without fear of arbitrary retaliation, their dreams will pinpoint the source of disturbance of their social selves.

During the watches of the night, our dreams survey, among other concerns, our social situations. A dream is a kind of night watchman, guarding, protecting, and watching over the safety of our associations, checking to be sure that it is safe to sleep.

Goethe, whose understanding of dreams greatly influenced Freud, employed this image to describe the healing function of dreams:

> Ye who surround this head with aerial wheeling,
> Here prove the noble elfin way of healing,
> Soothe now the wearied heart's contention dire
> Withdraw the searing arrows of remorse,
> Of horrors suffered cleanse his soul entire
> Four are the vigils of the night's dim course, . . .
>
> (*FAUST*, Pt. 2, Act 1)

This points us toward the concern for the health of the whole organism that is characteristic of the perspective of the dream work. To the extent to which we view the dream from this standpoint, our dream watches may be said to survey what I will call "night rules": those deep assumptions of our social unconscious, the root metaphors that represent to us the logic of our social identities.

Thus, although we might agree with Freud (1965) that in some sense the dream always points toward the ego, the individual, it is not clear that dreams are as he put it "completely egoistic" (p. 301). Freud himself wrote that he would "reject as a meaningless and unjustifiable piece of speculation the notion that all figures that appear in a dream are to be regarded as fragmentations and representations of the dreamer's own ego" (1959, p. 149). The individual is a social organism. In dreams we experience the personal and the social as overlapping transparencies, metaphors that are simultaneously ego- and sociocentric. Social myths, icons, and stereotypes are surveyed by our dream intelligence.

However, to explore the sociocentricity of the dream work is not to deny the existence of dimensions of dream experience that go beyond the immediacy of daily, particular social life. Dream appreciation always remains open-ended, reaching out to the broad periphery of human awareness, to the telepathic and parapsychological and archetypical dimensions of experience. Thus the study of our night rules is a particular practice and discipline of dream work which offers a perspective on dreams that can serve to combat the social ignorance of the dreamer.

In order to fully appreciate the social information in dreams, the dreamer must be able to share a dream in a context in which it is possible to become reflective about the conditions and circumstances of social life, to critically examine assumptions about self and society from the standpoint of the will to therapy (wholeness) which directs the dream. To work with dreams as tools for social investigation entails developing a group process. Ideally, a dream appreciation research group would be a voluntary association of equals who had a task in common and were committed to using dream information in an understanding of their own group dynamics.

In the sections that follow, I will work with the texts of several dreams, attempting to appreciate them as social information, as pointing out interpersonal, intersubjective, contextual dilemmas. We experience our social selves at many different levels of abstraction. Our most intimate associations and the most remote, mediated images find themselves together in our dreams. Such is the range of our social unconscious.

The Polaroid Camera and the Nature of Self-consciousness

After a student joined one of my classes I dreamed the following:

> I am watching a new student in my class trying to take a photograph of himself standing in the front row of a group of his fellow classmates. He is using a polaroid camera, and I see him both standing at the head of this group smiling at me, and simultaneously standing apart from the group trying to take his own picture. He looks at the picture which he takes and sees that he has had his thumb in front of the lens and this has blocked out his own face in the photo. He laughs nervously.

I am struck by the dilemma this dream poses: How can one picture oneself as part of a group of which s/he is a member? The picture the student is taking of himself places him in the front row of the class, grinning toward me and photographing himself at the same time. I see two of him: one facing me, the other trying to view himself as a group member. The split standpoint makes it impossible for him to get a clear view of himself.

Standing in the front row of the group, "at the head of the class" is a social image, the product of certain rules and relationships—principles of social organization—just as the polaroid camera is a product of a particular technology. The instant camera can provide us with an image of the relational appearance of our lives: here I am with Tom and Andy, or there with Linda on the steps, seen as "others saw us," outside myself in association with others.

In our attempts to get a sense of how we fit in a group we confront objective patterns of membership, structures of status and hierarchy (like the set of assumptions involved in being "first in the class") that provide a comparative standard by which one's self-image can be judged. In the dream, the student is smiling at me, not at the camera. It is toward me that his pose is directed, for I can determine who is at the head of the class. His self-image is split into two parts, one performing for me, the other trying to stand back and evaluate himself in terms of the group of his peers. In trying to get a picture of himself he is "all thumbs."

This dream points between us to a set of assumptions that structure our relationship. I am involved in his anxiety by virtue of my position in the classroom. The dream points to my own responsibility and emotional involvement, to my participation in the social images that structure self-consciousness in a common social situation. Here the dream can be seen as both ego- and sociocentric, exploring the tensions of status or role anxiety within a social body of which I am a part. Appreciating dreams as social information is like removing the thumb from in front of the camera lens. It opens a fuller picture of our social being.

Contemporaneously with the development of the polaroid camera, we have reached a stage in our group development when we can see that there is need for skills through which to give a group feedback on itself, so that it may come to reflect upon its process as a whole. In this dream we can see how difficult it is for a member of a hierarchical status-system to face one's position, to perceive oneself truly. Performance and status anxiety distract and split us, placing on the individual a contradictory demand. This might be called, following Laing (1982) and Bateson (1972), the schizophrenogenic aspect of group dynamics, the splitting of attention between the referee-leader-teacher and the rest of the class.

Here we see the sides into which the classroom is drawn, where the two perspectives of the student correspond to the structural separation of the seminar that I discussed in the "ultimate frisbee" dream above. There I, as both teacher and participant, referee in a game without a referee, the only one on my side, directing the discussion and giving the grades, am separated by objective contradictions from the rest of the seminar. The student's experience is split by this structural relationship, focused in two directions and organized so that the possibility of direct and instant feedback with regard to one's place in the group is negated. Where individuals within a group are split in this way, whatever such a group may accomplish will be distracted by the tensions in its organizational structure which these dreams point out.

Identity, Economy, and Society

Alienation from social information affects both our everyday familial interaction and our relationships with the larger economy in terms of which our familial identities are supported. Family and work are an interconnected web of meanings. Our intimate associations and emotions are matters of economic security. The organization of our workplaces, the divisions of labor that structure them, and the hierarchical specialization of information and position which defines the patterns of communication within them are all aspects of the context of meaning within which we experience family.

Familial emotions are economic transactions, exchanges within the *oikos* (Gr. for family, household, root of *economics*). Our intimate and extended economic activities are interconnected. How we work is inseparable from how we live, how we organize the production and the reproduction of life. How we distribute the satisfactions and responsibilities that define us in relationship to our economic identities and our experience of the quality and character of this distribution become apparent in our dreams.

Often it is difficult to distinguish the range of emotions in intimate bonds. Dream sharing within the family can help to sort out the psychosocial pressures that are released under conditions of intimacy. The following exchange of dreams took place between a couple shortly after the husband had lost his job:

> He dreams that his wife is suffocating him with the bed covers. He throws them off, wakes up lashing out at her next to him, waking her. Frightened, she screams. He realizes he was dreaming and tells her the dream. In the morning when they wake she tells him that she dreamed that he was being suffocated by the god of economic power.

Taken together, these dreams represent perspectives of partners in an intimate association. The problem is suffocation. He dreams that she is suffocating him. She dreams that he is being suffocated by economic power. Here is a dream-communication between them, free association between dreams. The dream information is that there is a connection between his feelings of suffocation by her and the structure of economic power, presented in her dream as a god.

The god of economic power is a metaphor to conjure with. If my anger at you is connected with and mediated by the generalized insecurities and contradictions of the larger economic order, then I can learn to distinguish how it compensates for the weight of a deeper societal powerlessness—which would otherwise be unconscious.

In addition to dream sharing in the family, dream information can clarify the affective connections between individual and work situation. Here is a dream that depicts the separation/relation of work and informal socializing:

There is a dinner at my home with people who I think are my work mates. It is an ordinary relaxed dinner. The day after, we go to work. When we get to the work place there is a circus. We talk and change clothes in order to work at the circus.

After working with this dream the dreamer commented:

> The circus is where I work. The dinner is false. It is a way of seeming to have something together, but it is over when the act begins and we have to change clothes. Then we go into an act to please the public, who are the people around me.

The tension involved in not acknowledging that the dreamer works in a circus comes to consciousness through appreciating the manifest content of the dream.

Here is a dream that depicts the pressure of conformity in the workplace:

I was swimming in a pool. There were lots of people around the pool. I didn't see any faces, only their heads. Suddenly they pressed down my head. Then I was very scared, but said to myself, "OK, let them press me to the bottom, then I will fly up again." Then I let them press me. I went to the bottom, then I flew up very quickly, and then I was relieved. I had no clothes on me. I swam like a fish. Children were behind me also swimming like fishes in the water.

They press down my head. They are faceless. Speaking of the work context that generated this dream, the dreamer commented:

> I felt everyone was telling me how to think. They were trying to persuade me to think along what they felt were the right lines. When I deal with them individually they are very nice, but when they become members of an invisible nameless group they can be terrible.

We all belong to this invisible, nameless group which composes the pressure of a diffuse and abstract sense of faceless authority and conformity, the force of normality and social opinion. Imaged in this dream are "heads without faces," hierarchical positional authority (as in "head" of department, class) which depress the individual, submerging her under an impersonal, fearful force that threatens to drown her. There are connections between hierarchy, impersonality, and depression manifest in this dream which suggest that being "pressed down" is a structural consequence of her work life. Here we can see that depression is a pattern of identification both economic and psychological, related to conformity in thinking and the repression of individuality. This pressure weighs down on the dreamer like the spirit of gravity. But her dream reminds her of her capacity to relieve the pressure. By recognizing her work situation in these metaphors she can identify the social tension, the faceless impersonality that depresses her.

In addition to metaphors which illuminate familial and workplace identifications, dreams can help us to focus the dilemmas of social-sexual (gender) role identification, as can be seen in the following dream:

I scolded my daughter for spending an exorbitant amount on stationery. My husband asked if I was going to complain. I located the manager, told him I had three daughters and was a longtime customer. He offered me a Barbie Doll. I replied that I was too old for dolls, and asked for my money back. *

This dream depicts a nexus of social-sexual identification—call it the "Barbie Doll complex"—which is coming to consciousness for the dreamer. Scolding her daughter, being perceived by her husband as "complaining," defined by the structural relationship of manager/customer—this complex is a logically interconnected whole. In the dream the resentment of the "longtime customer" who has "bought into" this complex is coming to the surface. The issue involves genuine satisfaction and maturation. The dreamer wants her money back; she will no longer be bought off with a Barbie Doll image of herself.

The Barbie Doll is both a personal and a social metaphor. It points to the relationship between a cluster of concerns—anger at one's daughter, recurrent complaining, the passivity of the customer for whom life is managed by others—and the patterns of satisfaction that are expected to compensate for being treated, as an adult woman, like a little girl. This social image integrates a set of tensions around familial, economic, and gender identification. It illuminates their interconnections. The dream indicates the possible rejection on the dreamer's part of this pattern of identification.

Processes of identification can be more or less conscious. We develop patterns of adaptation in reference to the history of our symbolic identifications. When we become aware of symbols that represent ill-adaptive identifications, we become capable of perceiving what is contradictory and self-defeating. We can become more open to the need for genuine satisfactions.

---

* The above three dreams are courtesy of Montague Ullman's dream appreciation groups.

Having explored the psycho-economic patterns of identity above, we can now broaden our lens to include the subject of political metaphors in dreams, searching to uncover contemporary images of political identification.

Spectacle Entertainment

Another dream of mine:

I enter the department seminar room, but instead of my regular class there is some kind of party going on. I remember that the class is being transformed into a special event. It is combination newsroom and offtrack betting room (a "bookie joint"). News reports fill the room from different radio and TV sets. When a piece of news come in, everyone gets excited and rushes to show it to others. Part of the group is following professional football results. The other is following the presidential election. Someone reads out this information to an old graduate student friend of mine who is typing it all down. Someone reads out a message: "If the Minnesota Vikings beat Dallas then Powell will win the election." I enter, several students give reports to me, but I feel unneeded. At one point I announce that if anyone has any questions they can ask me. I sit down for awhile, but nobody asks me anything. I feel very detached from the goings on.

What sort of party is this? The kind of party that is the special event of the dream combines images of two contemporary social activities, football and electoral politics, and connects these activities in a causal statement. If something happens in the Super Bowl, there will be a specifiable consequence in the realm of politics. Both activities seem to be treated similarly as objects of study by the seminar. Electoral politics is like professional football. There are rival and competing organizations, teams that make game plans. In the perspective of the dream, both are spectator events which happen at a distance and are "mediated," encountered as the sort of information that is brought to us by the evening news. "Beating Dallas" is like "winning the election"— special events which people follow, as fans and partisans: "Party" competition.

The seminar room is a bookie joint. People are placing bets on the basis of predictions. The activities of both football and politics are associated with the activities of professional gambling, and the "if, then" logical form of predictive knowledge of special events which happen at a distance and are experienced as spectacles is the same logic as the calculation of odds. So the sense in which politics is like football in the dream refers us to a way of thinking and a theory of knowledge that is like gambling.

Here of course we might recognize both the known familiarity between politicians and gambling figures and the increasing prevalence of gambling (lotteries) as generating "public" revenue. The dream also suggests that "class" (in the economic sense) is being transformed by this way of thinking.

This dream confronts me with my own distance from politics understood in this way and from a dominant research methodology in the study of political behavior based on statistical prediction. When I dreamed this I was teaching at a large state university in which I often could not judge whether my political scientist colleagues were discussing sports or politics, particularly when the seasons overlap as they do in the fall. In the dream I feel unneeded, irrelevant, outside, detached. These feelings of alienation depict my relationship to an academic work environment based on certain assumptions about politics and knowledge.

In Plato's *Republic* (Bk. 7), Socrates presents the famous allegory by means of which we are to imagine that we are prisoners in a cave, chained together so that we cannot see anything of each other save the shadows of icons that are projected on the wall in front of us. Plato notes that such prisoners might give a prize to those who are "sharpest at making out the things that go by," thereby most able to divine what is going to come. Such knowledge of what is "coming into being" is appropriate to prisoners for whom special events are to be watched, not done. The images on the wall of the cave, like media images, are the iconography of a particular culture, within which it makes sense to think of politics as if it were like football. Imagine a football over which is written: "Campaign '96."

Politics as a special event is also the social myth that focuses my dilemma in the classroom. I would like to be useful to those who are studying politics as if it were like football. This would be to talk about the political iconography of detachment, of the consequences, in Ellul's words, of "living in the news." The dream points to a particular political illusion with which I am in tension, to assumptions associated with a conception of politics as spectacle entertainment.

I am no longer identified as a political scientist in my work. In several of the dreams above I have worked with aspects of my own professional identification in the context of exploring those structural contradictions which they revealed to me regarding my work life. The last of these dreams occurred after I had been away from academic life for several years and was getting in touch with deeper contradictions than those of the immediate situation. In the following dream, images of class and racial privilege show us that despite our most cherished self-images to the contrary, we are objectively, deeply alienated from our fellows, across gaps of privileged, stereotypical identifications.

The View from Across the Aisle

While traveling on a Greyhound bus from Pittsburgh to Chicago I was reading a book on the Haymarket "riots" in Chicago at the end of the nineteenth century. Included were several examples of anarchist posters organizing workers to strike. Across from me was a young black man. I curled into the seat to sleep and dreamed that I was watching myself as I slept from his seat across the aisle. Above me as I saw myself sleeping, in the space reserved for commercial advertising, was a poster. It was composed of a series of columns of figures which computed my lifetime grade point average, from kindergarten through my Ph.D.: 3.9 was the total. Above these numbers was my signature, Jack Wikse. Someone walked over and scribbled "Jack Wis" over the poster.

Here the dream presents me with information about my signature, as seen from a specific perspective, my academic vita viewed as a lifelong, continuous record of my grades. The anarchist posters from my reading have been transformed into a self-advertisement of my academic achievements, a sign or signature for my persona, projected from the perspective of a stranger across the aisle. "I wonder how he sees me?" is the seed of the dream, projected by the social unconscious across the aisle of race, class, and privilege. The answer is mediated by the iconography of the lifetime grade point average, simultaneously a personal and a social image (perhaps even an institution). The dream tells me it is my signature, that is, the way that I am recognized by others. It is an image of privilege and success.

An off-kilter version of this identity is scribbled, across my self-image, a defacing of my poster-signature, "Jack Wis," something strange and feeling unfinished, partial. When I worked with this dream I felt that the transformation of my last name into "Wis" was an ironic way of saying, "You think you're so knowledgeable and 'wise,' studying the history of the working class, such a 'wiz' studying the anarchists, but cut off from the man across the aisle." Several months after having moved to Wisconsin, I saw the abbreviation "Wis" on my address, and thought that this was a perfect metaphor to organize my changing identity in an unexplored environment.

This dream confronted me with my unfinished self-image, challenging me to integrate this perspective on my social self, pointing me to explore the relationship between race and privilege and academia, those patterns of identification that had made it a dilemma for me to cross the aisle to another part of my divided social body.

Like race and class, deep in our social unconscious are images that probe the larger identification patterns of our collective lives—national and international symbols which allow a broader cultural unconscious to emerge as an object of awareness. In the following I will discuss certain structural characteristics of the social unconscious as they are revealed in a dream that I had in 1980 after traveling from Europe to the United States.

Seriality and Mediation

We are in a crowd of people, moving along a conveyor belt. Plastic tubes connect our eyes, ears, and mouths. We start up an escalator. "Second floor, France!" says a voice from a loudspeaker, "All French depart here." I see a sign on the wall with a list of the things the French hate, so that people can tell who they are. "Third floor, America, end of the line." I enter a weightless environment, where bags of potato chips and Coke bottles float in space. A young woman grabs a passing bottle, puts it to her groin, has a brief orgasm. It is like an airport lounge, but also like a department store, with goods for sale, and an amusement park, with arcades, and like a prison with separate cells, and a classroom with seats in rows. Everyone is waiting in line.

Along the sidewalks are slot machines which cough up ping pong balls and pairs of pants, toys, gadgets, and liquor. People are at work feverishly playing these machines, buying another chance, trying to hold Kewpie dolls and glossy magazines in their arms while catching the ping-pong balls at the same time. Occasionally short, nervous laughter is heard from the players. Members of the family cheer on their best players as they perform, calling out advice or consolation, threatening retribution against the losers. Someone says:

"It's a real good machine, this one. If you keep playing it, it will go on forever."

Let us proceed sequentially through the development of this set of interconnected metaphors. The first image is of being in a crowd on a conveyor belt: mass society. Sensory perception is mediated by plastic tubes which connect our organs of communication: the mass media. The nation-state system is organized around patterns of identification based on hostility and negative reference. We know who we are and where we belong by virtue of what we hate.

America is depicted in this dream as a weightless environment of junk food and consumer-good orgasms, part department store, amusement park, prison, and school. These overlapping images of contemporary institutions are characterized by seriality—gradation into series of rows. Work and play are mixed together, involve feverish, mechanical performances, compensated for with baubles and prizes. The family offers a range of emotion from consolation to retribution. The tendency of this mechanism is to perpetuate itself.

Seriality and mediation are experiences connected with mechanical organizations (conveyor belts, escalators, slot machines) and networks of communication that integrate patterns of meaning and identification. From the viewpoint of this dream, performance, compensation, retribution, and negative reference are patterns characteristic of contemporary culture.

To define mass society as the experience of being in a crowd on a conveyor belt (as the dream does) is to treat the image of the conveyor belt as a root metaphor for the experience of standardization and to highlight the institutional connections that integrate national identity—mediating our awareness of who we are. Here the dream definition can be a starting point for the exploration of the overall emotional tone of the dream, the feelings of competition, isolation, and stress in the midst of vacuous enjoyment, the feeling of gorging oneself mechanically, the feeling of the standardization of idiosyncracy.

Seriality, mediation, gradation, depression, conveyance: these are images of our cultural "night-rules"—the patterns of organization that provide the metaphoric background against which we can perceive our dream selves working through the dilemmas of our shared, social unconscious.

Why Is "the Social" Unconscious?

There is a richness, a density about dream metaphor, a playful intensity, full of import, pointing to what we need to know. In group work with dreams this density unfolds. Emotional and metaphoric realities interweave to knit together a more comprehensive awareness of the whole of our experience which we share with one another. In the dream appreciation group, social intelligence is at home with itself.

Social intelligence develops through inquiry, care, and involvement. It is not as detached spectators viewing others, problems, or social institutions as if they were external to ourselves that we discover our interrelatedness. The social is not external to the individual. Indeed, it is perhaps characteristic of our contemporary culture that the shrewd passive aggressiveness of the well-educated, lifelong customer, the cynical calculation of the odds by isolated individuals and the aggressive competition of what we call survival in the "global marketplace" encourage us to ignore and disvalue the healing interconnectedness so manifest in our dreams.

Some cultures, organized quite differently from ours, emphasize the interdependence and relationality of human feeling and place dreams at the center of social life. For example, the Kalapalo Indians of central Brazil consider that dreaming occurs when a person's *akūa*, or "interactive self" awakens and seeks out another. According to Ellen Basso (1992), the akūa is an "interactive phenomenon" (p. 95). A person's awareness of this interactive relational self is always achieved in a communicative context (p. 93).

On the contrary, we seem to believe that feeling is an individual, incommunicable matter. In a dream, I was once explaining the concept of "social feeling" to a group of people. When I awoke I wondered, isn't it obvious that feeling is social, that we experience feeling in relationship, that though we feel within, feeling is in between us, what we share? But then I thought, no, I suspect most of us would say that feeling is *mine*—that you have yours and I have mine and I can't really know what you're feeling. And that therefore, to be responsible, we must "own" our emotions. This possessive individualist view of reality is deeply embedded in our assumptions about identity (Wikse 1977). Thus not only have we privatized dreams, we have also privatized feeling. We must overcome this double illusion—itself sociocultural—in order to appreciate the sociality of feeling as evidenced in dreams.

By counteracting the occlusion of our social selves, working with dreams in a dream appreciation group opens a vantage point that Trigant Burrow (Galt 1984) called "applied anthropology" (p. 137). Burrow thought that the person whom anthropology wishes to study stands amidst controversy and contradiction, struggling within and with others. Such persons are ourselves. In seeking to overcome our social ignorance and neurosis, attempting to become conscious of our social selves, we are not looking elsewhere. As Burrow (1937) put it:

> The physician occupied with behavior-disorder may say, "Here is a sick or neurotic organism in the midst of a healthy society." Or he

> may say, "Here is a sick and neurotic organism in the midst of a society of sick and neurotic organisms." Finally he may take the ground: "Here is a sick, neurotic organism, but this organism is really an expression of society itself and I am, myself, of course, necessarily part of this ill behavior-condition affecting society." (p. 247)

Practical anthropology involves an attempt to develop more humane social forms, through which the healing wisdom of our dreams can speak more articulately, humorously, and openly to us. As we begin to appreciate the social significance of our dreams, we are able to locate our present dilemmas within a field of potential, through which we may yet learn to make our lives more responsive to the logic of free association.

References

Bateson, G. *Toward an Ecology of Mind.* New York: Ballantine Books, 1972.

Basso, Ellen B., "A Progressive Theory of Dreaming," in Barbara Tedlock, (ed.), *Dreaming: Anthropological and Psychological Interpretations.* Santa Fe, N.M.: School of America Research Press, 1992.

Beradt, C. The *Third Reich of Dreams.* New York: Times Books, 1972.

Burrow, T. *The Biology of Human Conflict.* New York: Macmillan, 1937.

Ellul, J. *The Political Illusion.* New York: Knopf, 1967.

Freud, S. *The Interpretation of Dreams.* New York: Avon Books, 1965.

———. "Remarks Upon the Theory and Practice of Dream Interpretation." *Collected Papers.* New York: Basic Books, vol. 5, 1959.

Galt, A. S., ed. *Trigant Burrow: Toward Social Sanity and Human Survival.* New York: Horizon Press, 1984.

Laing, R. D. *Sanity, Madness and the Family.* New York: Penguin Books, 1982.

Ullman, M. Discussion of Dr. Walter Bonime's "The Dream as Human Experience (A Culturalist View)." *Dream Psychology and the New Biology of Dreaming.* M. Kramer, ed. Springfield, Ill.: Chas. C. Thomas, 1969.

Wikse, John R. *About Possession: The Self as Private Property.* University Park and London: Penn State University Press, 1977.

CHAPTER EIGHT

Myths, Dreams, and Divine Revelation

From Abram to Abraham

JOHN A. WALSH

John Walsh brings both theological and psychological sophistication to the story of Abraham's covenant with God and its allegorical reference to the covenant one makes with oneself through dream work. He likens Abraham's struggle to the universal issue of individuation and the role that dreams can play in the struggle toward that goal. He compares the dream to an inner voice that points the way, a way beset with setbacks and trials.

Father Walsh's interest in dreams is related to his general concern with ministry. The title of his doctoral disquisition was "The Experiential Dream Group as Ministry." In it he describes his own experiences as a leader of a dream group of his parishioners.

My dream:

I am vested and preparing in the sacristy to offer Mass. I am wearing a new alb (a long white robe), and it is woven material of a magnificently soft fabric. The robe is seamless. I enter the small bathroom that is part of the sacristy and begin to wash my hands in preparation for Mass. I am standing at the small sink with the water running, and suddenly the toilet, which is behind me, makes a terrible roaring sound and begins to overflow spilling feces all over the floor. I am startled and very concerned that my robe will become stained. I try to stop the toilet. As I do this, the toilet grabs hold of my robe and with a roar begins to pull it down the drain. I am alarmed and angry. I struggle to prevent the robe from being flushed down the drain. A tug of war ensues, and by now I am using all of my energy to pull the robe out of the toilet drain. After great effort and anxiety, I finally succeed in retrieving the robe, and I look to see if it is stained or damaged. I discover that there is not a spot or stain on the robe. It is just as beautiful as when I first put it on.

Needless to say the experience of this dream has remained very powerful in my memory and imagination. While it is not my purpose to develop this chapter by interpreting my dream, it is my overall plan to incorporate my experience and understanding of this dream as a working example in developing the theme of dream appreciation and/or interpretation as significant in our spiritual growth.

On one level, the dream encompasses the metadimension of my life as I look back over the years. (I am now sixty-three years of age.) The metaphors of the dream reach all the way back to my early childhood when an inaugural vision of myself and my desires preoccupied me. Such a vision in its early stages was opaque and filled with energy. The metaphors contain the partial realization of the vision and my struggle to enflesh it in my personhood and world. They also comment on my lifelong struggle to avoid being swallowed up by both the personal pull and collective pull of dark, threatening forces. The metaphors are signposts of the struggle to put into positive operation the resourceful talents and gifts that are within me—the struggle to sustain and further an authenticity of my selfhood and the expression of such through my chosen role identity. Carl Jung describes such a process as the great alchemical work that is the innate purpose of life. As Jung writes, "The sole purpose of human existence is to kindle a lamp in the darkness of mere being."

Such a struggle is translated by the great teachers of spirituality as the ongoing agony and ecstasy of the experience of conversion, of making room for the emergence of the spiritual life within us. Within the context of this dynamic, particularly in the Judaic/Christian tradition, dreams, visions, and stories of God's doings have always played an essential role. This is true because the phenomena of these experiences have enabled people to touch a dimension of reality that is other than their ordinary contact with the physical world. Certainly my own dreams since childhood and on through the various stages of my life cycle have substantially influenced my sense of my own unique inner world, the growth demanded through conversion of life process for that inner world to reveal itself. Even now these wonderful events still occur and radically affect my sense of me and my connectedness to God.

This chapter, then, is devoted to describing the role of dream experience in one's religious development, and the contents of this chapter are written within the framework of the Judeo-Christian tradition. The limiting of these considerations to this tradition stems from two considerations: first, I am a devotee of that tradition and have been formed and schooled essentially within its framework. Second, the vast amount of material concerning dreams, myths, and images that continues to be developed from all the great religions, is far beyond the boundaries of this present work.

The Books of the Two Covenants—that is, the Old Testament and the New Testament—present the religious experience of people in terms of conversion. In other words, when a person or community of people turn to religion and to one extent or another, embrace Judaism or Christianity, they do so because they feel the need to convert, to change their life. The method and motivation that precipitate this turning to religion defy definition, for there are as many reasons for seeking conversion as there are people who convert. A synonym for the word *conversion* is our English word *repentance.* The word connotes a "doing of an act of penance" a changing of one's behavior or, colloquially, cleaning up one's act. This English word *repent,* is the translation of the Latin *poenitemini,* which approximately implies the same meaning. The Latin word, however, translates a word used in the Greek scriptures, namely, metanoia. This Greek word suggests that a person should radically (that is from their very roots) "think around" their life, or their life should do a complete "turnabout." It means that the direction toward which one's life is presently aimed should be so changed that the new direction is diametrically opposite to the present focus.

This Greek word *metanoia* is the translation of the Semitic derivative *shub*. This word suggests a sense of "returning." It is frequently used in the Bible in the context of a community or individual man or woman turning to God or turning to a religious interpretation of their life. It also connotes the process of turning to God as a returning home or to a more authentic identity. So, in the gospel of Luke, Jesus tells the story of the prodigal son. The story relates how the wayward son eventually came home to his father and was reconciled to him. On a deeper level, the narrative indicates how turning to God is actually a coming home. On a personal level, the plot traces the process of a young man coming to terms with his own identity. In the strength of that discovery, he is able to return to his geographical home or center. The word shub in its biblical use, describes conversion to the ways of God and experiencing one's personhood as connected with the divine. Therefore, to discover or rediscover the inner core of our personal identity—our true home—our center is to simultaneously uncover at the inner point of this center union with the divine, with the Creator-Spirit, referred to in the Old Testament as Yahweh, Elohim, or El-Shaddai and in the New Testament as Christ. *Shub*, therefore, means the event or ongoing experiencing of self-discovery and the discovery of God and the Kingdom. As the little prayer attributed to St. Augustine of Hippo states it: "Lord, teach me to know me so that I might know you." The implication here is not that finding or discovering this reality is an external mandate of God, but rather it arises out of the deepest law innately present in woman and man. To be a truly faithful man or woman, then, is to become that person who is in touch with their selfhood and with the Creator-God who is the ongoing author of that identity. The discovery is not a once-and-for-all experience, but rather a journey, and a nomadic journey at that, rather than a pilgrimage. This is a nomadic journey because the origin as well as the final journey is not always clear.

The role of dreams and visions can be essential to this process. The dream experience is uniquely able to enlighten a person on such a journey. Certain dreams or visions surface out of a transconcious source, a source that the religious person identifies as the movement or the "workings" of divinity. These occurrences illuminate one's search for self-identity; they shed light on the direction of both the exterior and interior paths one chooses; they confirm and confront us in our dealings with God, within ourselves, and with others. The robe dream, for me, was a confirmation, as I said, of my being involved in the struggle. The crude and raw image of the toilet and its contents strikes me as the dark, underworld, shadowy space of my selfhood with all its toxicity. The appearance of the seamless robe is a contradistinctive image of my life's vision; the tug of war speaks of the real battle that did erupt and continues to wage in my longings and yearnings for self-containment. The preservation of that extends far beyond my knowledge and specific goals.

I think of the third verse of the hymn, "Amazing Grace," "Through many dangers, toils and snares, we have already come; t'is grace that brought us safe so far, and grace shall lead us home." It is out of this conviction drawn from my dreams and visions, and the many such experiences that a multitude of people have shared with me, that this chapter now turns to the similar experiences of the prototype historical model of the person of Abram and the story of his life.

The origins of the Hebrew people are described in the Book of Genesis in terms of a family tree that is traced back to Adam and Eve. Although this book concentrates on the evolution and development of the Hebrew family, it also constructs a religious account of the creation of the human family. In language that is specifically concerned with the cosmic or physical creation, the opening pages describe the original act of God as a movement or conversion from the darkness into light, from chaos into order, and from void into meaning. Thus, the dark abyss that exists before creation becomes enlightened by the creature sound as God utters his creative word. Through such a flooding of light, chaos and meaninglessness become transformed into order and purposefulness. The same movement eventually is employed to describe the conversion process or the "coming to faith" of a person who turns their life in the direction of God. Such a person undergoes a transformation that is best described as the evolution from darkness into light, chaos into order, and void into meaning. Such a process happened to Abram, the least likely of candidates, as he lived in the status of a nomadic chieftain, serving the many natural gods of his life, who provided economic security for his shepherding business. It is chapter 12 of the Book of Genesis that introduces this man.

Through a series of visions or experiences of God, something takes hold of this man's life, something so new that it totally changes him. Through this experience a great religion was born, and a way of interpreting life was fashioned that became the "taproot" of the entire Judeo/Christian religious view of life. The process that so dramatically uprooted and shaped his life, converting him in a gradual but total manner into a devotee of the one God, has served as the model or paradigm for communities of religious believers and individuals within those communities. Abram's experience contains a universal format for the genesis of faith or, as the psychologist Jung would say, an archetypal blueprint that is the guiding force energizing people to discover their God-given identity and through that discovery to experience the mystery of God. The book of Genesis refers to the process as a creation and the Bible describes it as conversion. Jung, from a psychological perspective, refers to the process as "individuation" or the continuous reconstellation of the archetypal energies that govern the process of psychological and/or spiritual growth. Within the context of this chapter, the notions of creation, conversion and individuation will be used in a synonymous manner with appropriate distinctions where they may be necessary.

An essential and highly significant dimension of the account of Abram's conversion is the role that his visions or auditory experiences of the presence of God play in his journey. Morton Kelsey (1974) explains that dreams, visions, and supernatural visitations are "all of one piece" (p. 80); that is, it is difficult to separate and delineate the exact difference. Kelsey also points out that the content or meaning that comes before one's consciousness is more important than the exact state of consciousness in which the experience occurs. Abram's experiences of God will be interpreted along the lines of dream interpretation, although the Bible does not clearly indicate what state of consciousness Abram was caught up in when the visitations from God occurred.

Generally the "round-figure" date of 1850 B.C. is given to the time of Abram. His homeland was Mesopotamia, and his life was that of a nomad, a sheepherder. He resided with his family, his servants, and his flocks in an area then known as Ur of the Chaldees. Abram was a business person of his day. His investments consisted of his family, his servants, and his flocks. These were his security and his power. His experience of himself as a man, his own self-worth and dignity and the measure by which he gauged these things were dependent on economic success in his own eyes and the eyes of his clanspeople. All this required continual appeasement of the gods. Abram was a polytheist. He had to worship many gods, and his livelihood rested on their intervention. His gods were those of nature controlling the sun, the wind, the rain and, in general, those aspects of his life as a sheepherder, where he was in a posture of dependence and submission. As E. A. Speiser (1964) explains in the Anchor Bible, "All major decisions in heaven required approval by the corporate body of the gods. And since nothing was valid for all time, the upshot was chronic indecision in heaven and consequent insecurity on earth. Man's best hope to get a favorable nod from the cosmic powers lay, it was felt, in ritualistic appeasement. And as the ritual machinery grew more and more cumbersome, the spiritual content receded ever-farther, until it all but disappeared from the official" (p. 48).

To challenge the polytheistic religion of the day would demand a tremendous struggle against all the forces of society. To supplant polytheism with a monotheistic belief in one God demanded more than just the logic and vision of reason alone. For Abram to reach the conviction religiously of just one God without any known precedent for this realization implied a rejection of everything that was important economically. It meant going against society with all its rules and expectations. It implied standing alone with support emerging only from his inner convictions.

The most extraordinary aspect of this transformation in Abram's life was the loss of power, security, and success that were woven into his reliance on and worship of the gods of nature who afforded Abram economic stability. This is a challenge of almost insurmountable size for any person. A new vision, a new power, a new security, a new sense of self; all of this meant a new birth, a new beginning, in short, a re-creation. As recounted in the story of Genesis, the genesis process, conversion, happened in the life history of this man; he underwent a conversion. Through an experience, a happening, a process, his old ways took on the semblance of darkness, chaos, and void. The newness of his vision became light, order, and meaning. The process of creation began to occur in this man's life.

I dare say all of us are led by some vision, some dream that occurs, takes shape and form in various stages and multiple ways as we journey through all the stages of one's life cycle. In my dream, the spotless, stainless, seamless robe represents an image that has been imbedded deep in my spirit or soul since childhood. It is always there in some way or another, something felt most of the time, rather than some definite form, present as promised and filled with energy. The phenomenology of religion teaches that realization or fulfillment or full manifestation of hoped-for realities, dreams, visions, are only and always present by way of promise. The Latin derivative of the English word *promise*, *promitto*, literally means "I send me in front of me." A vision or dream is just that. It is the promise of ecstasy that is present to us by hint, hunch, or expectation. For me the robe of my dream is a manifestation of my personal dream; its origin was always there. Its fulfillment is always beyond my experience, cognitive grasp, and conscious awareness.

Abram, likewise, had a dream, and this is the way the Bible describes it: Abram's father, Terah, left the city of Ur with his son and family for the land of Canaan, driven by a vision of a better future for himself and his family. They settled in Hurrian country, in a place called Haran. It was at Haran that God spoke to Abram.

> The Lord said to Abram, "Leave your country, your relatives, and your father's house and go to the land that I am going to show you. I will give you many descendants, and they will become a great nation. I will bless you and make your name famous, so that you will be a blessing. I will bless those who bless you, but I will curse those who curse you. And through you I will bless all the nations." (Genesis 12:1–3)

A fundamental question concerning this communication from God to Abram is that concerning the manner in which it occurred. The scripture gives no clear indication. Was this a dreamlike experience that Abram remembered only as "divine audition," or did it occur while he was fully awake? Was the voice of God heard outside him, or did it erupt as an inner summons? These questions cannot be answered with certainty, but what is certain is that ultimately the "voice" touched Abram in the depths of his personhood. Whether or not he experienced the "voice" as coming from without or within, its resonance was heard from within the depths of his soul.

In the context of Jung's psychological thought, the voice is at once the voice of Abram's self-archetype and the voice of God. Jung describes the central power of the human personality as the "self" or "self-archetype." By this he means that this is the representation and central guiding force of the entire emerging personality. It is greater than our conscious ego-state, for it not only contains our consciousness and unconsciouness, but also has its roots in what Jung refers to as a universal or collective unconscious. It is within this universal collectivity of unconscious energy that the self is joined or related to the transcendent, divine and/or God. In other words, the selfhood is that reality within a person that bears the stamp and image of God. From a Jungian perspective, then, the central source of all consciousness arises out of the collective unconscious and is explained by Jung as having its root of origin in the God-image archetype or power. (This is human psychological language that points to a reality that is beyond explanation.) From a religious perspective the mystery of God which is over and above and beyond any human analogy reveals itself through this central power of potential consciousness in the collectivity and localizes itself in the human person through the self-construct or archetype. So the voice that Abram hears can be understood as both the voice of God and the voice of Abram's higher or greater self. (The conviction here on the part of the writer is that at any given moment there is always more to each of us than we are conscious of at the time.) In this sense, then, the summons or command can be understood as a critical moment, a crisis. (In the Greek, the word *crisis* implies a moment of decision!) The voice urges Abram to become more than he is conscious, and to enter into the greatest journey of his life, namely, self-expansion arising out of a faith trust in the voice and its promise. Jung refers to this process as individuation. Individuation can be likened to the profound experience of conversion or re-creation. One implication of this particular understanding of our dream experience, our imaginings, or even our reflective discourse within ourselves is that such natural phenomena often contain the impetus and direction for the development of our life and personal growth.

The Bible indicates the contents of the communication: Abram is instructed to "go forth," to take leave of his present situation, to take upon himself a journey. Jung describes individuation as a departure from one's familiar way of judging and resolving problems. It is a separation from the collective mindset of society in service of a greater sense of personal responsibility. Ordinarily, the familiar props of our lives afford us fundamental security and consolation. We cling to other people, to our comfortable surroundings and to the way of understanding life and the world that we have constructed over the years. We need to feel part of our society, to be included within its approved attitudes and ways of operating. When confrontation personally enters our life, when a demand for change happens that grasps us in the depths of our being and becomes a conscious conviction, the upheaval and anxiety occur in our inner world. The anxiety focuses on both the loss of supporting structures and the unknown aspects of new ways of experiencing ourselves. Individuation and/or conversion implies all of this and even more. If the journey is responded to in a positive manner, then we are thrown back on our own inner energies. Our personal sense of worth adds a value, our inner strength comes into play, we begin the long odyssey of separation, trusting in and depending on our own inner promptings (voice), in short, our selfhood.

The Bible states, "Abram went as Yahweh told him. . . . Abram took his wife Sarai, his brother's son, Lot, all the possessions that they had acquired and all the persons they had obtained in Haran. They set out for the land of Canaan and arrived in the land of Canaan" (Gen. 12:4–5). Abram obeyed his inner experience, the inner summons or voice.

In biblical ways, there is no conversion without the overwhelming sense of faith or trust. Faith is a response, a trusting surrender to one's discernment of an intuitive summons that supersedes all the other voices in one's experience. It implies a redefinition of one's values and securities and a clarification of "who" or "what" one deems worthy of trust. Abram's discovery of a new trust relationship enables him to start out. The new "god-like" voice becomes the source of energy that gives him overall direction. He is enlivened and quickened by a new-found hope arising out of his personal willingness to trust in a promise from a voice that appears greater to him than any other sound he has ever heard. It's almost as though, up to this intersection of his life, he has been deaf or as though the sum total of all the sound he ever heard has given rise to a new utterance that is totally different than any utterance he has so far known. His experience of the phenomena of Faith is born on the hearing experience of this new voice.

When we go on a trip, most of us carry "excess baggage." We pack too much. Railway stations, bus stops, and air terminals are a daily scene of people dragging their belongings, sometimes with a great deal of effort and frustration. These scriptures indicate that Abram took "all his possessions."

Individuation and/or conversion in its earliest stages is often not understood as a radical departure from one's familiar ways. Therefore, most of us, like Abram, decide we're going to have "the best of both worlds." This does not work! Abram's crucial task is to so travel the inner road of his selfhood that the Voice of command to "leave all" becomes clearer and clearer to him in its fullest implications. Comfortable habits, attitudes, and values, age-old fears and phobias, unreal and illusionary expectations of God, others, and life itself must be sacrificed in service of inner integration. In short, the process demands a new vision, a new way of receiving oneself and others. Abram begins both his inner and outer journey still holding on to what he thinks he needs. His subsequent hearings of the Voice and events in his outer world gradually change all of this.

Abram struggles to live on the strength of the promise, and the promise is presented under the image of a blessing. The blessing consists of multiple progeny, "I will make of you a great nation" (Gen. 12:2), and the possession of a new land, "Go forth . . . to a land that I will show you" (Gen. 12:1.) His trust and faith in this new voice and in the resonance of the sound of this voice within him is strong and for him. However, the completeness of the expectations of the inner voice are far from being enfleshed in Abram's consciousness. Abram and Sarai are childless; they are beyond the childbearing years. Where will this great nation come from, or how will it originate out of the barren womb of Sarai or the aging physiology of Abram?

Chapter fifteen of Genesis begins with another description of the Voice addressing Abram. Sometime afterward, this word of Yahweh came to Abram in a vision:

> "Fear not, Abram! I am your shield. Your reward shall be very great." But Abram answered, "O Lord Yahweh, to what purpose are your gifts, when I continue childless. . . . Since you have granted me no offspring, a member of my household will become my heir. "Then Yahweh's word came back to him in reply. . . . "None but your own issue shall be your heir." He took him outside and said, "Look up at the sky and count the stars if you can. Just so," he added, "shall be your offspring." He put his trust in Yahweh, who accounted it to his merit. (Gen. 15:1-6)

This time the scripture refers to the experience as a vision. Morton Kelsey (1974) describes the various connotation of Greek words used for the word *vision* in the New Testament. He states that the Greek word *horama*, used to translate the Hebrew words for both dream and vision, refers to the state in which one receives a vision, as well as to the dreaming state. Kelsey suggests that the word does not distinguish explicitly between dreams and visions. Whether Abram is sleeping or in an altered state of consciousness is of no great significance. He is experiencing something beyond his normal conscious state. The contents of the message are comforting and of a directional nature. They implicitly deal with an underlying issue of Abram's make-up, namely his ability to trust. This appears as "unfinished business" in this man's personality. Ullman and Zimmerman (1979) write of the dimension of honesty in dreams.

> While we are asleep and dreaming, our self-healing machinery propels us into a realm where feelings are displayed honestly. They shape images that may frighten or delight us, but that is not their intent. Their intent is simply to tell it like it is. . . . The change from dreaming to waking effects a radical transformation. We move from a realm of honesty to one in which honesty becomes mixed with expediency. While dreaming we have been given a clear lens with which to examine ourselves. When awake we often look at the same situation

through rose-colored glasses. And to make matters worse, we have no way of knowing that our vision is now colored. (pg. 231)

Abram's journey in one aspect consists of his being forced to confront himself. Shortly after his initial response to God and his new sense of self, Abram found himself to be in serious trouble because of his deceitfulness. Forced by famine to temporarily leave the land of Cannan, Abram goes to Egypt. There the Pharaoh desires Sarai and in order to save "his own skin," Abram pawns her off as his "sister." He then gives her to the Pharaoh who takes her into his household. The scriptures relate that Yahweh afflicts the household of Pharaoh with extraordinary plagues. The Pharaoh discovers Abram's deceitfulness and expels him from Egypt.

This is the first allusion in the Bible to Abrams darkness, a darkness that needs to be integrated, so to speak, into the light of his consciousness and a consciousness that needs to acknowledge the presence of this dark side, which always hovers, tentatively waiting to dominate the light and impulsively govern one's behavior. My struggle with the roaring, growling toilet and its attempt to devour my robe is an explicit image of my personal grappling with the integration of my own darkness, whether that darkness is uniquely there because of my personality or my ecclesical role and vocation or because of an unexplained force that attempts to overpower me. Dark, shadowy domination expresses itself through a lack of self-honesty or deceit at various levels. We use toilets in our culture to flush out of sight what is repulsive and toxic to us. It's a space and place that we take care of in secret. Parents with their young often express great anxiety and oppressive behavior until their child is "potty trained." For me, the toilet and its behavior in my dream is an honest commentary on my own deceit and denial dynamic. It confronts my struggle with the flush syndrome in my own life. The danger of inappropriate use of the flushing denial reflex is that this pattern has the potential to take over our selfhood so we flush away what actually is me and of great value and worth. The tug of war with the toilet is a statement of my investment of energy and effort to protect and preserve what is of authentic value within me. Such a struggle with the shadow side is Abram's anguish as he enters more deeply into his journey. The vision of Genesis 15 strengthens Abram's original resolve. It addresses his fear. Abram fears the alien powers of his outer world, yet he is also plagued with inner doubts about the process he has begun. Abram still resorts to relying on collective society; he has not yet been able to break from this security. Being deceitful as a way of dealing with ourselves in order to feel secure and protected is a major defense system we employ. It destroys self-honesty, which then alienates our relationships with others and with God. Doing truth, or as Ghandi of India said, possessing truth-force, is an uphill climb or battle. Truth is not something we possess as if it were an objectlike sort of thing that we could hold in our hand, but rather, truth as something greater than ourselves possesses us or we participate in its energy if we are willing to deal with the issue of self-honesty. Abram fears what is innermost to him, his new-found sense of self and the divine. Jung (1961) describes this state of the individuation process as an intermediary stage:

> It would therefore be wrong to regard this intermediary stage as a trap; on the contrary, for a long time to come, it will represent the only possible form of existence for the individual, who nowadays seems more than ever threatened by anonymity. Collective organization is still so essential today that many consider it, with some justification, to be the final goal. . . . Nevertheless, it may be that for sufficient reasons a man feels he must set out on his own feet along the road to wider realms. . . . He will go alone and be in his own company. (p. 343)

The motivating force of such an undertaking becomes the individual's secret. Abram is both motivated and frightened by his inner secret. Jung describes such a secret as reinforcing the person in the isolation of individual goals. God has spoken to Abram. Only he knows the experience; only he has felt the urgency and insistency of the promise. As Jung adds, many people cannot bear this isolation. The person who acts on the secret becomes totally engaged by its implication and begins to act as though "driven" by a new and frightening force. Jung says that a person driven by this secret "truly enters the untrodden, untreadable regions" (p. 344) where there are no charted ways and no shelter spreads a protecting roof over his head. In the religious realm, one spiritual writer describes such a journey of faith relying on a promise as a "journey without maps." Abram's vision with its dialogue between God and his soul brings into relief the conflict between the outer and the inner world. God demands fidelity of Abram, and Abram is concerned about the reward or fulfillment of God's promise to him. "Who will be the recipient of all my possessions?" asks Abram, or in another form, When will you and how will you fulfill your part of the bargain? The inner transformation so often gets detoured as we mistakenly look for the rewards of God in our experience of the outer world status, riches, power! This diversionary tactic is doomed to failure, disappointment, and disillusionment. Coming to grips with the inner movements of our spiritual development is often understood only through contact with our inner images and dream experience. It is precisely the intention of the dream to correct and adjust one's conscious misapprehensions of personal values and goals. The major themes of a person's life such as loves, hates, attachments, addictions, and so forth, appear in a stark state of reality within the images and movements of our dream state. Close attention to the feelings and movements of the dream images often reveals the fuller meaning and direction that should be given to one's life's themes. Abram, with his inaugural vision of himself and his God, with his inner secret of possessing a personal promise of fulfillment from God and with age-old habits of self-deceptive behaviors, finds himself caught. Only a series of dreamlike visions can clearly illumine the way out of this inner dilemma.

An additional consideration surfaces in this particular vision. Inner conflict between outer and inner strivings does not necessarily place one at odds with God. God's reply to Abram in this vision is one of acceptance and understanding. The vision is at once affirming and directing. The concluding scene of the vision attempts to express this relationship: "When the sun had gone down and it was very dark, there appeared a smoking fire pot and a flaming torch. . . . That day, Yahweh concluded a covenant with Abram saying, 'To your offspring I give this land.' "(Gen. 15:17–18)

The Bible often expresses the experience of God through the symbol of fire. Moses encounters God in the burning bush (cf. Exodus 3:2), and in the New Testament God is referred to as an all consuming fire (Hebrews 12:29). The strength and all-pervasive effect of fire speaks of the impact of covenant or union with God. It is, so to speak, the overall sense of being in God, in the grasp of the divine, that compensates for the inability of a person to perfectly live out the commands of God. It is this perduring inchoate "grasp" that enables people to struggle with conversion and transformation. What we are dealing with here is a "knowing" that supersedes all other forms of knowing. More than a "knowing," it is a profound, radical phenomenon of being known. The mind seeks to know, to fill itself with content, while the heart waits to be known, grasped, intimately wrapped in a presence. Such a form of communication grounds the person and confirms the significance and uniqueness of selfhood. Such an experience is expressed in the frailty of human language as a confession that a "transcendent Other" (that is, the mystery of God), has addressed me in my innermost being. This Other as the origin and source of my personhood, and even more, as the ultimate wellspring of my relational energy causes us to rejoice in our creatureliness and recognize God as parent and source of all life.The medieval mystic, Meister Eckhart, explains it this way: "The eye by which I see God is the same as the eye by which God sees me." So in this sense coming to a religious understanding of one's self and life itself is the discovery that "I am the you of God," that the fundamental meta level of my very being is that I am first addressed by the Other, or spoken into existence and the energy of life.

One might apply the words of Psalm 2 to this experience: "You are my son, this day I have begotten you" (vs. 7). The psalm expressed in language this identification of my selfhood with God. I experience within myself the sense of the Other as joined with me or the source of me. This communication of the Other as parent and initial source is put this way: "You are my son, my daughter—I am continually sustaining you, revealing myself to you through which you are always experiencing my energy of new birth, new life." The heart of religious mysticism in the Judaic-Christian tradition hinges to one extent or another on this realization—that is, life is ultimately from the Other; and that conversation is initiated by the awakening of the hint of this mystery—a hint that entices and urges me to begin exploring with fascination and terror this invitation. Jung's theory of the collective unconscious is helpful in this area. The transconsciousness or transpersonalism of one's conscious roots, although present in a person's experience of selfhood, is ultimately founded and grounded in God. The revelation or disclosure of God, then, can be experienced in our own self-discovery, in the coming out of ourselves and relationally entering into a world that transcends and is over and beyond my cognitive grasp or ability to control. God's covenant with Abram simultaneously affords Abram unconditional acceptance on the part of God and profound self-acceptance. Abram's faith or trust in the Voice reverberating within him is the medium or web site that transmits this message of graciousness and blessing. The great dreams and visions of our life often act out this inner mystery of gratuity. My dream graciously reveals that both the robe and the toilet are intrinsic to who I am. The graciousness of the inner fiber of the dream is that both images are me—with all that is implied in this revelation. Graciousness arises out of my recognition of the roar and terror of this animated flush-drain, the ongoing battle with the cthonic (underworld) dimension of myself and the hoped-for result of no major destruction of myself (no spot or stain), in the tug of war.

Jung explains that in such dreams the self, or the central archetype, often appears in images of wholeness or completeness. This is so because the self is the totality of the human person. Images such as a circle, a square, a quaternity, mandala, or child; something perfect and complete, any symbol that speaks of wholeness, reflects the wholeness of the self (p. 9398). Jung elaborates on the relationship between the self and the God-image archetype occurring in a dream:

> It is only through the psyche that we can establish that God acts upon us, but we are unable to distinguish whether these actions emanate from God or from the unconscious. We cannot tell whether God and the unconscious are two different entities. Both are borderline concepts for transcendental contents. But empirically it can be established, with a sufficient degree of probability, that there is in the unconscious, an archetype of wholeness which manifests itself spontaneously in dreams etc. and a tendency, independent of the conscious will to relate other archetypes to this center. . . . The God image does not coincide with the unconscious as such, but with a special content of it, namely the archetype of the self. It is this archetype from which we can no longer distinguish the God-image empirically. . . . One can, then, explain the God-image . . . as a reflection of the self or conversely, explain the self as an *imago Dei* (image of God) in man. (p. 395)

Abram's voice in his vision is both the utterance of God transcendentally and imminently present to him at the same time and the articulation of Abram's fuller self, self-archetype. The Voice, which speaks of wholeness and greater integration, takes on the same meaning as images of wholeness in dreams. The dream, then, in its religious dimension, potentially leads us far beyond that vision limited by human reason and discloses those "edge situations," blurred as such edges may be, where the divine intermingles with the human condition and through such imposition, reveals mystery. The promise given to Abram resides in his response to such revelation. It is precisely such a response that is promise-being-actualized and it is precisely in Abram's willing response that he becomes the biblical paradigm—the father—of all who enter into the great transforming power of such response in their lives.

Karl Menninger (1958), in describing approaches to the interpretation of psychoanalytic resistance, insightfully remarks that people spend a lifetime expecting the wrong things from the right people and the right things from the wrong people (p. 136). The story of the birth of Ishmael is a concrete example of this fact in the journey of Abram. Abram is psychologically and religiously driven by his desire for offspring. He feels the need for some concrete, permanent sign that the promises of his visions are being fulfilled. This is the classic temptation in the life of faith. As the song from *Godspell* says it, "When will God save the people?" Abram, in his outer world, is an aggressive business person of his own day; he knows how to "take things into his own hands and run with them"; he can "get things done." The Bible says he took Sarai's Egyptian maidservant, Hagar, with the supposed approval of Sarai (later the Bible says that Sarai bitterly regretted her benevolent gesture) and has sexual intercourse with Hagar in hopes of generating offspring. Abram is seeking the right thing from the wrong person. Hagar becomes pregnant and bears a son named Ishmael.

The Bible describes Ishmael as "a wild colt of a man, his hand against everyone, and everyone's hand against him" (Gen. 16:12). Later on, in the New Testament, Paul writes, "Man proposes and God disposes." Such is the case with Abram's folly. Turmoil entered his life in the form of marital dysfunction and human hurt. Sarai reverses her decision. She scornfully tells Abram, "This outrage against me is your fault! I myself put my maid in your lap. But from the moment she found out that she had conceived, she has been looking at me with contempt" (Gen. 16:15). In the life of faith, there is a tendency to put aside the inner vision and sense of God and choose what seems expedient and attainable. This urge reveals itself in motives of ambition, power, status, and achievement. Unconscious issues and urges operate without the control of the inner self's judgment and ultimately lead one to act in haste and without integrity. The result is usually damaging. In the case of Abram, family strife makes his life so miserable that the only solution is to banish Hagar and her son Ishmael. This Abram does with God's assurance that they will be taken care of under His protection. Abram had to learn that his sought-after fulfillment of the promise would happen in God's time and in God's way.

Religious faith rests on relationship—relationship that the scriptures refer to as covenant. Faith is a way of knowing that is characterized by an unusual sense of being-in-God and God-being-in-you. It is a knowledge that the pact or alliance with the divine has no finality to it but, rather, continues to unfold its mystery and experience as one enters more deeply into the union. Chapter 17 of Genesis accents a new consciousness for Abram in his covenant with God. In a visionlike dream episode, Abram experiences a moment of intimacy with God:

> When Abram was ninety-nine years old, Yahweh appeared to Abram and said to him, "I am El Shaddai. Follow my ways and be blameless. I will grant a covenant between myself and you, and will make you exceedingly numerous. . . . And this is my covenant with you: You are to be the father of a host of nations. Nor shall you be called Abram any longer: Your name shall be called Abraham, meaning that 'I will make you the Father of a host of nations.' . . . And this shall be the covenant between myself and you, and your offspring to follow, which you must keep, every male among you shall be circumcised. You shall circumcise the flesh of your foreskin, and that shall be the mark of the covenant between me and you." (Gen. 7:1–11)

There are many interpretations for the name El Shaddai. Traditionally it has been understood to mean the "Almighty." Another meaning given to the name is "self-sufficient." Our modern interpretation gives the meaning of *mountain*, implying the symbol of divinity (Speiser 1964). At any rate, the name implies the greatness and transcendence of the Divine One, who manifests himself to Abraham. The change of Abram's name surely implies not only a new sense of relationship with God but also a more expansive sense of selfhood. Symbolically, a name expresses identity. It is the ordinary way that people externally and concretely identify themselves and are identified themselves and are identified by others. One's name becomes so intimately wrapped up with one's identity that it becomes almost impossible to separate one from the other. In this vision, the man Abram comes to a new vision of himself. His name is broadened and lengthened, signifying self-expansion. Jung (1961) states that the selfhood of a person is beyond total comprehension of one's consciousness. "There is little hope of our being able to reach even approximate consciousness of the self" (p. 398). The new name is a turning point in Abraham's consciousness of himself. In his vision, he grasps himself in a far wider sense than his ordinary consciousness could afford him. He is in a sensitive partnership with himself and with God.

A dream can and does give us energy and power that we never knew we possessed. Some dreams are self-revelatory. They reveal us to ourselves. They picture us in a complementary image that stirs our inner sense of worth and value. Such an image breaks down our more narrow boundaries of self-estimation and challenges us or liberates us to risk experimenting with new modes of growth and development. Just as the change of name in many cultures and religious traditions symbolizes a new beginning, a new way of living, so too, Abraham, through the medium of a vision, is able to assume a far greater sense of his own identity.

The reference to circumcision, as the sign of the covenant relationship, speaks of change and integration and health. The word literally implies "to cut around" or "to cut away from." Within the context of the vision, it represents for Abraham a new sense of inner sojourn. He must shed his false self and bring forth new light, order, and meaning to this world. The symbol implies the creative process as it personally touches this man. He is called to be the generator, the father of many; he, himself, must first become the creator by cutting around and away from the false world that gradually will appear to him as darkness, chaos, and void. Again, the vision speaks of the "Genesis process." Abram becomes Abraham, therefore, not through the external lengthening of his name, but by personal consolidation and integration. The internal "coming together" of his selfhood, the experience of having, so to speak, "all the pieces fit," for a privileged moment, is the promise of the fullness of the covenant. His outer world of behavior has yet to adapt to his inner experience. Such a task takes a lifetime and maybe even more than that.

In a delightful scene, the Bible describes a banquet that Abraham and Sarah (her name had now been changed) put on for God and two angels who visited them in their tent. God and two figures appeared at the entrance of the tent of Abraham. Sarah was quickly ordered by Abraham to fix the food, and the visitors ate. During the course of this extraordinary occasion, the three visitors informed Abraham that Sarah, who is ninety years of age, was going to have a baby. Sarah, the Bible adds, had been listening inside the tent and when she heard the "men" talking, she laughed at their "naivete." God then confronted Abraham and asked why Sarah laughed. Sarah interrupted and denied laughing—or listening. God retorted, "Yes, you did" (cf. Genesis 18:ff). Frederick Buechner (1973) in his book *Wishful Thinking* elaborates on this event:

> When God told Abraham, who was one hundred at the time, that at the age of ninety, his wife, Sarah was finally going to have a baby, Abraham came close to knocking himself out—"fell on his face and laughed" as Genesis puts it. In another version of the story, Sarah is hiding behind the door eavesdropping. And here it is Sarah herself who nearly splits a gut, although when God asks her about it afterward, she denies it. "No, but you did laugh," God says, thus having the last word as well as the first. God doesn't seem to hold their outbursts against them, however. On the contrary, he tells them the

> baby's going to be a boy and that he wants them to name him Isaac. Isaac in Hebrew means laughter. (pp. 24-25)

Faith, in this instance, gives birth to laughter. What is the meaning of this story? It obviously has many levels. One interpretation would be that even the impossible is possible with God. On a deeper level, it implies the readiness and pliability that conversion affects in a person so that God can accomplish his will and design. Jung might interpret it as a scene of wholeness and integrity in the individuation process, a wholeness that is capable of creatively and enthusiastically giving birth to the unexpected, to a new possibility. Ordinarily, our love relationships contain projections that fill us with desires that express themselves in coercion and constraint. The individuation process enables us to withdraw such projections and to detach ourselves from the false expectations that cripple us as we attempt to relate. Another way of saying it is that individuation allows us to enter into relationships of giving and receiving. So often marriage and friendships are referred to as a "give and take proposition." "Taking" is the offspring of unrealistic expectations toward one another. Healing unions with others necessarily become the peaceful and expansive occasion of learning how to freely give and freely receive. This dynamic between persons produces life. It causes us to lovingly celebrate our own freedom and the freedom and dignity of others. Abraham seems to have reached this stage in his development; he is ready to give birth, along with Sarah, and such a prospect causes laughter in both of them, and from them is born the child of laughter, Isaac. Abraham's faltering attempt with previous behavior "to force the issue" (Hager and Ishmael) through his unconscious, manipulative ways, seems or appears to be just that, the faltering of a man who did not know himself.

The banquet suggests union and communion. The covenant, or partnership, is consummated by eating together. Food and drink are passed and shared; conversation accompanies the process, and the union or oneness is celebrated. This sense of oneness quickens and energizes Abraham. Similar, then, to the Spirit that fertilized the dark, voidlike womb of creation and brought forth life and light, so too, Abraham and Sarah fuse their energies, and the womb of Sarah stirs. And lo and behold, the child of Faith is conceived. Isaac, the embodiment in the flesh of God's promise and God's laughter, is born to two noble people, and the promise of Abraham's dreams and visions is well on its way.

Separation from others is never an easy task, and yet a major theme of human development through the life cycle consists of this process. As John S. Dunne (1972) writes:

> It is difficult to grow out of the relationships formed in one period of life and to enter into those appropriate for the next period; to leave behind those of youth for those of manhood; to leave those of manhood for those of old age; to leave behind those of old age for those of the dead. It is also difficult to allow someone to leave a relationship with oneself behind as he grows and moves onward, because a familiar relationship is being abandoned for an unknown one. (p. 44)

Usually, we will resist with the greatest of effort the severance of union with those who have played an intimate role in our life. In the process of psychoanalysis, writes Menninger (1958), one criterion for the success of an analysis is when the "analyzed person" comes to realize in his relationship with others that he "has no need to find satisfaction for childish wishes" (p. 167). He continues "The 'analyzed person' either comes to realize that he can be gratified without such exertions as he had previously made or that he does not need to be gratified or that he has no further feeling of need for such gratification or that there is no prospect of gratifying them and hence they must be renounced without regrets" (p. 168).

In my dream the washing of my hands at the sink in the bathroom is something of the process of renunciation. In the celebration of Mass, just before the priest proclaims the great Eucharistic Prayer of blessing and consecration over the bread and wine, the priest washes his hands. While washing his hands, he prays, "Lord wash away my iniquity, cleanse me of my sin." Washing symbolizes many things. For me it is always something of a purification, a cleansing. In the dream, while attempting to wash my hands, a catastrophe breaks forth behind me with the eruption of the toilet. The washing and the eruption are something of the "coincidence of opposites." What I need to be washed, the iniquity and sin to be removed, is not the toilet with its uproar and aggressive behavior, but more so the unwillingness to see that and all that it implies, as part of me, as connected to me. The refusal to deal with this in my conscious world is what causes such an uproar in relating to myself and others. I say "the coincidence of opposites" because the robe and the toilet are related—they are part of me. Recognition and acknowledgment of both lead to the assurance of keeping the robe spotless. So often opposites come together in our dreams to balance out the lopsided view we carry into our conscious life.

Chapter 22 of Genesis narrates the drama of Abraham's renunciation and separation from his only son, whom he loves. The content of this chapter constitutes a passion and suffering, such a ripping away from, that every human being shudders from and is repulsed by the very thought of God's demand. "Take your son, your beloved son, Issac, whom you hold so dear and go to the land of Moriah, where you shall offer him up as a burnt offering on one of the heights that I will point out to you" (Gen. 22:1–2).

The Book of Hebrews in the New Testament states: "It is a terrifying thing to fall into the hands of the living God!" (Heb. 11:31). Abraham is caught, not by some outside force that will violate him and his family, but by an interior knowing that has become all-pervasive in his life's judgments. Jung's (1961) teaching on the "inner secret" is extremely applicable here in understanding Abraham's dilemma:

> But if a man faced with a conflict of duties undertakes to deal with them absolutely on his own responsibility, and before a judge who sits in judgment on him day and night, he may well find himself in an isolated position. There is now an authentic secret in his life which cannot be discussed if only because he is involved in an endless inner trial in which he is his own counsel and ruthless examiner and no secular or spiritual judge can restore his easy sleep. . . . In this case, the court is transposed to the inner world where the verdict is pronounced behind closed doors. . . . Nothing so promotes the growth of consciousness as this inner confrontation of opposites . . . the inner world has gained that much weight by being raised to the rank of a tribunal for ethical decisions. . . . The ego becomes ambivalent and ambiguous and is caught between hammer and anvil. It becomes aware of a polarity superordinate to itself. (p. 345)

For Abraham it is no longer a question of whether or not he should obey. He undergoes the anguish of giving up the last vestige of reliance upon the satisfaction of human companionship as the ultimate answer to anything in life. The Bible simply says, "He laid him on the altar on top of the wood. He put out his hand and picked up the cleaver to slay his son" (Gen. 22:9–10). "But an angel of the Lord called to him from heaven, 'Abraham! Abraham!' 'Here I am,' he answered. And He said, 'Lay not your hand upon the boy, nor do the least thing to him! Now I know how dedicated you are to God, since you did not withhold from me your own beloved son" (Gen. 22:11–12).

A characteristic of childhood, writes Jung (1961), at least in the eyes of adults, is the way that this stage of human development represents paradise; childhood is a time of being carefree, playful, taken care of, provided for, and cherished without anxiety or responsibility (p. 244). This aspect of childhood lingering in our adult consciousness causes us to expect and unconsciously await the fulfillment of childish dreams in the future. It is the longing to find the "pot of gold" at the end of the rainbow. In an acutely terrifying moment, Abraham tears himself from such fantasies. His son, Isaac, was not to be sacrificed for his personal growth, but rather to show a readiness to relinquish that naive world of paradisaic solutions to the hard problems of human living. The purity, innocence, and goodness reflected in the child Isaac and God's unwillingness to have the child harmed mirrored for Abraham a more complete picture of himself and the ultimate demands of trusting in a promise.

Conclusion

Faith then is born from heeding dreams, visions, and voices. It begins with a leave-taking, a journey that actually guides us. It is a series of creative moments that gradually change or convert the way we view ourselves, others, and the world. Abraham's sojourn teaches us that such a process opens up an experience of life that is more vast than "counting the stars at night" or "measuring the sands of the seashore." It is learning to live with a promise whose fulfillment seems to continually be changing. Such a promise is continually reinforced, reshaped, and rephrased by the inner movements of our images, voices, and dreams.

The inner power modeled for us in the personhood of Abraham empowers us to give new life, new birth to ourselves and to others. It causes us genuinely to erupt with laughter in response to the surprise of discovering new life at the strangest times and in the most uncommon of places. Living life in this manner allows us to understand the stumbling, faltering uncertainties of our travel as okay and necessary.

"From Abram to Abraham" is the story of a man who found out that the "promised land" of his voices and visions lay in the discovery of his own identity. Through that discovery, he came to know and trust in God, who weaves His creative voice into our selfhood. Through that discovery, Abram came to realize the shortcomings of an abbreviated name. With the help of God, he took ownership of the name that fully expressed his identity—Abraham.

References

Buechner, F. *Wishful Thinking*. New York: Harper & Row, 1973.

Dunne, J. S. *The Way of All the Earth*. New York: Harper & Row, 1972.

Jung, C. G. *Memories, Dreams, Reflections*. New York: Random House, 1961, 1962, 1963.

Kelsey, M. T. *God, Dreams and Revelation*. Minneapolis, Minn.: Augsburg, 1974.

Menninger, K. *Theory of Psychoanalytic Technique*. New York: Harper & Row, 1958.

Speiser, E. A. *Genesis—The Anchor Bible*. New York: Doubleday, 1964.

Ullman, M., and Zimmerman, N. *Working with Dreams*. Los Angeles: Jeremy P. Tarcher, 1979.

CHAPTER NINE

Dream Work and Pastoral Counseling

Steps toward an Educational Program

SVEN HEDENRUD

I first met Sven Hedenrud during my initial stay in Gothenburg from 1974 to 1976. As he describes in this chapter, this led to a close working relationship that has lasted until the present time. He was most responsive to the way I taught about dreams and, most important, was in a position to do something about it. As the head of a training center, he invited me back repeatedly to work with both the faculty and the students. He gained the respect and support of the church authorities in his endeavor to include dream work as an integral part of pastoral counseling. His untiring efforts went beyond Sweden to include Finland as well. He has from the beginning played an important role in the development of the leadership training program under the sponsorship of the Dream Group Forum, a national society in Sweden to propogate group dream work.

In the late seventies I got to know Montague Ullman in Gothenburg, Sweden. I had heard about him from some friends and invited him to our staff to introduce the new way of working with dreams in groups that he was developing. For over ten years I was director of a growing center for psychotherapy and pastoral counseling, the St. Luke's Foundation, where we also had a recognized and well-known psychotherapy training program. Our orientation included an interest in existential and religious matters. I am also an ordained minister of the Church of Sweden.

All the staff was very much taken by the effectiveness of the process, working with our own dreams under Monte's leadership. Loving care of dreams—and of dreamers! We had experienced something matchless. We could not do without it! We would have to learn. There was a growing feeling that traditional psychoanalytic theories were plainly not sufficient. Also, we soon saw how we could use the method beneficially in our training program. Now we had a better means of understanding the nature of dreams and reaching their hidden message. We just had to include it in our psychotherapy program. This addition was welcomed by the students.

As my own view of dreams deepened, I realized that we are all continuously working through our heritage from the past as we relate to those closest to us, to others, to ourselves, to nature and animals, to existence as a whole. This inner activity continues to confront us with what we are doing to our fellow creatures, to ourselves and, yes, with what we are making of our lives. Gentle or tough, often with a playful humor, the dream brings us to new insights and, in some cases, speaks so forcefully as to change our lives.

Again and again we just marveled at the richness of expression in our dreams. As priest and pastor, working also with pastoral counseling, in addition to psychotherapy, I recognized this inner force, driving us toward maturity and fairness in our dealings with other people. The overflowing joy, the power of shame and guilt, if excessive, so disabling but basically necessary for a humane, social life—they are all there in our dreams. (The relationship between dreams and conscience would be an interesting subject to explore theoretically.) What is the aim of pastoral counseling but to assist people in their striving to be more truthful, to be in dialogue with their guiding inner voice, to gain a better perspective of their life, to find a ground for self-acceptance and an active and caring responsibility for fellowman and for whatever is entrusted to you in life?

Spiritual leaders of every age have regretted that people don't care much for such essential questions. According to recent research in our country, people are much more occupied with existential problems than has been the case for some decades. Modern man is not as in earlier times searching for solutions in a traditional religious context; he tends to create his own view of life out of elements from different traditions.

In any case, now as always, the basic questions for any spiritual guidance worthy of its name, must be: What is genuine, what is just taken over without reflection, what is turned away in disppointment or defiance? How can we meet?

There is always one reliable personal inner authority. Everybody has dreams that are pondering, questioning, challenging, healing. I have to say to myself: "This belongs to a spiritual life!" And if dreaming is an expression of spiritual life, everybody is, in a way, spiritually alive. One problem is that too much of it remains unconscious because our culture, in contrast to many earlier ones, has been neglecting dreams and now lacks a way of dealing with them on a large scale.

People in biblical times, for example, did not. Nor did the ancient Greeks. Among the latter I have found only two who despised dreams, namely Democrit, who was atomizing instead of synthesizing and Aristotle who ontologically was a materialist. So, in the very fundamentals of our Western, Judeo-Christian culture, there is considerable respect for the kind of life revisioning and reorientation that goes on at night.

If the first practical consequence of my encounters with Monte was to modify our psychotherapy training program, the second was to bring dream work into pastoral counseling. There were two problems to consider. First, is it possible to do dream work in a confessional context, without betraying the principles of the method? Second, how much is dream work a pastoral concern?

First, we look at the dreams as welling up from a level of consciousness offering a more comprehensive overview of our life. To marvel at this inner wisdom and creativity you do not need the hypothesis of God. But if you have a religious orientation, of course it should not be excluded from your understanding of dreams. Maybe you can be responsive to religious projections from the group and spiritual interpretations from the dreamer, on one hand, while seeing to it that no pressure be exerted, on the other.

Second, how much is dream work a pastoral concern? To me, all human communication that brings us closer to truth, love, righteousness, and beauty is of pastoral value. Dream work certainly does. To be pastoral in a more specific sense, it has, by definition, to be performed in a church context and with the common intention of bringing about or deepening the personal communication with your inner life and the religious interpretation of your life in the context of a religious tradition—specifically, in my case, with the Biblical texts. If so, it must be very important to consider how dreams are valued in the Bible.

No book, ever, has been so thoroughly investigated as the Bible. Uncountable treatises and papers have been written about its many different aspects. Still, you can find commentaries that don't say a word about dreams. This reflects, of course, the lack of interest in dreams despite how rich and important they are both in the Old and in the New Testament. Theology has been dominated by prevalent epistemological theories. According to them, what knowledge could you get from your dreams?

I had to go through the Bible anew, from the dreamer's point of view, and I had to study what became of the dreams in the traditions of the Church. There was some help, specifically from Morton T. Kelsey in his valuable book God, Dreams and Revelation (1974.) It was rewarding.

In the Old Testament I found a view of dreams that was clear and consistent. Man receives knowledge in dreams. God speaks through dreams. Some individuals are specifically called to mediate God's will to the people. That will is often given to them in dreams and visions. In Numbers 12:6 it is directly said: "Hear my words: If there is a prophet among you, I the Lord make myself known to him in a vision, I speak with him in a dream." Dreams and visions are spoken of as actual events, often powerful in their meaning and consequences. Dreams were God's best means to make a caring connection with his people.

Of special interest is the dream theology of Elihu in the book of Job, chapters 32 and 33. "For God speaks in one way, and in two, though man does not perceive it. In a dream, in a vision of the night, when deep sleep falls upon men, while they slumber on their beds, then he opens the ears of men, and terrifies them with warnings, that he may turn man aside from his deed and cut off pride from man" (32, 14–17). Even in Job's nightmares there is a message, a warning.

As dreams were so important, there were also charlatans, false prophets who pretended, in their own interest, to proclaim God's will. So there are also warnings for false religions and false religious leaders.

In the New Testament this tradition is kept alive. When Joseph was told in his dreams to remain at Mary's side, although she was expecting, or, to flee to Egypt, and to come back home again, he obeyed (Matthew 1 and 2.) According to Acts 10, what caused Peter to overcome the order not to associate with pagans was a vision he had. This made it possible to spread the Gospel to non-Jews as well. These may suffice as examples. That the dreams of the Bible were taken seriously is obvious. What has become clearer to me, with awe, is that such visionary dreams are by no means restricted to ancient times.

Through the years I have been lecturing about dreams and dream appreciation all over Sweden. Nearly every time, someone comes up to me after the lecture to tell me a dream she or he has had, ones just as spectacular as those from the Bible. Often a dream is confided to me, one that the dreamer never dared to tell anybody before, for fear of being considered crazy, or because it has been so special in its holiness.

I think it is important to combine respect for the dreamer with a sound amount of skepticism, and to be aware of the possible influence of mere chance or subliminal perception or the possible occurrence of telepathic communication or misrememberance, yet there remain some that seem to be of the same paranormal type as those reported in the Bible. I do not see any difference in the quality of some modern dreams, compared to those in the Bible. It is just a question of who had the dream and in what frame of reference you interpret it.

There are several reasons for a pastoral counselor to get help from dream work. It is not only compatible with old traditions; it belongs to basics. And now, supplied with an extraordinary method, he has a means available. In order to bring about an encounter between dream work and the pastoral context, I decided, together with my colleagues, to invite the public to a Dream Week at a church where there are retreats and courses and all kinds of inspirational activities, a place where there was a sound devotional life going on, independent of us but accessible. Every participant would be free to work with a dream as we do in a dream group. There would be no pressure whatsoever to make any religious interpretation, but the environment was chosen in order to enhance connections with the religious dimension. This occurred in the fall of 1981.

We received enough applications to have four groups of six to seven participants. As to be expected, the great majority were women. Various professions were represented, with some emphasis on the caring professions. The first year we had two dream sessions a day, and everybody felt it was enough. There was plenty of free time in between. We also had two evenings free for general discussion where all kinds of questions were raised about dreaming and dream work and about connections with ordinary life and the religious dimension. We also had a social evening on the last night.

The evaluations were very positive, and we were encouraged to continue on this path. Several dreamers had new insights about the healing aspects of dream work and religion. Some had been using traditionally religious metaphors in their dreaming; others had discovered their confessed religion meant more to them than they had thought or, that they had their own personal ways of expressing matters of ultimate concern.

Originally, I had proposed that the church center make the Dream Week a "joint venture" with the congregation of the Church. They declined but were bold enough to offer us the place and allow us to make the arrangement ouselves. The Church was represented among the participants, and any reservations about dream work in the future was dissipated.

In 1997 we had our seventeenth Dream Week, always at the same time of the year, the week after the Swedish Midsummer Feast. In the last four years the Dream Week has also been extended to include training of dream group leaders, with the participation of the Dream Group Forum, our national association for promoting dream work according to Monte's method. (I am one of its founders and its first secretary.)

For some years from 1982 on, our yearly Dream Week was used as one alternative form of further education for priests of the diocese in southern Sweden, where it was located. For five years eight to ten male and female priests attended. The arrangement was also open to the public, so the groups later were mixed, including both clergy and laymen. Some clergy returned for another year at their own expense. One man said: "I have got another view of my fellow men. I realize everybody is a dreamer, artistically depicting her life situation every night, the unconscious trying to convey healing insights every night. I have a new respect for the personal." One woman expressed herself this way: "I marvel at our abilities as dreamers. After looking at a TV show I counted the names of the production cast, 163! In my dreams I do it all myself, from the script and the directing to all the actors involved!"

One of the participants of the first Dream Week returned after three years as a missionary in Zaire, Africa (now, again Congo.) I learned a lot from what she told me about dreams and dream interpretation in that culture, specifically about fundamentalism. There dreams are given much attention and are considered as conveying literal truth to the extent that, if a man dreams that his children have stolen, they have—and they get punished for it! If a man dreams that his wife has been unfaithful, he has the right to divorce! (The same is not true of a woman's dream.) On one occasion a man spoke to the missionary in deep anguish. He had awakened that very morning with a terryfying dream. He had been dreaming that earth had been filling up around him, higher and higher. He could not move. When the mud finally reached his mouth, he woke up in cold sweat. Now he was convinced he was about to die—maybe even be suffocated by earth! The Swedish woman asked him about his life. It turned out that he was a very intelligent man and that in his village he had been entrusted with many assignments, so much so that he felt heavily burdened. That day he was liberated from the "dream fundamentalism" of his culture. A metaphorical understanding of the dream left him very relieved. Dream work à la Monte in a village of Zaire!

I am not telling this just as a good story. Fundamentalism can certainly be a problem in pastoral counseling as in dream work. In fact, living religion and dreams have use of playfully constructive metaphors in common. There is and must be this inner space for connecting outer reality with inner reality. That is where creeping thoughts learn to walk. My professor of philosophy at the University of Lund, Gunnar Aspelin, once said that religion is more similar to art than to science. As a student I was disturbed by that, being at the same time a believer in science and in Christ. I now see he was right. Art and religion are akin. They are creatively working with wholeness, interpreting reality using symbols and metaphors. On the most personal level, this is also what dreaming is about. Winnicott, 1971, talks about "transitional objects" filling the gap between the little child in its beginning separation from its mother. He describes the"transitional area" as an "area" created by the child to connect outer reality with its own inner reality. This is where fantasy and playing take place. With adults the remaining transitional area is the growth place of art, music, religion, and, to a large extent, science as well. The abundance of it is blooming in our dreams.

The immediate consequence would then, evidently, be to include dream work training in the educational programs for pastoral counseling. In 1992 I decided to leave my position in Gothenburg to take on new responsibilities, as teacher of pastoral counseling at one of the two official training institutes for priests of the Church of Sweden at Lund, in the southern part of the country. With a university degree the students come for one year of practical training before their ordination. One of the main subjects is "pastoral care" or "pastoral counseling."

What are the chances for me now, to deal with dream work in this context? Within the structure, there is room to reach every candidate with lectures on the nature of dreams and of dream work. The students are also informed about some settings where they can gain experience on their own. They are challenged to keep a record of their own dreams. Some are interested in taking part in a dream group I have outside the institute. They are welcome to do so when our teacher-student relationship has changed into one of being colleagues.

At present, I think the proper context for a more elaborate training in dream work is in the further educational programs being offered by dioceses or other units of the church. I value such an official recognition. First, it gives status to dream work recognizing that it really deserves to be considered as a tool in pastoral care. I am aware there are and will always be skeptics to question the significance of dream work generally and in pastoral counseling, specifically. Secondly, the financing would be done by the church and not be dependent on personal resources.

The other option, also a good one, is to attract clergy and deacons to dream work and training opportunities offered by members of the Dream Group Forum. This would be fully dependent on personal initiatives both from leadership trainers and individual priests and deacons. The advantage would be working together with other professions, while perhaps missing the specific elements of pastoral counseling.

The kind of structure I am developing at present is the following:

1. I make an agreement with the arranging body (diocese, e.g.) about time and place. I would prefer to have five days at our disposal but accept three days. The best location is a church conference center, with a devotional life going on, independent of our course but congenial with dream work.
2. The main content is ordinary dream work in groups. Some may have prior exposure, others may have no earlier experience.
3. In an introductory lecture I outline the motivation for dream work generally and for dream work in pastoral counseling specifically. I talk about dreams in the Bible and the Old Church—and what became of personal dreams in the further history of pastoral care. I sketch out how dreams can reflect and foster spiritual maturity and the genuineness of personal faith. Finally, I describe opportunities for going further and how to learn and be trained in the dream group process. I also, somewhere during the course, note some of the restraining factors, what can still be seen as possible dangers in connection with dream work. (See below.) I find

this can be of help in understanding the general neglect and suspicions about dream work.

4. Somewhere in the middle we have one session to discuss general questions about dreaming and dream work. This is done with the groups meeting together. On this occasion we can bring issues arising in the various work sessions.
5. At the end we have an evaluation of what has been learned, how to use it further and what opportunities there are to get leadership training with the help of trainers of the Dream Group Forum.

If our dreams represent such healing potential and if all known cultures but our own pay so much attention to them—why are they so neglected, even ridiculed, as they have been for such a long time?

I can see several reasons. First of all there is this characteristic strength and weakness of our Western civilization, namely the stress on rationalistic science and technology. What can be measured and constructed is what can make you wealthy and happy. Dreams cannot be weighed and measured, not even manipulated. From the point of view of common logic they are senseless. I have even met persons who are afraid of their dreams. *Am I crazy?* they wonder. Sometimes people have asked me this question directly. Others have not dared to tell a dream to anybody, because of fear of being labeled "strange." The language of dreaming is not self-evident!

To a less serious degree is the fear that one would be so involved in dreams as to lose interest in the outer world and use them as an escape. Theoretically that might happen, but only if it is not understood that dreaming really is an invitation to participate more fully in life.

As it becomes clear that physics and technology have made it possible for us to come to the brink of annihilation and that chemistry is close to poisoning us all, there is again greater need for other subjective values. We can start looking at dreams again, for example. Now perhaps other risks may become apparent.

Dream work may be looked upon as just another field to exploit. There is money to make. We live in a free society. Values based on respect for human integrity and ethical consciousness have to compete with the values of those who are more interested in exploiting the dreams of others for their own gain.

Dreams can be approached and used in a magical way. There have always been those who pretend to be or even believe they are talented with special insights and the ability to tell another person what a dream means or even proclaim that their own dreams reveal truths about others or bring messages to the world. The Bible has many warnings against false prophets.

We have already mentioned the literal understanding of dreams. One variety of "dream fundamentalism" is the practice we know from many cultures to employ dream dictionaries, where you can look up the image and get its meaning revealed. I find it moving to study these efforts in history to make dreams understandable and to bring order into a world of overwhelming richness and variation. But they are of little or no value and are sometimes harmful.

No wonder there has been a clash between those in positions of power or authority and the ordinary dreamer. The one in power wants control. But how can you control dreaming? I think this has been a fundamental problem for those in power, in some periods of human history. Above all I think of the change of attitudes on dreaming, which took place in the transition of the Old Church to a well-organized hierarchical structure, where the officials were managers of the Truth and where lay people no longer could have direct access to God through their inner life if it was not sanctioned by the Church. *Extra ecclesiam nulla salus.* Outside the Church no salvation. That happened around the year 600 under the leadership of Pope Gregory the Great, who, by the way, was great even as a dreamer. The religious value of dreams had to be decided by the priest, the "expert."

Over different periods of history there have been efforts to limit the understanding and use of dreams to experts. Whatever the alleged reasons may have been, whether they had to do with the power of the Church, concern for the health of the dreamer, economic reasons, or other thinly disguised, self-centered interests, I think the time has come to recognize these limitations for what they are. As in psychotherapy, only by overcoming resistance to change can we go forward toward the goal of stimulating a wider interest in dreams and ability to work with them.

If we let pastoral counseling and dream work meet, one might ask as a dream worker, is it possible to accept religious projections and religious interpretations in dream work? The answer must be yes, as long as the basic rules of dream work are respected.

Looking at it the other way around one might ask, What are the reasons to include dream work in pastoral counseling? Let me put together some conclusions about what dream work can contribute to pastoral counseling and why dream work training ought to be promoted by the church.

First of all, it is, as we have seen, totally in accordance with the Bible and spiritual experience.

Second, in all pastoral care, whether we call it pastoral counseling, spiritual guidance or something else, there are basic values at stake. In dream work they are the same, often more concretely and experienced.

1. *Genuineness.* When St. Luke tells the story about the prodigal son in his fifteenth chapter he uses, in Greek, the expression that, "he came to himself" (in The New English Bible "he came to his senses"); that is, he stopped escaping. And when he became genuine, his wasted life made a turn. Dream work helps a counselor to get in touch with what really matters to herself and gives her an instrument to assist others in the same process.

2. *Truth* is a central religious value. Working with dreams confronts us with aspects of truth about ourselves that we have neglected but need to see. Dreams are given to us gently or dramatically and often with humor reveal that truth.

3. *Hope.* Dream work does not only help us to recognize wounds and conflicts and weaknesses. Dreams are composed in our depth to heal and to guide us. Above all they point to our resources and possibilities. If they are listened to, they strengthen self-knowledge, self-respect, and self-confidence. There is always something new in a dream, little or much, pointing out or hinting at a personal way forward.

4. *Love.* Dream work confirms that a dream in itself is basically a gift of love. It makes it clear to us how much our relationships to other people mean, how important they are to our well-being. Monte once expressed it this way: "If we look around the world and see all the conflicts and wars, we cannot but wish that humans had a special organ to guide the way to good and constructive interaction—and we do have one such organ, expressing itself in our dreams. If we just could learn to listen to them!" After many years of experience of dream work, I agree.

5. *Faith.* Dream work shows that we need to live in trust. It shows us what to trust and put faith in and what not. In a more direct religious sense, dreams tend to show the liberating and rehabilitating power of the message, not to be bound by shame and guilt and shortcomings but to be set free, trusting forgiveness and atonement. That is the existential essence of the Gospel. Furthermore, working with dreams makes us more at home

with the symbolic and metaphorical language of our religious documents rather than the literal.

6. *Communion.* Dream work is not an individualistic performance. Its effectiveness depends on the common endeavor and contributions by the group. From the start a dream group can be an encounter with others on a deep personal level, one that rarely happens in other contexts. Group members often say they feel like they are on holy ground when working with their dreams.

7. *Growth.* Dream group work usually goes on for a limited amount of time. A group can also decide to work together for several years. Even with a limited amount of time, it may initiate a continued capacity to listen to dreams. A process of growth has started. This can happen to a dreamer on his own with a dream, but it is facilitated in a group.

One woman of seventy-five told a dream she had in her thirties. She was on a train. The conductor came to punch her tickets. She gave them to him. He looked with warmth at her and said: "You still need another one, the ticket of heavenly joy." She started digging in her handbag, and, finally, at the bottom, she got hold of a slip of paper and handed it over to the conductor, who seemed full of love. It was the ticket of heavenly joy. This dream triggered a renewal of faith, she said, and a transformation from a legalistic, fundamentalistic person into a more generous, warm, and positive being with much more joy in life.

Another woman of forty-five had a dream where she was sitting alone at a big table, trying to catch slippery fish, several of which were powerfully jumping around on the table. She was unable to get a grip on them and felt a growing despair. After a long while, she got a hold of one, and then of all of them, and was able to put them all in a beautiful basket she had on her lap. She woke up with a strong feeling of happiness. She had been struggling for a long time with issues of faith and now she felt at one with a healing faith, the fish being an old Christian symbol.

I see dream work as a free gift to any church, synagogue, movement or organization that wants to promote mental and spiritual well-being among people, as long as the rules of dream work are respected and followed.

In the Church, pastoral care is the field where dream work belongs. That is why dream work should be included in the training programs. This is not to say, however, that leading dream groups in the Church should be restricted to its ordained ministers, but that this key group should be knowledgeable in the method. Dream work can be a complement to pastoral counseling. Interested lay people can be trained. Special dream groups can be set up. Existing groups, like prayer groups and Bible study groups, youth groups, or even the church choir can temporarily be changed into a dream group, to be enriched, strengthened and made more effective and bear more fruit.

I am convinced that the Church does well in adopting dream work as a means of expressing itself. For the sake of truth, hope, love, faith, communion, and growth, for its own inner peace, credibility, and effectiveness, I hope dream work will be included in the training of all ministers working with pastoral counseling.

References

Kelsey, M. T. *God, Dreams and Revelation.* Minneapolis, Minn.: Augsburg, 1974.

Winnicott, D. W. *Playing and Reality.* London: Tavistock, 1971.

PART III

Applications in Psychology and Psychiatry

CHAPTER TEN

Working with Dreams in Group Psychotherapy

INGE WIDLUND

Inge Widlund, a group therapist, has participated in many of the leadership training programs I conducted in Sweden over the years. These sessions were designed to prepare the participants to lead experiential dream groups. The principles and rationale of the process were considered in great detail as were the problems that arise at each stage of the process. Sensitive to how different this approach was from group therapy, Inge was quick to respond to what it had to offer the group therapist. He is one of the few group therapists to master the process and to feel equally at home in the experiential dream group and in psychoanalytically oriented group therapy. Based on his long experience with both he shares with the reader his assessment of the similarities and differences.

Psychoanalytic Background

Working with dreams and their meaning in a group using the method developed by Montague Ullman has provided me with important and profound experiences—both as a member of a dream group and as its leader. For quite a long time I have been occupied with the question of how these experiences—this way of looking upon and dealing with dreams—could be of use in my work as a psychotherapist. How could my experience with dream groups be implemented into the kind of group analytic therapy that I am engaged in?

It has occured to me that dreams no longer seem to be at the core of psychoanalytic therapy. I find a resistance against dreams within the psychotherapeutic profession. In my own experience and in the experience of others it has become apparent that work on the interpretation and understanding of dreams is almost neglected in the education and training of psychotherapists. Candidates and colleagues have often confessed their insecurity with regard to dreams (as if it were a speciality lying outside their therapeutic competence). How can this be? I return to Freud and the origin of psychoanalysis to get a perspective on this development.

Freud's *The Interpretation of Dreams* (1900) is generally considered one of his most—if not the most—important work and a solid ground for psychoanalytic theory. His analysis of his own dreams and those of others are exciting reading of lasting value. He had discovered "the royal road to the unconscious," a road that he expected would become of great importance in the years to come, both in clinical practice and in establishing psychoanalysis as an acknowledged science. But only five years later, in the description of the Dora case, Freud shifted his emphasis to the exploration of what he had earlier seen as the greatest obstacle; namely, the transference, which he now considered "the most powerful ally."

The patient's projection of aspects from early significant persons onto the analyst—the transference—has since then been in the foreground in psychoanalytic therapy. Moreover, the analysis of the resistance also came to assume greater importance. Working with resistance and transference has ever since—with no doubt good reasons—dominated psychoanalytic technique.

In short, one could say that the dream and its importance was incorporated by Freud into the psychoanalytic domain only to be overshadowed later on and to become of minor interest relative to the growing attention to transference reactions and resistance. In general, however, at least for the western world, dreams and dream interpretation are highly connected with psychoanalysis. This state of being may be understood in view of the relative exclusivety of the psychoanalytic enterprise and also in light of what Fromm describes as modern man's inability to wonder. "Whatever the merits of our high degree of literary and universal education, we have lost the gift of being puzzled. Everything is supposed to be known—if not to ourselves then to some specialist whose business it is to know what we do not know." (Fromm 1951, p. 3)

Freud considered the manifest dream in terms of distortions and disguises. The puzzle of the dream became a complicated cipher for which he looked for a code or key. The key was psychoanalytic drive theory, and the process of interpretation resembled detailed detective work. It is without doubt that Freud's work was far reaching, sophisticated and brilliant. It may be easy to understand why Freud's followers seem to hesitate before setting foot on the domain that Freud so supremely mastered.

This might be one of the reasons why so few clinicians have more critically examined Freud's theories about dreams. His analysis and interpretations were so detailed that they seemed to exclude any alternative way of understanding the dream at the same time as they distracted attention from the feelings and the striking power of the manifest content to shed light on the immediate experience.

One of Ullman's great merits is that he has extended dream work beyond the psychoanalytic field to society at large. The main thought behind his dream group is to return the dream to the dreamer and to reduce the alienation that exists between the dreamer and the dream, and to fully understand that he or she is the responsible director for this inner captivating night drama that has meaning for waking life.

In Freud's view, the dream was a way to understand neurosis. The dream, however, does not exist because of neurosis but exists in its own right. It does not only depict our secret wishes, as Freud believed, but also our situation in life, our relations to other people, our conflicts, fears, rivalries, ambitions, ideals, and so forth.

Thus, there are reasons to once again investigate the possibilities for using the language of the dream as a tool for widening our consciousness in psychoanalytic therapy. In the following I will consider the form of therapy that may be the closest to the dream group, namely group psychotherapy.

Dream Group and Group Analytic Therapy

The dominant kind of group psychotherapy, at least that which is practiced in Sweden, has its roots in psychoanalytic theory. That doesn't mean psychoanalysis in a group but rather using psychoanalytic theory to understand the inner world of individuals through their relations to one another, to the group as a whole, and to the leader. To understand the dynamics and the process in the group is the primary task. This application in a group is called group analysis or group analytic therapy.

The group analytic approach does not have leadership in its general sense. The therapist, who is called *conductor* by (Foulkes and Anthony 1957), follows what is going on in the group and when he believes it may be helpful to the group, he may interpret what he understands is going on. Thus, there is no structure, no special order of the work. But the conductor also has a role as administrator and as such he is responsible for the rules concerning the framework; namely, agreements about time, place, confidentiality, payment, and so forth. There is only one basic rule for the work in the group, which is to speak about what you feel and think while you are sitting in the group with as much frankness as possible. An underlying reality is that each member soon will begin to act as a therapist towards his group mates. One of the cornerstones in group analysis is that everyone has the ability to interpret or, in Foulkes's words, "translate" the communication from another person. What characterizes a structureless group, without direct leadership and with seven or eight members, at least in the beginning, is that it sometimes can provoke feelings of getting lost, of uneasiness or anxiety, as well as regression to earlier developmental stages, resulting in more primitive behaviour. This can be seen as a powerful therapeutic tool and at the same time as a defense that hinders more realistic coping with the problems at hand. Usually the group undergoes different states of being. W.R. Bion (1961) has created a well-known theory about such different states in a group that occur as defense towards a threatening underlying primitive anxiety. He describes four different modes of defense, *Basic Assumption Groups*: (1) Dependence, (2) Fight/Flight, (3) Pairing, and (4) a mode of a more realistic character he calls Work Group.

Working with dreams in a group using Ullman's method demands that the group be on the level that Bion designates as work group. In my opinion this is possible because the dream group is richly structured. This doesn't exclude the essential emotional part of the dream work. One of the cornerstones of Ullman's ideas about working with dreams in a group is safety. The dreamer is not forced or manipulated. He must feel safe. The fulfillment of this is dependent on the leadership. The leader does not just let things happen, but on the contrary, he sees to it that things happen in the right way. The principles for a dream group are founded on cooperation between the group members in order to focus solely on the one who has presented a dream. The dreamer's presentation of the dream, the group members' contribution of feelings and metaphors, the reaction from the dreamer, the dialogue about this material, and the orchestration intended to offer connections between the dream and the dreamer's life situation are all parts of a structure aimed at bringing the dreamer a greater understanding of the dream. To this aim, the structure appears to be an equally genial and effective invention.

The structure has another important function, namely to prevent group regression and to maintain a realistic level of working. Despite that, regressive tendencies can of course occur. (Ullman and Zimmerman 1979) gives an example of a transference reaction that hindered the work with a dream. In the work with dreams and the feelings and associations that are evoked in this context, there is a need for access to what are called primary processes, that can be viewed as a form of partial, individual regression in the service of the dream and the dreamer. But this is far from a group regression as described earlier.

There are considerable differencies between the dream group and the therapy group. To a certain degree they even have opposite ground rules:

The dream group	*The therapy group*
Rich, firm structure	No structure
The individual is at the center	The group as a whole is at the center
Attention to the dream and the dreamer's life stuation	Attention to the "here and now," communication, interaction
Leadership limited to maintaining structure	Withdrawn, neutral leadership
Participating leader	Nonparticipating leader
No group regression	Group regression
Limited, specific goal	Wide, open, manyfolded (both common and individual) goals

Some differences may seem obvious: the dream group has no specific therapeutic goal (yet it starts therapeutic processes); the group analytic therapy has a completely different base, theoretically, clinically, and traditionally. A vast and significant difference is that in the dream group the dream is the center of interest and the dreamer controls the amount of information he or she wants to offer, whereas in the therapy group it is the free-floating dialogue and the interaction between the group members that are the objects of attention. The free-floating discussion in the group is the equivalent to the free-floating association in psychoanalysis. Such interpersonal interaction is not given any place in the dream group.

Considering what has been stated above, our conclusion might be that there are few possibillities for using features of the dream group work in group therapy (or the opposite for that matter). That is true both for the structure and when it comes to the thorough treatment of the dream. In group therapy any installation of structure would counteract its foremost tool, free-floating dialogue. On the other hand, any thorough treatment of a dream would force the analytic group to stay focused on the dream of one dreamer, with the effect of neglecting the group process. How does the dream come into group analytic therapy?

Theory

The following summarizes the theory expressed by the originator of group analytic therapy, the German-British psychoanalyst, S. H. Foulkes (1898–1976). He emphazises the importance of the communication that occurs in the group. He claims that both individual and social integration is furthered by the basic human need to communicate. As communication over time becomes expanded and refined, underlying conflicts can be expressed verbally instead of by symptoms. Foulkes compares this process with the transition from dreams—symbols and metaphors—to the spoken language, from the primary process to the secondary process. The communication process is essential as the vehicle for making the unconscious conscious and thus functions as a bridge between the conscious, the preconscious and the unconscious.

An important concept in Foulkes's theory is that of a group *matrix.* Matrix, originally meaning (lat.) womb, is a hypothetical web of all communications and relations in the group, both manifest and latent. Compared with the individual mind it is the "group mind." The history of the group and all experiences in the group exist in this matrix, and thus influence what is happening in the group, and are also the source of meaning behind the activities in the group. In this context it is important to keep in mind Foulkes's view of the group as "the group as a whole."

The group analytic theory also includes noting specific therapeutic factors that are at work. One of them is *socialization*, a process referring to the integration of the individual into society. In the group this means that the individual is brought from the isolation that characterizes many patients into participation with other people. To be understood and to understand other human beings and to share the basic conditions of life are important ingredients in this process.

The mirror phenomenon is another factor. It implies that the patient can see aspects of himself in others, in their behavior and problems (it is easier to see the problems of others than one's own). Mirroring also includes identification or contrasting in the process of getting a better image of oneself. Mechanisms like projection and introjection are naturally at work in the mirroring process, which often leads to relief from feelings of guilt or anxiety.

The collective unconscious of the group is manifested under the surface of the free discussion, by material that is now and then expressed by symbols, dreams, common fears or phobias, and the like. Foulkes refers to this as the *condense phenomenon.*

Still another factor is called *exchange.* It includes the lively exchange of information—facts, advice, opinions—that goes on between the members of the group. Foulkes compares the group members to siblings, who are more willing to accept from each other what wouldn't be accepted if it came from the parents.

So, we notice that the dream has a place in what Foulkes calls the *condense* phenomenon. The dream is a "discharge" from the collective unconscious of the group, and it is what Foulkes terms a "group dream," that is, a dream that in some way or another throws light on something that has happened in the group, an actual situation in the group or the relationship of a single member to the group.

However, the dream does not have a central or natural place in group analysis. Similiar to what has been said earlier about psychoanalysis, resistance and transference are more at hand for analysis and interpretation.

Yet, Foulkes could be seen as somewhat contradictory in this case. On the one hand Foulkes (1964) claims that the dream is an individual creation that is not meant to be published or communicated to others. He refers to Freud, who pointed out that even the self refuses to accept the dream as an internal, intrapsychic communication. On the whole, the telling of dreams in a therapy group is considered an expression of resistance and should be treated as such. It would therefore be a quasi-psychoanalytic stance if the therapist were to play into this resistance with the consequence that the group members would continue to produce dreams for analysis (instead of other material).

On the other hand Foulkes says that the group analyst obviously does not reject dreams but treats them according to their dynamic meaning. First of all, every dream that is told is the property of the group.

Groups intuitively differentiate group dreams from other dreams. Foulkes further notes that these group dreams sometimes communicate relevant information concerning interpersonal relations, attitudes towards the group leader, or insights into the common, unconscious resistance of the group. A dream that is told in the group is left to the group to analyze. Group dreams are valuable in this context. Foulkes states that a continuous rendering of dreams by one individual is a sign of withdrawal from contact with other human beings and is therefore significant as resistance. Thus, it seems as if Foulkes speaks both as the psychoanalyst, confessing his belief in Freud's view of the dream (with the accompanying demands on unveiling the latent content) and as the group analyst seeing the significance of the manifest content as an important communication about the patient and the group.

Comment

In my opinion Foulkes overlooks the function of the dream with regard to several of his group-specific factors. The factor he calls socialization includes the value of sharing experiences, the need to be understood and to understand others. I have found that exactly to be of the greatest value in dream groups. The accepting of one's seemingly chaotic world of dreams, the understanding of one's own dream, and learning to understand others through their dreams is an effective part of what is called social integration. The mirror phenomenon covers mechanisms like projection and identification, which according to Foulkes serve to relieve anxiety and feelings of guilt. These mechanisms are to a high degree at work in the dream group. Also with regard to the factor called exchange I think that there is plenty of space for the dream. The willingness to give and to accept, which Foulkes considers central for this factor, is also significant for the work in the dream group.

In my opinion the dream and the telling of dreams is a natural part of and has an obvious function in group analytic therapy, and my view is based on my own experiences of both dream groups and group analytic groups. Then, what is the problem?

It may appear that the problem is that the dream demands quite special attention. Behind Foulkes one may hear the voice of Freud: the analytic task is to uncover the latent content of the dream behind the disguises and distortions that show in the manifest. Since this is not supposed to happen in a group analytic group (as it would then be psychoanalysis in a group), analysis of the resistance will come even more to the foreground.

Foulkes's ambivalence seems to grow out of a conflict between an orthodox psychoanalytic view of the dream and the fact, as he himself mentions, that members of the group have both the sensitivity and ability to understand the manifest meaning without any support from experts. It comes natural to me to take the latter opinion as a starting point. That also fits with the confidence in the ability of the human being and the radical spirit in which Foulkes created the group analytic group. It seems strange to me to believe that attention to dreams would push aside the interpretations of resistances and transferences. On the contrary, the dream actually supports this effort with descriptions of transference reactions and resistance that are often far more effective than interpretations by the group therapist.

In my experience, most of the dreams that are told in the group are, in Foulkes's vocabulary, group dreams. His own example of a typical group dream is a dream about the group leader as a lion tamer. In an example from a group of mine I am the owner of a restaurant. The member who presented the dream had been absent for some time and was reluctant to pay the fee about which there was a mutual agreement. Shortly after his return to the group he told a dream that had touched him deeply: he is in a bar or a restaurant, it's dark and shady, there are other people but he doesn't know what's going on. The owner asks for money. The only thing he will get in return for the money is that he may go down into one of two dark holes in the floor. He pays the owner and goes down into the left hole and slides down to a basement. To his astonishment, there is a funeral. Some other people are there, silent. The group, listening to the dream, was also silent. It was a newly formed group that didn't have any experience working with dreams. I said: "I am the owner of a restaurant who asks for money for going underground." Laughter and a short silence followed. Another group member called attention to our argument about money. Yet another made some remarks about what the left hole meant (the dreamer had now and then panic anxiety expressed through heart symptoms) and so it went. The dreamer, with a little help from the group, could understand the essence of the message from the dream: his resistance against being confronted with his feelings (or, his responsibility for his feelings). The dream contains elements of transference and resistance, which is ultimately resistance against encountering painful experiences. All this came from a dream that was so elegantly concentrated and striking. With the support of the other group members the dreamer could appreciate the meaning of the dream, a meaning that would have taken considerable time to reach in the "usual" ways. The group participated because it felt involved and because the dream pointed out something that had been latently present in the group. This group continued to bring dreams to share and work with. One could say that it included dreams into its culture.

We must however also consider that there exist certain conditions in the group for meeting a dream with interest and understanding. That has become obvious at times when I have tried to initiate work with a dream with less success than in the example above, mostly because of my lack of attention and sensitivity to the psychological state of the group. The following circumstances may occur: group members have negative reactions towards the one who presents the dream and therefore don't offer any contributions; the dream has not concerned the group or the dreamer has not—directly or indirectly—asked for help or, most commonly the dreamer turned to the therapist as the expert. It is also quite common for a person to tell a dream despite the fact that the group at the moment is not at all interested but is working with totally different processes. At such occasions I point out that nobody seems to be interested in the dream and wonder why this is so. Often a spontaneous analysis of the state of the group will then occur and the dreamer's resistance to participate can be interpreted and understood. On one such an occasion the group confronted a member who had just told a dream with the fact that she never seemed to care if anybody else was listening because she never listened to others; she did her own thing, *not relating* to the other members of the group. This became an important turning point for her work in the group.

These experiences of my own are different examples of the resistance that Foulkes refers to. But the dream and its content can also, in a liberating way, illustrate the resistance. In one group a member went on telling dreams with a recurrent theme. She dreamt about a house with a high fence—sometimes it was a wall. She sometimes could manage to get inside and thereby protect herself from persecutors outside. As time went by she could tell that the fence or the wall had diminished. In another series of dreams she described that she had gotten a new apartment, which pleased her, but whenever she would enter it there would always be someone ahead of her, somebody who had taken the best seat, or, in one dream there was a subway running through a room. These dreams made visible the resistance, defense, and transference to the group in a way more effective than verbal interpretation or analysis could provide and, perhaps most importantly, in a way that was possible for both the dreamer and the other group members to understand and accept. One can easily recognize and share the experience of fear and the tendency to withdraw as well as the vital necessity to struggle for one's own place—a self of one's own, acknowledged and respected—a struggle that goes on in every human group.

Another Way of Listening

I have found that my interest in dreams—and my participation in dream groups—has given me not only a greater ability to listen to dreams but also, as a kind of by-product, an ability to listen with a keener ear to the unconscious communication that is going on in the group.

The discourse of the group contains of course not just dreams but also images and references, more or less disguised, more or less unconscious. This is most obvious in the beginning of the life of a group. There are often discussions about the room where the group is meeting, how high or low the ceiling is, whether the colors are warm or cold, if it's too light or too shady, or the chairs are not very comfortable. This kind of communication goes on, often in vague or sophisticated ways.

Robert Langs (1982) has criticized the failure of psychotherapists to listen to the unconscious communication between patient and therapist. The result, he claims, has become a therapeutic conspiracy between the two that blocks understanding and the success of the therapeutic efforts. Langs names the unconscious communication primary process communication or codified communication. Another psychoanalyst who has been interested in the communication between patient and therapist in a similiar way is Patrick Casement (1985). Instead of meeting the patient with theories and ready-made conceptions of the therapist, Casement pleads for an active listening for suggestions from the patient that unconsciously are woven into the manifest communication. Matte Blanco (1975) claims that the two systems—unconscious and conscious—cover different logical principles, symmetric logic and asymmetric logic respectively. The symmetric logic throws light on the equivalence between things or persons belonging to the same class of phenomena; for example, mother and child can change places in their internal relation. Another sign of symmetric logic is timelessness. These are phenomena we can recognize from the world of dreams. Matte Blanco also states that the unit of a human being consists of two different fundamental forms of being: symmetric (unconscious) being that is in a dynamic interaction (tension, cooperation, or even union) with asymmetric (conscious) being. In other words, there are developmental tendencies in psychoanalytic theory that quite convincingly point out that what we call the unconscious is not far away from our waking, daily, and conscious life and that, through careful listening to the manifest expressions, we can understand much of the latent (I am tempted to say the real) meaning as we can explore the truth in a dream.

In a group of group therapists that I supervised, one of the therapists said that he felt confused and irritated by a female group member who told a detailed and long-winded story in the group. He did not understand his own feelings. The woman's story included a theme about her trying to get in touch with a man that continuously rejected her. The man was married to her sister. I suggested she might be talking unconsciously about her relationship to her therapist in a disguise. This interpretation was supported by the cotherapist (a female), who had noticed the movement and glances of the patient. Together they could recall situations where there were more open attempts to move closer to the male therapist, who now was able to understand what he earlier had resisted seeing. The patient had communicated with the unconscious of the therapist in a not too unusual way. However, the other members of the supervision group mildly protested my way of interpreting the communication. One of them quite strongly expressed her doubt about her ability to adopt this way of understanding communication in a group. It occurred to me to ask her to think of the story as if she had heard a dream being told and she understood with visible relief what I meant. I have offered this example to demonstrate how close the interpretation of dreams is to interpretation of other kinds of communication. If the aim in a group analytic therapy group is to make the unconscious conscious, then attention to the unconscious communication, the codified messages is one of the most important tasks for the therapist.

(Foulkes and Anthony 1957) also says about group analytic therapy that it "uses this manifest content to arrive by a process of analysis and interpretation at the latent content, in a way similar to that by which psychoanalysis uses the manifest content of a dream to discover the latent dream thoughts" (p. 37). Helping people reach a higher level of consciousness evolves via the manifest expression of the unconscious, inclusive of the dream. I cannot think of any better way of learning to listen and understand the manifest expressions in a group situation than to learn from work with dreams in a dream group. That has been my experience, and I wish to share it with more colleagues.

Conclusions

Important aspects of the dream group experience from a dream group are useful in a therapy group. One cannot use the structure of the dream group, and one cannot treat the dream so thoroughly in detail. For this goal there is the dream group. What a therapist can take from dream group experience is the interest, the attention, and the ability to appreciate dreams. The attitude of the group leader towards dreams in the therapy group sets the norms for the group. The important thing is that people in a group can understand dreams both of their own and of others if they gain the confidence and time to do so. The group throws light on and enriches a dream by their manyfold contributions more than any single individual, expert or not. For dreams to be told depends on whether they are welcome or not. To interpret the telling of dreams as resistance in therapy should be done very rarely if at all, since the reactions from the group members and their involvment are the most important indicators. It can be easier for a member of the group to communicate via a dream than directly. Learning to work with the language of the dream provides a better ability to listen to other kinds of metaphors and other kinds of unconscious communication that continuously go on in a group.

In the dream group you become skilled in abilities such as emotional identification and empathy. You are finding out what different feelings a dream evokes. You associate and "play" with images, symbols, and metaphors. This "play," with all the pleasure and benefit it provides, is exactly what it is in the play of children, a serious matter. You might even say that the task of the group is to play.

This leads me quite naturally to think of Winnicott's playing area that he thought of as a experiential and transitional space, a potential space between the inner world of the individual and the outer environment, the space that both unites and differentiates mother and child. Winnecott sees this as the base for the creative development of the whole of our cultural life. I think that the dream group is a brilliant example of such a playing area. The dream belongs to the inner world of the human being. As he or she tells a dream, it is brought out and belongs to—at least for a while—neither the inner world, nor the outer. It becomes the potential space where the play can occur, that both unites and separates—the transitional area. Winnecott further says that psychotherapy is about two individuals who play together. When this is not possible the work of the therapist must be to get the patient to a state where this is possible. The group analytic group is a splendid place to establish this playground, with the dream as splendid a way to play as there is.

References

Bion, W. R., *Experiences in Groups and other Papers.* London: Tavistock, 1961.

Casement, Patrick. *On Learning from the Patient.* London: Tavistock, 1985.

Foulkes, S. H. *Therapeutic Group Analysis.* London: Maresfield Reprints, H. Karnac, 1964.

Foulkes, S. H., and Anthony, E. J. *Group Psychotherapy: The Psychoanalytic Approach.* London: Penguin, 1957.

Freud, S. *Drömtydning.* Stockholm: Månpocket, 1974 (translation from Die *Traumdeutung,* 1900). (*The Interpretation of Dreams.* Standard edition, vols. 4 and 5, J. Strachey, ed. London: Hogarth, 1953).

Fromm, E. *Escape from Freedom.* New York: Rinehart & Co., 1951.

Greenson, Ralph R. *The Technique and Practice of Psychoanalysis.* London: Hogarth, 1985 (1967).

Langs, Robert. *The Psychotherapeutic Conspiracy.* New York: Jason Aronson, 1982.

Matte Blanco, Ignacio. *The Unconscious as Infinite Sets.* London: Duckworth, 1975.

Ullman, Montague, and Zimmerman, Nan. *Working with Dreams.* New York: Delacorte, 1979.

Winnecott, D. W. *Playing and Reality.* London: Tavistock, 1971.

CHAPTER ELEVEN

Dream Work and the Psychosomatic Process

A Personal Account

CLAIRE LIMMER

Although the basic principles of the experiential dream group process were worked out with Nan Zimmerman before I left to teach in Sweden in 1974, it was while I worked with students in Gothenburg that the process emerged in its present form. On my return to the United States in 1976 I was invited to co-lead a course in dreams at the William Alanson White Institute in New York City. It was my first opportunity to try out this newly developed approach in this country. Claire Limmer was a member of that class and has been associated with my work with dreams ever since, as a participant in weekly dream groups, as a member of many leadership training workshops and as a co-leader with me. She has developed dream workshops of her own.

Some people are "naturals" in dream work. Claire Limmer is certainly one of them. In this chapter she addresses the healing dimension of dream work in relation to physical illness. Presented in part as a personal narrative she describes her encounter with two life-threatening illnesses in the seventies and eighties and the role she feels that dream work played in her recovery and in the maintenance of health in the years since.

Not only is this a very moving account. It was also a harbinger of the more recent resurgence of interest in the role of emotional disorder in psychosomatic illness and the initiation of new approaches such as hypnosis in the amelioration of breast cancer.

It had not happened before, nor did it happen again that my mother told me a dream. That February morning in 1977, entering the kitchen still visibly moved by the power of the dream fragment that disturbed her sleep, mother described how she had awakened, surprised to find her arms outstretched, as they had been in the dream. All that remained of the dream was the memory of her dream voice, speaking in her native French, calling with tenderness, "Seigneur, Seigneur" ("Lord, Lord").

At the time I was a member of a weekly dream group and was also involved in ongoing psychoanalytic therapy, two types of activity for which mother had little patience. She had been strictly raised in a Calvinistic home in Switzerland where strength of character was valued above all and acquired, it was believed, through deprivation and discipline. She spent most of her adult life married to a Presbyterian minister, never overcoming her natural timidity and need for seclusion, very much valuing the dignity of privacy.

It would be rather an understatement to say I was feeling enthusiastic about my involvement in psychoanalysis and group dream work. More accurately, I was feeling myself coming alive as I began to share inner thoughts, to allow myself to be known in both the private and group settings. I learned, however, not to share that excitement with mother. She had closed the subject abruptly with a statement quite harshly spoken, "We have no right to meddle with dreams." As for psychoanalysis, she wondered after all how anyone could stoop to talk to a man she paid to listen to her.

My mother's dream has stayed with me all these years, moving in and out of my thoughts, the one small glimpse into her unconscious. What had been on her mind that night as she slept in my home? Had some thought of death sparked a dream vision of life after life? Did the dream reflect not only mother's spiritual yearning to be relieved of the burdens of her life, to be allowed in final form the dependency long sought? Was the Seigneur she called both her heavenly Lord and her husband, long gone, who had always been very much her lord?

The guessing and the need to guess are lifelong patterns in me, reaching back as far as I can remember to when I was a small child searching my mother's face carefully for some hint of feeling. That morning no more was said about the dream. There was no sharing of inner thoughts in this family. Emotions were controlled and contained, as was any material that might stir up feeling. Mother rarely spoke of her childhood, how many brothers and sisters she had, who her parents were. These were basic facts I never knew. As for the happiness and unhappiness of her adult life, the joys and difficulties of her marriage, these were all concealed by dignity, patience, self-denial, and, I suppose, a fear of what she felt.

It is clear to me now, why at forty-two I began writing for my daughters, drawing from dream material of my own gathered over a ten-year period to tell them as much as I could about my struggles to grow. I suppose some of us live out our lives correcting the past, no doubt overcorrecting at times. It was in that year that I was hospitalized with breast cancer, an event that followed too closely a previous hospitalization with another form of cancer, a melanoma. Both illnesses had been preceded by experiences of loss, the first, a pending divorce after nineteen years of marriage, and the second, an attempt to terminate seven years of analytic work with a most caring therapist. I had viewed the first bout of illness as a coincidence. The second made it clear to me how my body responded to the threat of separation from a loved one. Now my daughters too were threatened with loss as they feared for my health. I wanted them to know me, as I had not known my mother, to sense how they were like me and how they were not. I felt intuitively that the psychosomatic process, the breakdown of body rather than mind, was connected to a style of relating to loved ones in a merging form that left one endangered by any threat of abandonment. I hoped that if my daughters knew me better, perhaps their adolescent struggle for separation, threatened by a mothers's illness, would be less difficult and protracted than mine.

There was no way of knowing whether or not I would stay well, how I would fit into the cancer statistics I was up against—a 75 percent chance of making it five years, a 50 percent chance of making it ten, taking into account breast cancer alone. By day I felt optimistic, but at night my fears took over, filling my mind with apprehension about what would happen to my girls and with questions about what I could leave them. The answer to this grew increasingly clear. What I had to give was my work with dreams. Mine would be a legacy of dreams.*

For four months, on sick leave from my work at a children's psychiatric hospital, I spent four days a week at Memorial Sloane-Kettering Hospital, waiting anywhere from two to five hours a day for the few moments of radiation treatment prescribed as a follow-up to surgery. In

*Legacy of Dreams (manuscript unpublished)

waiting rooms I studied the dreams recorded over a ten-year period, eventually choosing sixteen in chronological order to best describe the struggles I underwent and wanted to share with my girls. Upon my return to work, I concentrated all my writing in the summer months when I was on vacation from teaching. I wrote over a five-year period, working on dreams of the past and new dreams generated by the writing itself and by current life issues, completing a final manuscript in 1983.

During this period there were a number of forces at work. I was systematically reading the current psychoanalytic literature on the psychosomatic process, paying particular attention, as it interested me most, to the writing coming out of the Paris Psychoanalytic Society. I was involved in an experiential dream group, led by Montague Ullman, and had begun to try my hand at leading a group. I was also beginning an important, final phase of therapy marked by a capacity to speak with a new sense of freedom. It had taken seven years of analytic work and two hospitalizations for me to begin to speak as I did. There was, it seemed, little more to lose. The psychoanalytic literature gave validity, as words and ideas do, to what I was finally beginning to touch, both in dream work and in the analytic setting—that central disturbance which the experience of illness had uncovered. The writing for my daughters on dreams served to begin the process of integration and health.

The dream images I was examining had made me suspicious of a core emptiness, often reflecting as they did, painful extremes of experience. They helped me see I had not found a comfortable middle ground between an aggrandized sense of self and a depleted self. In one dream there was the image of a single peony, a pink flower of delicate beauty that crumbled before my eyes into a heap of petals. In another, the image of an elegant woman, more fashionably dressed than I have ever been, wearing long skirts and boots, fades to become the figure of a crazy woman, walking on the grounds of a mental hospital in a sacklike dress and socks. There was a dream of a handsomely wallpapered room being painted over in black. There was another of an exquisite mansion facing a river on the other side of which are city streets filled with garbage. I dreamed of small candlelit restaurants, the metaphoric expression of the warmth and intimacy I felt at moments in my life. I also dreamed of barren lunchrooms as I struggled with a sense of meaninglessness and emptiness. Dream color shifted back and forth from white to black in a long dream series of weddings and funerals that suggested I either felt alive and connected or alone and dead.

What this was all about was what I wanted to convey to my daughters in the hope that they would grow to be stronger than I. Putting this into words seemed important, though I did not yet have a full grasp of the urgency I felt. Through dreams I began to write about my primary family and the issues that growing up in this strange home had brought about. There was my father, born in 1883 into a well-to-do Italian banking family, who ignored his family's ambitions for him in the world of finance to enter the Roman Catholic priesthood. At the age of twenty-seven he was brought to trial in a civil court in Rome, a trial involving Pope Pius X himself, to defend himself against accusations of libel. He had publicly stated that the sacred sacrament of the confession had been violated by a cardinal of the Church. The Church, he believed, had wished to uncover the activities of a group of young dissident priests of which father was one. This was my father's final act in a career filled with doubt about Church theology and practice. He left Italy, exiled and excommunicated, arriving in Geneva to study Protestant theology. He came to America just before the Depression, a Protestant minister with many talents but without a church. I grew up frequently reminded of the heroism of my father's actions, the courage he had sustained, above all, in the face of serious personal loss, for he never saw his family again.

Mother was Swiss, a young girl of twenty, when she rode her bike briskly from Geneva to Lausanne one spring day to be interviewed for a position as governess to a well-to-do Connecticut family planning to tour Italy. She arrived, pink cheeked and excited, and got the job, as well as an offer at the end of that vacation to return with the family to the States. She said quick goodbyes to her family and left despite her own mother's foreboding that they would not see each other again. Four years later grandmother's premonition came true. My maternal grandmother died at an early age of a massive heart attack, leaving mother in New York grief stricken, feeling guilty perhaps, certainly depressed and lonely. Two years later she married my father, twenty years her senior, and began her life as a minister's wife and mother of three. She worked hard to supplement her husband's meager income, taking jobs in the clothing district of Manhattan, a much too tough milieu for such a timid woman. She sang in the church choir and polished the floors of the chapellike sanctuary, always remaining shy and remote. Her view of her role as a minister's wife—to be an example for others—set her apart from others, meshing with her own schizoid tendencies to withdraw into herself. She could not unburden herself to a friend, though I believe she was up against some serious problems in the marriage. She grew more and more removed from human connections, relying on intense spiritual sustenance. She kept up correspondence with one sister in Europe whom she did not see for more than thirty years.

It is no wonder that I bound myself too closely to her, that I learned a style of relating where all psychological functioning is dependent on another person, be it mother, husband, or analyst, where there is always fear of abandonment, danger of collapse. Because of my mother's origins, her own emotional damage, and because of life circumstances—the loss of her mother, the distance between her and her primary family, the growing disillusionment in the marriage—she drew me too closely to her. I suppose she found purpose for her life and a sense of identity, not so much in her role as a minister's wife, where she never felt comfortable, but in her role as mother, particularly with her last child and only girl. This child helped to repair a loss, providing a reunion of mother and daughter. She applied all her Swiss discipline to the act of mothering, exerting control over her child's bodily functions and proudly depriving the child of gratifications she felt might cause me to become spoiled. In terms of physical caretaking she was not just a "good-enough mother" (Winnicott 1966) but an "over-good mother" (McDougall 1980a), responding to me almost as an extension of herself, leaving little psychological space where an independent self might develop. There is no question in my mind that my mother's relationship to my father took second place to the mother-child unit, that the mother-baby relationship replaced the husband as the primary source of love and comfort. There was in the relationship to me that strange blend of "deprivation" and "impingement" (Guntrip 1969), of too much or too little emotional space which is written about in so much of the psychoanalytic literature. These words describe both a quality of overdiligence in a mother's caretaking, as she fulfills an intense need to be a good mother, and a strange unresponsiveness to the child's own particular needs and moods. In the home in which I grew up there was much dedication, zealous caretaking, much worry over all three children, and too much control. We were told what to do and how to feel. There was a dulling of all inner life.

At twenty-eight I was only vaguely aware of a strange possessiveness I felt guilty about when my first daughter was born, as I watched my mother hold her grandchild and feared she would not let me be mother to my own child. In later years I felt the same possessiveness about my home, as each of my mother's visits left me fearing her overpowering presence. There was danger of fragmentation as I felt my physical and emotional boundaries invaded. If I was aware of any anger, I did not know what to do with resentment toward a much loved mother with soft green eyes who had never hurt me deliberately, who had lived a hard life of considerable self-sacrifice. If there was discomfort, it was the sense that I could never be as selfless, as patient as she, or as Christian as my parents.

At thirty-five, with my marriage bankrupt, I began therapy, speaking of love for my mother to an analyst who eyed me a bit skeptically but responded to me patiently. There was surprise in the dreams that followed over the next few years. In one a child is vomiting, made sick by the pounds of Swiss chocolate she had consumed. In another an infant is crying because the milk in its bottle is too hot.

The analytic relationship was, of course, fertile ground for the development of a similar connection, the difference being that this one was evolving before our eyes and could be examined with care. Each separation from therapist made clear how attached to him I had become and how difficult it was for me to sustain a sense of connection on my own. Dreams before even a week-long vacation contained numerals denoting in precise countdown fashion how many days were left before separation would occur . . . four . . . three . . . two . . . one. How fragile I was in terms of ego development was not clear, however, until it came time to say good-by, to terminate seven years of analytic work that had given me many insights, made me feel alive, and altered the quality of my life. I had known for a long time that the analytic work would have to end. I tried to look at this positively; the ability to end would be proof of the success of our efforts. I was training to become a psychotherapist myself, so there was some need to test my mental health. I was most of all eager to please a loving therapist who had given me a second chance to grow up, and I hid from him what strain I was feeling in the months before our last scheduled session. I did not pay attention to several dreams that were predicting illness, dreams in which my breasts appeared strangely beautiful but vulnerable. Within days of that last session I was hospitalized for surgery and began the treatment for breast cancer described earlier.

This was a period of considerable crisis. The psychoanalytic work I had prized so highly seemed to have played a strange trick on me, for I had exchanged emotional illness for physical illness. I was disturbed by the anger I felt toward a much loved therapist, rage I would not have survived had I not had an analyst with much courage who assured me we would both get through this.

The psychoanalyst, Joyce McDougall (1974), has written:

> In the attempt to maintain some form of psychic equilibrium under all circumstances, every human being is capable of creating a neurosis, a psychosis, a pathological character pattern, a sexual perversion, a work of art, a dream, or a psychosomatic malady. In spite of our human tendency to maintain a relatively stable psychic economy and thus guarantee a more-or-less enduring personality pattern, we are liable to produce any or all of these diverse creations at different periods in our lives. Although the results of our psychic productions do not have the same psychological, nor indeed the same social value, they all have something in common in that they are the product of man's mind and their form is determined by the way his psyche had been structured. They all have inherent meaning in relation to his wish to live and to get along as best he can with what life has dealt out to him. From this point of view it is evident that the psychosomatic creations appear the most mysterious since they are the least appropriate to the overall desire to live. (p. 438)

My own psychosomatic "creations" were evident to me, though most of my friends argued with the notion of emotionally induced cancer. I knew I had had a physical crisis in my life instead of a mental break brought on by a level of stress I had not been able to identify in time, a struggle clearly connected to separation and loss.

During this period the image of a Christmas tree figured in at least a dozen dreams, a dream image borrowed from an actual photo of my daughters, taken when they were five and eight, looking at a Christmas tree that had been moved from the living room to the backyard. The ornaments had been put away in boxes and replaced with orange hulls filled with peanut butter and bird seed, a postholiday feast for the birds. I had used this photo in a visualization exercise to help me fall asleep at night when my level of anxiety was heightened, the image of all three of us, hand-in-hand, forming a circle around that small tree, a circle I was now determined to keep unbroken. The tree of my dreams, the Christian symbol of birth and celebration, expressed the dilemma I was in. Therapy had filled me with a dazzling sense of rebirth, perhaps, I know now, still all too new. Like the holiday tree filled with splendid ornaments, I too looked good, but I felt cut off from what all trees and people need to survive—a source of nurturance. Like the tree without roots, I could not stand on my own and I might die. This long dream series produced interesting variations. The Christmas tree of one dream is threatened by a smoldering fire, just as the anger in me threatened to destroy me. In another, a small fir that I embrace is found to have a great hole in its center, just as I was becoming aware of a core emptiness within me.

Lawrence LeShan (1977), who has been a therapist to terminally ill patients, has written that the basic emotional pattern of the cancer patient appears to have three major parts. The first "involves a childhood or adolescence marked by feelings of isolation" such as I had known. "There is a sense that intense and meaningful relationships are dangerous and bring pain and rejection. The second part of the pattern is centered upon the period during which a meaningful relationship is discovered, allowing the individual to enjoy a sense of acceptance by others (at least in one particular role) and to find meaning to his life." The analytic relationship had been this to me. "The third aspect of the pattern comes to the fore when loss of that central relationship occurs. Now there is a sense of utter despair, connected to but going beyond the childhood sense of isolation. In this third phase, the conviction that life holds no more hope becomes paramount. And some time after the onset of the third phase the first symptoms of cancer are noted" (p.70).

For me the loss of a central relationship was postponed for a few more years. The decision to end therapy was undone, more than a secondary gain to illness. As my analytic work continued, I began to speak with much less restraint, relying on dreams above all, for I had learned to value their honesty. I was determined to get to the bottom of this, for I was fighting to stay well. In the dream group I presented dreams as often as I could, unafraid to go public with any issue the dream might reveal. The group gave me new thoughts to bring back to the individual therapy setting. The writing for my daughters kept me thinking about the past and sparked new dreams that shed light on my beginnings as well as my present situation.

But it was the research I was doing on the psychosomatic process that excited me most, helping me see that in an intuitive way, through the dream processes with which I was involved—my own psychoanalysis, the group dream work, my own writing about dreams—I had stumbled upon a path of healing. It provided a link, offering me understanding of what I was feeling inside. I tempered my excitement, a bit apprehensive of challenging the gods with hubris. Yet over the months and years that passed I was surprised by my capacity to sustain a new sense of peace. I sensed that an inner change had occurred which would help me stay well.

On the Psychosomatic Process

Before I can explain this further, it seems necessary to try to summarize the writings on the psychosomatic process that were important to me, as complex as they are. Joyce McDougall, a New Zealander who trained as a psychoanalyst in Paris where she practices, writes that our psychic processes are on the side of life, that we create whatever psychic structures we do in order to manage as best we can whatever life has to offer. "The structure of the psyche is a creative process destined to give each individual his unique identity. It provides a bulwark against psychic loss in traumatic circumstances, and in the long run in man's psychic creativity may well lie an essential element of protection against his biological destruction" (1974, p. 438).

It is for this reason that the psychosomatic process is so curious. It may well serve to deflect an impending sense of psychic loss, but it certainly does not protect us from biological destruction. It can leave us, as it did me, a patient in a hospital, facing serious illness. It seems to pop into use when we lack some capacity to manage the pain life brings using mental processes. There may also be a limit to the intensity of pain any individual can manage, "a threshold beyond which his psychic defense-work can no longer cope, at which moment the body bears the brunt" (p. 445).

There are, however, individuals who seem less well equipped in general to encounter emotional pain, who are incapable of tolerating the suffering that comes with that pain and of working it through. This working through of pain is an important concept that needs elaboration. Federn (1952) makes a subtle distinction between "feeling pain" and "suffering pain." Suffering is the active inner experience of pain, pain that we allow ourselves to take in, to feel as present, and to endure. It involves a full realization of whatever event caused the pain, such that the next time thought or memory of the event occurs, that pain will no longer be felt to quite the same degree. This is what is involved in normal grief and mourning—the repeated realization of the loss incurred and the gradual lessening of pain connected to it. "The acceptance of pain," Federn writes, "is the tribute we pay to normality" (p. 268).

In the case of "feeling pain," the individual doesn't work it through but takes flight from it, short-circuiting psychic activity, much as someone who uses alcohol or drugs to flee from his problems. Some developmental failure leaves this individual unable to tolerate or endure pain. It is viewed as an existential threat that has to be warded off at once, for what is feared is psychic disintegration. Afraid that he will fall apart, this individual protects himself with what McDougall (1980a) calls "psychic armour plating," by a refusal to yield to anguish or depression. He does not allow painful feelings to come into awareness and is often quite unaware of the level of stress he is experiencing. To his friends he appears remarkably hardy. He looks as if he copes with difficult situations amazingly well. In an important sense, however, this type of individual is left passively exposed, always in danger, for no inner change has occurred. Thought of the painful event, when it is permitted, produces feelings similar in impact to their original intensity, or with anger connected to them.

What we are talking about is a fragile self, a psyche that has not emerged into maturity, one that is not strong enough to process the knocks that life brings, particularly ones connected to loss. We are also describing a type of individual who finds his sense of identity not within himself, but externally—in activities and relationships sought out because they enhance his sense of self. Because he needs another person to feel like somebody, he clings symbiotically, seeking merger with another, losing a sense of separateness. He remains sensitive to any threat of loss that would leave him feeling once again like nobody. McDougall (1974) writes, "What should be an internal conviction—of narcissistic integrity and individual identity—has constantly to be confirmed externally" (p. 452).

Related to this are two phenomena noticed in the psychosomatic individual. One is a characteristic mode of thinking, first termed "operational thinking" by Marty, M'Uzan, and David (1963). It consists of a preoccupation with the minute details of daily life, an attachment to facts and things in external reality with thoughts that are pragmatic in aspect rather than a reflection of one's inner life. The second phenomenon, termed "alexithymia" by Sifneos (1972), involves an inability on the part of the psychosomatic patient to speak about his feelings. When asked to try, as in the analytic setting, he seems to have little or no vocabulary available, frequently responding with such statements as "I can't find the words." When pressed to try, he often responds with a description of the external events in his life—what's going on—rather than how events or individuals in his life touch him inside. He has difficulty getting in touch with his fantasy life, often denying he has any fantasies. He may also say he never dreams.

It was this material that interested me, especially as I was so much involved in dream work and in writing about dreams, finding words for feelings and fantasies, drawing from material coming from within me for the first time in my life. The importance of dreaming and fantasies in maintaining emotional equilibrium has been noted by many writers. I was experiencing a kind of equilibrium previously unknown to me.

What makes someone feel so fragile? When does an individual learn a style of relating to others adhesively, remaining so vulnerable to loss? How and when are the types of mental processes described above, that is, being in touch with one's inner life, enduring pain, learned? It is difficult, of course, to speculate about the origins of any type of emotional disturbance, especially when it seems rooted, as this does, in the early relationship of infant to mother. It is in that first dependency, at the beginning of life that *psyche* evolves out of *soma.* It is then, as infants, that we experience life in such extremes, with either a sense of well-being when our needs are responded to, or with the threat of annihilation when they are not. To understand this we have only to picture the panic-filled infant, suddenly hungry, who cries as though he had truly been abandoned.

What the growing baby seems to need to learn from his mother is a dependency that does not compromise autonomy but nourishes it and sustains it. The empathic mother who responds sensitively to the infant's nonverbal expression of need, giving validation to what the baby is experiencing, is allowing both dependency and separateness, helping a young self grow with increasing autonomy and self-esteem.

A mother's ability to respond empathically to her child originates, however, in the experiences of her own infancy that are reanimated when she herself becomes a mother. A mother who has herself been deprived, whose own hunger and need for love are reactivated in mothering her child, may respond with overprotection and possession of the infant, exaggerating the normal functions of mothering, doing things to a baby out of her own need. What the child seems to need is a mother who provides protection against the stimuli in the world that would overwhelm the unprotected infant but who is not overindulgent in the function out of her own need to find a "good-mother self" (Benedek 1959), that is, a sense of identity in the function. It is the careful modulation of care, not being too close or too far away, being there to respond to the baby's needs yet not impinging on the baby, which appears to aid the growing individual in the development, as well, of certain mental capacities. The baby can permit herself to feel whatever is there to be experienced because she is neither overwhelmed nor ignored but is supported. She is helped to know what she feels because her own feelings have been responded to. Perhaps she has learned through the mother the verbal representations of feelings, as the mother expresses her own emotions or mirrors those of the child. The baby begins to attach some meaning to what she experiences.

Fain (1971) described a study of infants so overprotected by their mothers that they were unable to fall asleep unless they were rocked continuously in their mother's arms. The mother's overprotection had left the infant unable to conjure up some image of mother that would connect him to her, soothe him, and allow him to sleep—the beginning of a self-sustaining self. Commenting on this study, McDougall (1974) writes, "Instead of the development of a primitive form of psychic activity akin to dreaming which permits most babies to sleep peacefully after feeding, these babies require the mother herself to be the guardian of sleep" (p. 446). Anxiety that touches this infant is experienced as a global threat, involving a sense of annihilation and disintegration. "The baby who cannot create within himself his mother's image to deal with his pain is a lonely island. One way out is to turn oneself into a rock. Thus many psychosomatic patients continue on their unwavering tight-rope, ignoring the body's signs and their mind's distress signals" (p. 458).

Is it this capacity for symbolization, for making connections, for creating links, that is damaged in the psychosomatic adult, so out of touch with his inner experience, unable to distinguish feelings, to find the verbal representations for emotions, who is fearful of relationships that leave him in a vulnerable position, yet who knows no way of relating other than symbiotically? Ammon (1979) writes of a "hole in the ego" which the psychosomatic symptom serves to fill. He portrays psychosomatic illness as the expression of a structural ego illness that leaves the individual unable to move beyond a symbiotic dependency to a demarcation of his own identity. His efforts to relate to others break down because he uses relationships to repair a psychic gap. When loss does occur, the psychosomatic process takes over. As McDougall has noted, pain bypasses the psyche, unequipped to deal with it, and affects the body (1974).

Perhaps in some pitiful way even the psychosomatic process is on the side of life. For me, a lifelong fear of emotional fragmentation was replaced by a fear of death. As I was on the edge of psychic annihilation, illness occurred to push out all concerns but the wish to live. At Memorial Sloane-Kettering Hospital I pleaded to be allowed the privilege of using an outside terrace, basking in a sun that felt warmer and more wonderful than

I have ever known, looking thoughtfully at the blueness of the city sky and the changing shapes of the clouds I felt connected to.

The Healing Aspects of Dream Work

In the early weeks after discharge from the hospital I dreamed of a serious fire rising up through a wooden fire tower perched high on a lookout. I was standing at the top of the tower very much in danger of being enveloped by smoke. The dream image of a fire tower, itself in danger, trouble at that lookout, was a poignant metaphor for the analytic situation which had expanded my view, very much protected me over the years, but where I was now in serious danger. The fire was the anger I was feeling; the smoke was the confusion I could not see beyond in the rage I felt toward someone who had cared so consistently for me.

McDougall (1974) speaks of the psychosomatic patient as one who "tends to react with either psychosomatic maladies or increased sensitivity to infection and a tendency to bodily accidents, when faced with traumatic events and conflictual situations arising from the past or the present *including the psychoanalytic situation*" (p. 450, italics mine, C.L.). I had responded to the prospect of ending treatment that had given meaning to my life with a life-threatening illness no one could have predicted. The illness brought perspective to the crisis of completing my analysis. If I was torn about the pending separation from my therapist, I found myself far more torn about the threat to my children. I was determined to stay well, just as in the dream I was determined to climb down the tower and find my way out of the smoke.

In the analytic situation the way "out of the smoke," paradoxically, was in allowing a deeper transference to occur, permitting myself to feel and express for the first time the full depth of my dependency on another person and to begin to understand the anger that is bound to occur whenever anyone's psychic existence is so dependent on another. I was beginning to see reflected in that transference the symbiotic quality of my need for mother, a relationship where independence had not been encouraged.

In a 7:30 A.M. session, an extra session I had worked up to for days, I talked nonstop for an hour, amazed at how easily and clearly words came, packing in one illustration after another to make certain I conveyed fully the urgent quality of my caring, the great need I felt, the anger it contained, and the fright of expected loss.

Feeling embarrassed or humiliated by such admission no longer got in the way. I could feel the power of my words to heal. The more accurately and honestly I spoke, the more relief I felt. What seemed to matter was a new integrity I felt in presenting myself *exactly as I was.*

Looking back on this point, I know now that my involvement in dream work—in private therapy, in group dream work that complemented that therapy, and in writing about dreams—had helped me work up to that day, gradually creating structural changes, giving me new ego strengths to work through the transference, and in so doing, to stay well. In the remainder of this chapter I describe what I mean—a growth that cannot, of course, be proven but which is deeply felt.

I have been a participant in an experiential dream group since 1976, a regular member of a Monday night group. Men and women have joined the group, learned dream skills, and left while I stayed on year after year. I wondered sometimes why I continued. I only knew the work was important to me.

The process outlined in chapter I of this volume did not come easily to me. In Stage IIA (p. 9), when members of the group begin working on the presented dream, making it their own, trying to identify the feelings it evoked, I was often silent, unable to do this, just as I had sat in analytic sessions, unable to begin, feeling the panic of silence mounting with the minutes that passed. I would long for a question about what had been going on in the days since my last session, so I could begin to narrate events or describe a set of circumstances. It was talking about what I was feeling at the moment that I couldn't do. In the dream group, if I had difficulty responding to a dream and even more difficulty finding words for my responses, I could be silent and listen to the responses of others and begin to acquire a richer vocabulary for emotions. The process, as it is structured, gives us an hour and a half to work on a handful of images in a single, brief dream. The slowness of this exquisite process was always on my side, permitting me to move deeper and deeper into a level of consciousness somewhere between waking consciousness and the dreaming state, eventually allowing some feeling, however vague, to float to the surface and be felt.

If the initial stage of the process left me feeling inadequate, Stage IIB (p. 9) left me excited and deeply moved. At this point each member of the group is asked to draw upon his own imagination and unconscious to consider what possible metaphoric meaning the dream images conveyed. In dream work it was always the creative metaphor in dream imagery that stirred me. I was touched by the force and beauty of the dream metaphor just as, many years ago, as a literature major, I had been moved by the felt connection of thought and feeling in a literary metaphor. This should have been a clue to me. I know now that I have always been affected by such moments of connection, experiencing in them an aspect of healing.

Whether it involved work on a dream of my own, or work on another person's dream, the gentle pace of group dream work and the non-intrusive approach of the process, a combination that succeeds in lowering defenses, had offered me long-term practice at feeling my emotional response to a dream and at staying with that response until I could give it some verbal form. From the first words group members used, as they made the dream their own and responded to the feelings evoked by the dream, to the play with the visual images of the dream, to the final integration offered by the leader—throughout this long process I was gaining experience at tapping into the resources of my psyche to identify emotions and stay with them. I was learning not to short-circuit psychic activity but to develop whatever capacities for mental creativity I could, getting practice in managing whatever emotions were evoked, however painful they might be.

Joyce McDougall (1974) has written that the "psychoanalytic processes are the antithesis of psychosomatic processes" in that they "re-establish separated links and also forge new ones" (p. 439). I encountered this concept with excitement, for I was beginning to understand the need and importance of such links and the power of such connection to heal, and to appreciate the many connecting forces available in dreams and in dream work.

If I had been overly cerebral, a bit "operational," functioning impressively in all aspects of my day-to-day life but out of touch with my inner world, I was now connecting to the naturally creative part of myself, to the strange beauty of the visual images we all produce at night. If I had been somewhat "alexithymic," I was learning to find meaning for these images at an emotional and informational level and to give that meaning some verbal form. Writers on alexithymia have questioned whether an alexithymic patient can acquire a vocabulary for feelings. I certainly had. As I began writing about my dreams for my girls, I was astonished at how much I could draw from within myself, a self I had long experienced as shadowy and empty, in need of reliance on what others had written, certainly lacking in fantasy and creativity.

I felt the power of the dream to make many connections—to bring together past and present, thought and feeling, visual and verbal, to compare the myths we hold about ourselves and reality, to perceive our commonality to others and the ways in which unique sets of life circumstances have made us different. Finally, in the exquisite moment when the dream comes together at all levels of our being, when we experience the "feeling of fit that goes beyond linguistic categories and defies analytic approaches" (Ullman, p. 123), I felt a beginning connection of mind and body, of psyche and soma.

Out of moments such as this, repeated again and again, as I had made a commitment to dream work, something new and important was evolving that I would begin to use in the psychoanalytic setting as in every aspect of my life. In waiting for the "fit" to occur, I learned to rely on something within myself as the measure of the accuracy of that fit. The group was there to help, each member tapping into his own unconscious, his own imagination and life experiences, making an offering that might give the dream richness. The leader was there with his resources of intuition and intellect to help pull together the threads of the dream, but only the dreamer herself could know when the "fit" was accomplished. The knowing was felt inside, as a gentle release, like the relief of being able to take a deeper breath, a quietly felt truth, spiritual and aesthetic in impact, that is felt in the mind and in all of one's tissues.

For me this was no small achievement. There was a beginning sense of internal connection such as I had never known, a budding appreciation of my own authority after a lifetime of looking to others for authority. The pattern had begun in childhood with the formidable figure of my father in his pulpit and with my mother who loved me as herself, which was the problem. I strove to please her by being like her at a cost to my own individuality. The pattern had extended into the present and was readily apparent in the transference to analyst, another major figure in my life whom I tried to please. The change, when it came, was a subtle shift, strangely quiet and undramatic. It was the sense of peacefulness connected to it that made me take notice. It had, however, the power to alter the quality of all my relationships, leaving me less needy of approval, less defensive, less apt to try to prove my point, less threatened by the authoritarian stances of others, more understanding of the struggle with which any individual is involved when he takes such a stance. Most importantly, in the analytic setting, it offered a new independence with which to confront the core of my dependency. I could begin to approach the very needy quality of the connection to my analyst because I was also feeling the beginnings of separateness.

"The freedom to let oneself be known," Ullman (1984) has written, "is also the freedom to be oneself." I was feeling a new freedom to let myself be known and to be my own self—in the dream group where I had been given "privileged glimpses deep into the souls of other people" and had seen there "the same mix of vulnerability and strength" that I came to see in myself, where I had "the rare experience of human beings who come together as healers for each other" (Ullman, p. 124). I felt that freedom in the writings for my daughters. I felt it as well in the private analytic setting where I was looking at my most ancient and most current struggles with new honesty and clarity. In the struggle around dependency I began to acknowledge the anger toward a dearly loved therapist, anger long familiar to me from the past. It was the anger that occurs when we are fragile and needy, when we remain bound to others emotionally. As that connection was made, the anger could be relinguished—not quickly or entirely but eventually and sufficiently, leaving me stronger in the years that followed, more peaceful than I have ever been, and well.

References

Ammon, G. *Psychoanalysis and Psychosomatics.* New York: Springer, 1979.

Benedek, T. "Parenthood as a Developmental Phase: A Contribution to the Libido Theory." *Journal of the American Psychoanalytic Association,* 7 (1959): 389–417.

Fain, M. "Prelude à la vie fantasmatique." *Rev. Franc. psychanal.* 35, (1971): 291–364.

Fain, M., and David, C. "Aspects fonctionels de la vie onirique." *Rev franc. psychanal.* 27 (1963): 241–343.

Federn, P. *Ego Psychology and the Psychoses.* New York: Basic Books, 1952.

Guntrip, H. *Schizoid Phenomena, Object Relations and the Self.* New York: International Universities Press,1969.

LeShan, L. *You Can Fight for Your Life: Emotional Factors in the Causation of Cancer.* New York: Harcourt Brace Jovanovich, 1977.

Marty, P., M'Uzan, M.de, and David, C. *L'investigation psychosomatique.* Paris: Presses Universite de France, 1963.

McDougall, J. "The Psychosoma and the Psychoanalytic Process." *International Review of Psychoanalysis,* 1 (1974): 437–59.

———. "A Child Is Being Eaten." *Contemporary Psychoanalysis,* 16 (1980a): 417–59.

———. *Plea for a Measure of Abnormality.* New York: International Universities Press, 1980b.

Nemiah, J., and Sifneos, P. "Affect and Fantasy in Patients with Psychosomatic Disorders." *Modern Trends in Psychosomatic Medicine* vol 2. O. Hill, ed. London: Butterworths, 1970.

Nemiah, J., Freyberger, H., and Sifneos, P. "Alexithymia: A View of the Psychosomatic Process." *Modern Trends in Psychosomatic Medicine* vol. 3. O. Hill, ed. London: Butterworths, 1976.

Sifneos, P. *Short-term Psychotherapy and Emotional Crises.* Cambridge: Harvard University Press, 1972.

Ullman, M. "Group Dream Work and Healing." *Contemporary Psychoanalysis,* 20 (1984): 120–30.

Winnicott, D. "Psychosomatic Illness in Its Positive and Negative Aspects." *International Journal of Psychoanalysis,* 47 (1966): 510–16.

CHAPTER TWELVE

Clinical Work with Dreams

MONTAGUE ULLMAN AND CLAIRE LIMMER

I was a practicing psychoanalyst well over two decades before I began to devote my time exclusively to experiential dream group work. For Claire Limmer this sequence of events was reversed. Claire has been closely associated to me in the development of this approach to dream work ever since she joined the first group I started in the United States in 1976. She continued her participation in a weekly group and in a number of leadership training sessions over the years. During this time she also undertook her training in psychoanalysis which was completed in 1988. During these years she has been in psychoanalytic practice.

As we planned this current revised edition, it seemed logical to combine forces in a joint chapter with me focusing on those aspects of group dream work that were applicable in one-to-one therapy and Claire providing examples from her practice of how her experience in group dream work enriched the work she did on dreams with individual clients.

Part 1. Teaching the Basics (M.U.)

In September of 1974 another psychoanalyst and I were invited to Gothenberg, Sweden, to teach a group of young therapists in training the art and practice of dynamic psychotherapy. The students were mostly psychologists completing their graduate work at the Psychological Institute of the University of Gothenberg. Because of my special interest I was the one to give them the course on dreams.

It seemed to me, based on earlier experience,[1] that the teaching of dreams to psychoanalytic candidates failed to prepare them for the kind of interaction with a patient that could systematically expose the associative matrix of the dream. Theoretical and practical knowledge about dreams came about in a piecemeal fashion that generally included one or more clinical seminars on dreams, a reading course on dreams, and exposure to dream work in personal analysis and supervision. In the clinical seminar the candidate presented a session in which a dream was worked on along with a brief account of the past history and progress in therapy. The focus was generally on the way the dream can shed light on the ongoing dynamics of the treatment situation. The problem with this approach is that we are working with a "dead" dream. Discussion is limited to the information the candidate obtained from the dreamer. There is no opportunity to learn how to engage the dreamer in a way that might have produced more material.[2]

The reading course in dreams that usually accompanies the clinical seminar is essential but is still heavily oriented towards Freud's theoretical constructs and the patient's task of free associating and not on the active exploratory role of the therapist. For the beginning therapist, theory is fascinating and readily mastered. When he discovers that in practice the spontaneous free association of the patient is not enough to do justice to a dream, then what does he do?

Much can be learned about dreams through one's personal analysis and in supervision. The final results, however, can be variable depending, as they do, on the skill and interest in dreams of the analyst conducting the therapy and the supervision.

It was the shortcomings and uncertainties built into programs of this kind that led me to consider a radical departure from the traditional approach when I arrived in Sweden. To have a "live" dreamer in the room and to be able to do dream work experientially transformed the situation from a clinically oriented one to one designed simply to teach the basics of dream work. The latter included the recognition of the precipitating factors in the current life of the dreamer, the way relevant aspects of remote memory come into play, and the view the dream provides of certain realities that have not yet found a place in the waking life of the dreamer. My task was to conceptualize and teach the skills I had learned in practice (see chapter 1). The task of the students was to engage in learning about dreams experientially by sharing a dream. Once the basics were learned the student could then gravitate toward any particular theoretical orientation they found helpful in integrating dream work into the practice of psychotherapy (see Ullman 1996 for a more extended discussion of the process and its connection to therapy).

There were none of the trappings of a clinical situation. The students were not there as patients. There was no obligatory contract. They were free to share a dream or not. If they chose to share a dream they were free to choose any one they wished to share. The extent of learning would depend on their own curiosity about what the dream had to say and the degree of trust they felt. I was not there as their therapist but as a participant while teaching the process at the same time. They were there to learn something about the technique of dream work that would later prove helpful in their practice.

There are seven basic premises underlying this approach.

First Premise

Dreams are intrapsychic communications that reveal in metaphorical form certain truths about the life of the dreamer, truths that can be made available to the dreamer awake. Dreaming consciousness serves the nighttime needs of the dreamer. The experience of dreaming itself is generally not intended to be a public communication. The dreamer awake can, of course, go public with it. Dream imagery is potentially metaphorical. To realize that potential, the dreamer is faced with the task of sparking across the metaphorical gap between dream image and waking reality. Our dreams have an incredible way of zeroing in on who we really are instead of who we would like to think we are or who we would like others to think we are.

Second Premise

If we are fortunate enough to recall a dream, we are then ready, at some level, to be confronted by the information in the dream. This is true regardless of whether or not we choose to do so. Freedom and truth are inextricably linked. The more accurate our perception of an issue, the more freedom we have in coping with it. To experience freedom in that sense requires a level of honesty not always easily available to us while awake. Situations arise where, consciously or unconsciously, we act out of expediency. The dream offers us the opportunity to confront an issue with greater clarity and a deeper honesty. We get a bit closer to ourselves and a bit freer.

Third Premise

If the confrontation is allowed to occur in a proper manner the effect is one of healing. The dreamer comes into contact with a part of the self that has not been explicitly acknowledged before. There has been movement toward wholeness. Healing is simply another name for being more in touch with our own historical past and its influence in our relationships with others. It is as if the dream furnishes us with the connective tissue needed to repair areas of disconnection with our past and with others.

Fourth Premise

Although the dream is a very private communication it requires a social context for its fullest realization. The dream is the waking remembrance of the raw content of our nighttime dreaming consciousness. Once removed from its natural environment, it has to undergo a socializing process if the information embedded in the imagery is to play an explicit and active role in our waking life. That process begins with taking the dream seriously and engaging in the work necessary to allow the metaphorical potential of the imagery to unfold.

Fifth Premise

Dream images arise out of the unique life experiences of the dreamer. The fit between image and meaning is something that the dreamer alone can validate. The dreamer is the only one who can judge the effectiveness of the help offered. He or she alone has that resonant gut feeling when a truth strikes home. There is a distinct difference between intellectual acceptance and the spontaneous and richly generative response to a true fit.

Sixth Premise

Everyone's life experience is unique. Any symbolic image can be used in a highly idiosyncratic way. No a priori categorical meanings are assumed. One has to have a certain humility in dream work and realize that there is more to learn from the dreamer than we have to offer to the dreamer. The reason is simple. Nothing in our prior learning and experience is a substitute for the work that has to be done to discover how these particular images emerged out of the idiosyncratic life experience of the dreamer and why they came together to shape the dream on that particular night. The task is to help the dreamer uncover the answer.

Clinical dream work. Before discussing the carry-over from the experiential dream group to one-to-one therapy, there are important differences between the two situations to be noted.

First, there are differences in motivation. People seek therapy for relief from emotional distress. People seek dream groups out of the interest they have in their own dream life and their desire to learn more about the unique features of dreams. There are occasions when someone drifts into a dream group when they are really in need of therapy, a fact which should be recognized and acted upon early. There is no intrinsic incompatibility between being in therapy and in a dream group at the same time. In fact, they can very well complement each other.

Second, there are differences in the training and skills of the helping agency in the two instances. The psychotherapist undergoes rigorous training in preparation for the management of the various manifestations of emotional disorder. Therapy involves, among other things, the recognition of and techniques for dissolving the defensive structure of the patient—for example, the transferences and resistances that arise. By virtue of this special training, the therapist is in a unique relationship to the patient and operates with a body of knowledge and techniques the other is not privy to. The dream work is geared to and incidental to this therapeutic task. It is only one of many therapeutic tools and one not always optimally available to use in the crowded therapeutic hour. Dream work is time consuming. The therapist is at the mercy of how much time is available to make the best use of the dream. Other items on the patient's agenda often crowd it out. A dream presented ten minutes before the end of the session leaves no time for any indepth exploration of it.[3] There is also the problem of the many ways in which the patient may use dreams in the service of resistance—for example, offering it compliantly or as a gift without any genuine concern about its message.

The therapist as an authority, the one-sidedness of the situation with regard to dream sharing and the hierarchical arrangements this engenders, is precisely what is lacking in the experiential dream group. In the latter an egalitarian arrangement prevails where everyone, including whoever may be responsible for teaching the process, participates in every phase of the process, including the sharing of dreams. There is no hidden agenda, and the rationale for everything that goes on is known to everyone. Once the process is mastered it becomes the responsibility of the entire group to carry it out.

There are, of course, other specific features of the therapeutic situation with regard to dreams that distinguish it from the experiential dream group. The therapist listening to a dream has at hand an historical perspective on the life of the dreamer, as well as a knowledge of personality patterns as they have unfolded in the course of therapy. This offers the therapist the freedom to test out ideas based on prior knowledge and to offer broadly based interpretations. In the group process it is the work with the current dream alone that leads us into the past.

There is a final and most important point and that is that the patient in presenting a dream has the freedom from the very beginning to offer his or her associations and ideas about the dream. In the group process this amplification of the dream is delayed until after the group has offered their projections in the second stage. In therapy, while the therapist is free to offer a projection of his own if he feels it might be helpful, it is not done as a separate stage as in the group process.

There are, however, aspects of the group process that can be carried over in a helpful way in individual therapy. Take, for example, the dating of the dream. In the dream group we make a specific point of asking the dreamer when the dream occurred before hearing the dream. Preliminary ideas can then begin to germinate as one listens to the dream. A dream dreamt after a work day may be different from one dreamt on a weekend or holiday. In therapy, a dream dreamt after the previous session or just before the present one is apt to have some reference to therapy. A dreamer may, of course, spontaneously date the dream prior to telling it. If this does not happen and if only an approximate date is given, the dreamer can sometimes be helped to zero in on the actual date. It may take a little time and encouragement to more accurately locate the dream in the context of his or her life.

The various steps in the dialogue that take place in the dream group can all find a useful place in individual therapy. I place great emphasis in what I refer to as the search for the emotional context in the life of the dreamer connected to the occurrence of a particular dream on a particular night. The dreamer may spontaneously describe events going on in his or her life around the time of the dream. It is my experience, however, that in almost every case a good deal more can be elicited by systematic questioning designed to elicit further feeling residues, particularly ones that seemed too fleeting or incidental to be spontaneously recalled.

In the group, after the dialogue the dream is read back aloud to the dreamer in the hope of eliciting further associations. In therapy this can be done very much the way it is in the group or the therapist can simply call attention to specific images that have not yet been clarified. The techniques for helping a dreamer go further with elusive imagery are the same as described in the group approach. The effort is designed to reconnect the felt aspect of the image to feeling residues past or present in the life of the dreamer. Calling attention to the feeling aspect of the image or simply helping the dreamer move from the literal image to its more abstract metaphorical potential is often enough to help the dreamer see the image in a new and more helpful way.

Walter Bonime (1962), an analyst who has written extensively about dreams, refers to his role in dream work as offering "interpretive hypotheses." This is a most important statement about the role of the helper, either in clinical work or in the group. It indicates the helper's awareness that all interpretive efforts are hypotheses unless they resonate at a feeling level with the dreamer. The term I use to convey this in the group approach is *orchestrating projection.* This occurs in the final stage of the process where any member of the group may offer projected thoughts about the dream images and waking reality that they think might be helpful to the dreamer. Again, it is only the dreamer who can truly judge the fit and reject what does not fit.

Any therapist who has been exposed to experiential dream group work will become more aware of the many pitfalls that lie in wait when a patient seeks help with a dream. Two in particular are worth knowing about. The first is an overreliance on theory in lieu of an adequate search for the data. This results in a priori assumptions of what certain dream images mean as symbols derived from a particular theoretical orientation.

Aside from the features of the group situation that can be carried over to therapy there are beneficial results for the dreamer and for the therapist. For the dreamer the group process has the effect of demystifying the dream. The dreamer learns how to develop the relevant associative context which, in turn, results in an increased ability to do more on his or her own in gaining leverage on the dream. Much of the same thing will happen in therapy as the dreamer learns how to go about recovering the information that he or she put into the dream while asleep. The task of the therapist then becomes easier as learning takes place. A specific benefit to the therapist is the increased sensitivity he acquires in group dream work to his own projections in working with dreams in his practice.

In the presentation of dream work in the next section I want to call attention to the care the therapist takes in dating the dream, pursuing the search for the recent context by simply encouraging the dreamer to gather further details about recent events and playing back images that have not yet been clarified. In the first instance she notes the extent to which Helen managed to work out the dream. The orchestration served as a helpful summation that validated the very fruitful work Helen had done. It also conveyed to the dreamer, as orchestrations often do, that the dreamer had really been heard.

In the second instance, the therapist notes the wisdom of holding her own ideas in abeyance until the data have fully (as fully as possible) emerged. Her sharing this with the dreamer was a good example of what true collaboration is and how salutary it can be for the dreamer (as well as for the therapist). The therapist's summary statement at the end, carefully constructed on and limited to what the dreamer herself had disclosed, is a good example of an interpretive hypothesis or, had it occurred in a dream group, an orchestrating projection. The session with the dream also did what dream work should do, namely, lead to behavioral change. The dreamer had the insight and support she needed to face up to a difficult step.

When time does not allow a more extended exploration of the dream, Walter Bonime (1962) resorts to what he refers to as "Headline" interpretation. This is an attempt to identify the one most helpful metaphorical statement pertinent to the work going on.

In the early fifties I began exploring an idea that later became part of the dream group process I now use. I would begin the seminar by suggesting that we initially limit our knowledge to the age and sex of the patient, duration of therapy and the dream itself. The class and I would then offer our own projections of what the dream might be saying about both the dreamer and the dreamer's relationship to the therapist. Despite some initial resistance to saying anything about a dream before the associations were at hand, it proved to be a surprisingly helpful exercise.

Part 2. The Clinical Use of Dreams (C.L.)

The effectiveness of my work as a therapist has almost without exception depended on developing with the client a sense that we are embarking on a *collaborative* effort to look at the present-day concerns that brought him into therapy against the background of his personal history. Therapist and client together will attempt to come to an understanding of the way the client's life has been shaped by his history. This way of working has grown out of a realistic assessment of my therapeutic skills as well as an ever-renewed appreciation of the complexity of human existence, of how much there is to learn, and an openness to learn *with* the client about his life.

Nowhere does the spirit of collaboration shine more brightly than in the work therapist and client undertake with a dream. For this reason, I view the initial phase of treatment as a period of preparing the groundwork that is needed with a new client, a process that includes some teaching about *how* we will work together in order to create the kind of rich medium I think we should be digging in. This includes teaching the client how we will be approaching dreams. This holds true when working with teenagers, adults of any age, and with couples as well.

Clients come into treatment with a variety of preconceptions about dreams. Some think of dreams as new-age, flaky stuff. Others think of dream symbols as something you look up in a book. Others have had previous periods of therapy with good or not-so-good dream work or very differing orientations. There may need to be a process of reeducation. Sometimes I find myself sharing my view of the dream as a *shortcut* to understanding the work we need to do. This is reassuring to the client who fears the mention of dreams means we are embarking on a very long process.

It is important to clarify for the dreamer right from the start that the therapist does not have immediate insight into what the dream is about; that is, he or she does not know what the dream is about at the moment it is presented. Sometimes this is exactly what the client both hopes for—some magical insight—and fears—that the therapist knows something about him that he doesn't and is keeping it from him. That dream images have meanings idiosyncratic to the dreamer is a new concept to most clients. If we work together, hopefully we will come to understand the dream's meaning, or better yet, with the help of the therapist the dreamer will arrive at the meaning of the dream himself. The therapist's experience in working with dreams is what she brings to the effort.

Just as an experiential dream group coming together needs to be taught the process of drawing out the contextual data that will illumine the dream, the individual client learns (through the questions the therapist asks as well as through moments of actual instruction) that the meaning of the dream will come to him as he makes connections between the concerns and emotions he fell asleep with as well as any other feeling residues of recent experiences *and* the dream images, in short when he can answer the question, Why did I have *this* dream *that* night.

Gradually and naturally, if he's lucky enough to wake with the memory of a dream, he will have trained himself to think about what was on his mind as he fell asleep. He notes the day of the dream (because he knows this is the first question I will put to him). Hopefully, if the client's early experiences working on dreams are *felt* ones, he learns to value his dreams,to appreciate their beneficial effect, and to give them priority in a session.

This point of view did not evolve out of my own training as a psychoanalyst, and perhaps something needs to be said about this. I had been a member of a dream group and leadership training groups preceding and concurrent with my training as a psychoanalyst in the seventies and eighties. I had an advantage over my classmates whose insecurities about becoming therapists showed themselves mostly in working with a dream. To my mind they had every reason to be insecure. The curriculum, although otherwise an excellent one, provided only two courses on dreams. These were devoted to reviewing the massive literature on dreams, with no readings at all, however, on the phenominological approach to dreams; that is, working with the manifest content. There were one or two occasions in class for each of us to present a dream of a patient. Some background about the patient was offered, the dream was presented, questions were asked about the session in which the dream was presented, and the class was left to speculate about the dream's meaning. The focus was always on uncovering the latent content; that is, viewing the manifest content as a disguise of the latent content rather than seeing the manifest content as being the *dream* with no disguise intended. Some connection was made to day residue, but the focus in working on a dream was almost always on returning to the patient's past and the origins of his pathology, with little or no focus on the dreamer's present-day struggles as illumined in the dream. No effort was made to systematically derive more information about the immediate context of the dream, and it was never made clear that if the dream's meaning remained obscure it was because not enough data had been acquired about what triggered the dream. The analyst was viewed as the authority. Analysts in training often felt they were supposed to know with very little effort what the dream meant and that their clients believed they did. The idea of *collaboration* was not conveyed. Apart from classwork, the only other experience analysts in training had in working with dreams was in their own psychoanalysis and in supervision where the same hierarchical inequality may or may not have been conveyed.

I knew as a student that I was miles ahead of my classmates in this area, not only because of the years of work on my own dreams in psychoanalysis but because of my years of training in working with the dreams of others, focusing on the manifest content and the context in which the dream emerged including connections to the past. One has to learn the skills needed to draw out information from the dreamer that would help make his dream come alive.

I have made one or two rather weak efforts to teach courses on dreams at this institute. I have not been persistent because I'm aware I'm up against a wall. In the first place, to maintain the hierarchical system, there is a need on the part of many therapists to augment, not diminish, their positions as authority figures. In my opinion, the issue of power as a motivating force in becoming an analyst is not sufficiently addressed. Secondly, and most importantly, the training of psychoanalysts in institutions such as mine places the student in a fiercely and precariously defensive position. He or she faces one committee after another in the course of training, committees that are always on the look-out for countertransference issues to cause the analytic candidate grief. This leaves the student uncomfortable about any self-disclosure that might come up either in presenting a dream of his own or in the projections he might offer in working experientially with the dreams of others.

How then does individual dreamwork differ from experiential group dreamwork? For one thing, the dreamer has many life issues, and oftentimes crises, he needs to talk about. He may not be able to give the dream priority, although experienced dream workers come to recognize the dream as the "royal road to the unconscious" and give it precedence or certainly try not to leave it out. He may remember the dream in the middle of a session or close to the end. Assuming, however, that the dream has been offered early in the session, it can be worked with methodically using many of the principles of group dreamwork. After the dream is recorded I will begin to ask questions to uncover first the immediate context and then the extended context in the effort to shed light on the connection between image and reality. This is generally the longest part of the work, to follow up one bit of data after another with questions that will draw the dreamer out as fully as possible. When there is a sense that the context of the dream is fully known, there are often interesting results if the dream is played back aloud to the dreamer at this point . . .with a bit of drama or emphasis or even humor: "So - - - after all you told me about last night, why do you think you dreamt you were in a subway going to the west side?" or "Why, last night, of all the hundreds of people you know, do you think you brought Jessie into your dream?" The questioning (dialogue) continues, becoming more and more refined in terms of the specific dream imagery and its metaphorical meaning until the dreamer begins to get in touch with his dream, to experience a *felt* connection between his emotional state at the time he fell asleep, the pertinent historical data, and those curious personages and settings of the dream. Most often, and especially with a patient who has worked on his dreams for a long time, this is enough. Nothing more needs to be said by me. At other times, when the client is just beginning to close in on the meaning of the dream—that is, when the connections he's making feel tenuous or uncertain—it seems helpful, if possible, to offer an orchestration to bring together the work the client herself has done in a more integrated way. This is often experienced as an affirmation of the client's effort. If the context has been fully developed and the client still cannot connect to the dream, I will try to orchestrate it for him. I always make it clear that what I am saying is offered in the spirit of a question. "Given what you have said about what was going on in your life yesterday . . . or what you fell asleep thinking about (with highlights offered briefly), do you think your dream might be saying something about. . . . "

The beauty of all this, especially with young adult patients who are often in conflict with their parents and society, struggling with issues about their own emerging identities and the crises of growing up, is that they start to experience an inner sense of their own authority. One is teaching the young person to wait for that *felt* sense, oftentimes a clear feeling of relief like that of suddenly being able to take a deeper breath that is experienced when the dream's meaning becomes known. This may be one of the first experiences the young person has had of knowing *inside* what he is about. He can learn to rely on that felt sense in other areas of his life, to know when he is acting truly in advocacy of his own integrity or not.

What are the advantages and disadvantages of individual dreamwork? First, the disadvantages, and there are basically only two. The first is that there are only two of us in this consulting room. We do not have the benefit of the input of eight or ten individuals who are there for the sole purpose of working on a dream, the rich input of Stage II when the group members play with the feelings the dream evokes and the possible metaphorical meanings of the imagery. The dreamer does not experience the wide band of support and caring that the dream group offers as it participates in his dream. The second is the issue of timing. In contrast to a dream group where there is an hour and a half set aside for each dream, in an individual session we have at best a half hour or forty minutes to work on a dream, assuming time has been taken up with other matters. Sometimes the dream is not presented in a session until a few minutes before the end.

What then are the advantages of individual dreamwork? For some, the privacy of the setting and the longstanding relationship between client and therapist allow for fuller disclosure and less discomfort. The sense of safety is implicit in the setting. In fact, if in the dream group there is a need to follow the structured process carefully to preserve safety, in the individual setting the issue of safety is implicit and the therapist may feel he can confront the dreamer with greater boldness about what the dream might be saying. We know, as an important principle of dreamwork, that the dreamer is generally ready to confront the issues in a dream that has been remembered. It is always the ongoing sense of respect for the dreamer's ultimate authority in working with a dream that makes such confrontation possible.

In addition, the therapist knows a great deal about the client's life. They have worked together on many dreams. Dream images are frequently repeated—horses figure into one client's dreams over and over again, elevators in another's. The question centers on how the same image is presenting itself *now*—with what variations, with what indicators of growth. It is for this reason that even when a dream is presented close to the end of a session, with only ten or fifteen minutes remaining, we can often get to the heart of its meaning. We can also work with a dream over a number of sessions.

Perhaps what I have taken from group dream work is already clear, but let me restate briefly the important points I use daily in my practice with clients. First is the belief in a collaborative effort. This requires careful listening and following on the part of the therapist to *everything* a client is saying about the dream with no prejudgment about what is important and what is not. This is sometimes very hard to do, and self-reminders never cease. The client may have presented many dreams. We know a great deal about him or her. The dream may be similar to others, but the important question is what is *this one* about. Second is a conviction that the meaning of a dream will unfold when we have made a thorough effort to search for the contextual material that prompted the dream. When the dream is not clear it simply means we have more work to do. The techniques for conducting a dialogue apply here—drawing out the context, asking open-ended questions, following the dreamer rather than leading her, emphasizing the dreamer's own idiosyncratic associations to the dream images, and waiting to see if the dream's meaning will come to the dreamer himself. As therapist, one has to discipline oneself to work in this structure. It's such a temptation to jump in with an interpretation we are convinced fits, especially when a dream seems simple. They never are. The benefit for the therapist in holding back his or her own ideas is the reassuring knowledge that this method works, that the dream will come alive with much richer meaning than the therapist might have anticipated if s/he just gets to work. This knowledge does wonders for the therapist's own level of anxiety which is attenuated when both s/he and the client have learned how to collaborate. If the dreamer is experiencing difficulty connecting to the dream, there is opportunity to remind the dreamer of the key contextual issues she developed and then to play back the dream in the hope that connecting links will be made then. Finally, just as one does in a dream group, there is opportunity to offer an orchestration, using the material that has been presented and all that is known about the dreamer. Sometimes the dreamer needs reminding of one piece of context often ignored—an earlier session. If the dream occurred after a session and the dreamer does not mention the session, it is often helpful to ask the client what thoughts the session produced.

Now for some dreams.

Helen's Dream

The first dream I would like to discuss was that of a client who has been in therapy for a number of years. She has learned how to work with a dream, how we focus first on the events and emotional state preceding the dream, and then look at the imagery together.

The dreamer is about fifty. She was born in Europe right after the end of World War II. The family was stateless for the first eight years of her life, and she grew up in a household oppressed by her mother's countless recollections of the horrors of the war. She saw her role as the one to bring "sunshine" to the family, and her reponsibility to try to be the pleasing child. She has struggled with depression most of her life, been hospitalized twice, and made one suicide attempt.

The dream occurred on a Monday morning. "I was in a chair, confined, paralyzed, incontinent. I felt myself to be my grandmother. I was wearing something like a corset around my waist. It was strangling me. I couldn't move my legs, couldn't have sex, couldn't function as a woman."

Nothing much was needed from me at this point except a question about what the weekend had been like. "We had had a conversation with some close friends on Saturday night,a couple we've known a long time, about gender differences—how males deal more in a world of ideas rather than emotions. Sometimes with Will (husband) I feel my own perceptions are not tolerated—like they are being squeezed, pushed out of me. When I have a view that is different than his, it's not allowed—I can't really be myself. I was saying to Will as we went to bed that we should keep talking to our friends about this since we trust each other."

A simple question from me followed: "Did anything else occur?" Helen responded.

"My Mother called (calls every Sunday). Within a few minutes it felt like oxygen was being knocked out of me. 'You're doing it again,' I thought; 'You have no regard for me.' I had the unsettling feeling afterward that I had married my mother . . . when Will looks at me and refuses to listen to what I am saying or when I don't mirror his admiration for something."

"Anything else?" I asked.

"It had been Tom's (her son) birthday earlier in the week. He told me my mother had called him to wish him a happy birthday. I said, 'That's nice.' I didn't want to diminish his pleasure in her call. But Sunday after I got off the phone with my mother I wanted to talk to Tom, to tell him there's a side of grandma you don't know. I wanted to say 'Do you know she doesn't call me on my birthday or your sister, just you and your father?' I wanted to ask 'What do you make of this—the different ways she treats girls and boys?'

"I had also been working on my thesis. My wrists were hurting from working at the computer."

At this point there were four strong bits of context developing—the conversation with friends about gender differences, the call from her mother, thoughts abut Tom, and the work on her thesis. I suggested we look at the dream and asked her to think about why she had dreamt about her grandmother that night. Helen began to speak about this woman. "She was such a joyful young person. My grandfather adored her. She loved to dance. I thought of her as the *keeper of the heart*. When she got sick, she never complained. She would look out the window for beautiful things to see. But when she got sick my mother had total control of her as she always controlled me. She made me stay in after school and take care of my grandmother. I did my homework after school and wanted to go out and play. At times grandmother also yearned to die. She had lived long enough, and she needed relief. That's me too (Helen had made one suicide attempt). I am not going to let that happen to me. I wanted to dance as a teenager. My mother wouldn't let me. I want to live now. I don't want her to have that power—that numbing power. So much pleasure was robbed from me—including my sexuality as a girl. It was okay for my brother to have fun—not me . I was so involved in pleasing her."

Helen had arrived at the meaning of the dream herself. There was no need for an orchestration from me except to bring together all that Helen herself had come to see and feel that weekend, the heightened awareness of male/female gender differences that emerged from her talk with friends, the way this had been played out in her family of origin where males were valued and females devalued, the way this was being repeated in her mother's relationship with Helen's husband and son, the problems that existed along these lines with Helen and her husband, the telephone conversation with her mother that left Helen feeling suffocated, the physical tightness she experienced in sitting at her computer (as well as the constrictions being imposed on her creativity by her faculty adviser). All of this had contributed to the dream image that helped her see herself like her grandmother—in her capacity for joy, warmth, and largeness of heart, her role as keeper of the heart, and in the way constrictions to her spirit had been and still were being imposed on her.

Emma's Dream

The dreamer is a seventeen year old who had been in therapy only two months when this dream was presented. She is a beautiful young woman, highly intelligent, an outstanding student, extremely shy, with high ideals and a strong need to see herself as a "good" person. She had experienced some months of depression a year earlier that she had endured alone, but as this depression began she feared she could not tolerate its duration and asked her parents if there was any way they could get help for her. She was a "natural" for dream work as she saw herself becoming a writer someday and kept a daily journal, which included some of her poetry and in which she now kept a record of her dreams. The language of metaphor was not foreign to her but something she responded to spontaneously. On the surface the dream Emma presented did not appear to be an especially difficult one. I found I needed to control the impulse to offer ideas too quickly. It is given here as an example of what is gained by not jumping in too quickly, by waiting for the dreamer's own thoughts to unfold. Able to do that, I saw once again the much richer vista offered by the dream than I had anticipated.

The dream was brief and was presented toward the middle of the session. It had occurred on a Saturday afternoon waking Emma from a nap. "I was going to the prom with a group from school. I was wearing the wrong clothes, a shirt that didn't match. I decided to stay behind and said I'd meet up later. Then I was in a car, driving, feeling lost, trying to find the way. A dead body was in the passenger seat. I woke up thinking, *That's a perfect description for how I feel.*"

Emma was sleeping a lot during the day, and I knew that she was preoccupied with suicidal thoughts. I asked her to describe the day up until the point she napped. "I had been trying to write a paper for school. I couldn't concentrate. I didn't understand why I felt so bad. I didn't know how to put it into words. I was carrying around something terrible." (She was already connecting to the dream imagery.)

I encouraged Emma to say as much as she could about that afternoon. "I felt I had bumped up against a wall. I started thinking about the school newspaper (she works on it), about something I hadn't done, what Mr. X (faculty adviser) would say to me, (the beginning of feelings of self-criticism).

"Was there anything else?" I asked.

"It was my first day taking P- - - - (an antidepressant). I felt sad about having to take it. Maybe my depression isn't bad enough" (to warrant taking it). Stronger feelings of self-criticism were emerging. "I feel so bad about being depressed."

At this point my thoughts turned to Emma's relationship with her father. I knew he was having difficulty with his daughter's need for medication, being someone who believed in wholistic and nonpharmaceutical treatment. I got off the track; that is, I began leading the dreamer a bit rather than following her own thoughts as Emma had not yet mentioned her father. I asked her how he had seemed to her the morning she began taking antidepressants. "He seemed sad,"she responded, "but I had decided I wanted to give P- - - - a try."

At this point I had formulated some ideas about the dream. Emma's decision to take antidepressants had been an act of independence (like driving—an act of independence most teenagers long for) but she would have to bear the burden of her father's sadness about this (the dead body next to her.) But I held back my own thoughts and began playing back some of the images.

"Why do you think you were going to the prom on this particular afternoon, wearing a shirt that didn't match?"

"I think it says something about all my difficulties getting involved in school" (her shyness and reticence to speak in social situations and her almost total shutdown when she gets depressed). "Also, its probably a representation of my own self-criticism. I was thinking about Mr. X saying to me 'What's wrong with you? Why are you still so shy?' What *is* wrong with me?"

"And what about being in a car driving?" I asked. At this point I was surprised to learn that Emma had not gotten her learner's permit to drive, that she didn't feel ready to drive, she felt it was too much of a responsibility—supposing she hurt someone? "So . . . "I asked her," why do you think you were driving in this dream?" "Well," she replied," if I think of driving as a kind of independence, I don't like the idea of being dependant on anything. I don't like the idea of *having* to take a drug. I could decide *not* to take P- - - —I could *force* myself to do the driving (that is, not take the medication) "but I'd be lost and carrying a big burden" (the dead passenger).

It became clear Emma was struggling with issues of dependency (wanting to force herself to be independent). In fact this was one of the central themes beginning to emerge—the style she had developed of smiling, being good, not causing trouble at home, repressing anger and hiding her own needs in order not to burden her mother (who struggled with serious illness) and her father (whom she saw as unhappy). In short, she was having difficulty accepting dependency on them, letting them see her depression (rather than singing to cover it), asking for help (getting a therapist) rather than trying to manage it on her own, and wanting medication despite her father's feelings against it. Even her suicidal thoughts had much to do with not wanting to be a burden to her family. She wasn't a very good daughter, sister, etc. She was too depressed for that. What stopped her was that she knew an act of suicide would hurt them. She wanted their permission to end her pain. The dream was an important one as it helped Emma see clearly the heavy weight she had carried by trying to force herself to manage her depression alone. A week or two after this dream Emma allowed herself to be hospitalized briefly. I use the word *allow* in the sense that she experienced more fully than she had previously permitted herself the need to be taken care of—by doctors and nurses certainly, and by her family who began the process of family therapy to support her work with me. Shortly thereafter she withdrew from high school, relieving herself of the expectations and pressures she placed on herself, and she entered a hospital day treatment program for the weeks remaining in the school year.

As we concluded the session I took a moment to tell Emma what had just occurred for me—that I had initially seen the dream in a more superficial way—her decision to take P- - - - was an act of independence (which in fact it was) that might distress her father—but that in holding back my own thoughts we had come to a much deeper understanding of her struggles with dependency. I did this to reinforce for her the emerging sense of her own authority and the power of a dream to do just this. She smiled with delight.

"It makes all the difference," Jung wrote, "whether the doctor sees himself as part of the drama or cloaks himself in his authority." Nowhere is this reminder to therapists more fitting than in our work with dreams.

Notes

1. Faculty member, The Comprehensive Course in Psychoanalysis, New York Medical College, 1950 to 1962.

2. In the early fifties I began exploring an idea that later became part of the dream group process I now use. I would begin the seminar by suggesting that we initially limit our knowledge to the age and sex of the patient, duration of therapy, and the dream itself. The class and I would then offer our own projections of what the dream might be saying about both the dreamer and the dreamer's relationship to the therapist. Despite some initial resistance to saying anything about a dream before the associations were at hand, it proved to be a surprisingly helpful exercise.

3. When time does not allow a more extended exploration of the dream, Walter Bonime (1962) resorts to what he refers to as "Headline" interpretation. This is an attempt to identify the one most helpful metaphorical statement pertinent to the work going on.

References

Bonime, W. *The Clinical Use of Dreams.* New York: Basic Books, 1962.

Ullman, M. *Appreciating Dreams.* Thousand Oaks, Calif.: Sage, 1996.

CHAPTER THIRTEEN

Dreams and Society

MONTAGUE ULLMAN

The relationship between the private lives of individual members of a society as revealed in their dreams and the overt and covert nature of that society is an intriguing subject. Cultural anthropologists have had a go at it in their studies of primitive and preliterate societies but have hardly gone very far in exploring how the fallout from modern industrial societies shapes the dream images of their citizens. This chapter suggests one possible approach through noting and understanding the appearance in dreams of images that betray the existence of social stereotypes characteristic of a particular society. Were greater attention paid to imagery of this kind, the individual dreamer might gain a deeper awareness of the role such stereotypes play in his or her life. Through dreams we get at what the individual sweeps under the rug. Dreams may someday make us more sensitive to how societies do this as well. Trends suggesting the need for a sociology of dreaming will be noted.

The images that appear in our dreams speak to us of our most private concerns. They have much to tell us of the true nature of our encounters with others and with ourselves. They are particularly adept at pointing up distortions and deceits while being equally concerned with uncovering dormant resources and strengths. They derive from two sources, the natural world and the man-made world. We are familiar with the way these images are fashioned idiosyncratically to say something significant about the dreamer. Do they have something significant to say about the historically fashioned social world in which we live? First a few words about the general nature of dreaming.

Dreaming Consciousness

Dreaming consciousness can be looked upon as analogous to waking consciousness, but different in form and content. Its language is imagistic and metaphorical rather than discursive. Using a different language, we are also saying different things. Awake, consciousness is influenced by an external reality and helps us find our way through that reality. Asleep and dreaming, we are temporarily disconnected from the world and begin to experience ourselves from a profoundly altered perspective. We forsake the logic of time and space that frames our waking life, replacing it with an historical view based on the emotional contiguity of past events. Asleep and dreaming, we move into the feeling dimension of our existence. The emotional residues that linger with us at the end of the day do so because of their connection to still unresolved issues in our life. Our feelings act as a kind of fluid matrix that connects present concerns to their roots in the past.

Dreaming consciousness may be looked upon as a steering mechanism that orients us to the future by offering both a wider and a more honest perspective on the current scene. Awake, our passions often chart a devious course for themselves. Far from being devious our dreams reflect this deviousness honestly. While dreaming we are not concerned with deceiving ourselves. We are concerned with showing, in no uncertain terms, that we are deceiving ourselves, if that be the case. The dream is a kind of emotional range finder that locates our deeply felt and true position amidst those influences, good and bad, known and unknown, that impinge on us from within and without. This is what makes their pursuit more than a game and more meaningful than fantasy.

To understand the essence of dreaming we have to consider the unique and versatile role of metaphor. While dreaming we seem to have turned all our resources into a metaphor-making operation. Whenever we find ourselves in the Rapid Eye Movement stage of sleep (REM), we come upon a spontaneously generated flow of visual metaphor. In some way we have transformed a primitive imaging capacity, one with the ability to reproduce literal pictures inside our heads, into an emotionally expressive metaphorical language. Metaphor is more than a figure of speech. It goes right to the heart of whatever it is we mean when we speak of creativity. It seems to be a way of moving into new and unexplored areas, cloaking them with analogous, original, and sometimes fantastic creations. It is a vehicle that helps us absorb the emotional thrust of new experience. An original metaphor (live, as contrasted to a dead one, such as "the heart of the matter," "the foot of the mountain") is a conceptual leap into the mysterious.

The Dream and Society

Cultural anthropologists have long viewed dreams as useful instruments for studying the mores and value systems of exotic cultures. Logically, they should be as useful in the examination of our own society. Social in origin, our dream imagery has an intrinsic bidirectionality that points inwardly to the innermost and often hidden aspects of our personal being and outwardly to the source of their origin and to their possible connection to prevailing social realities that otherwise tend to be obscured from view. Just as dream work in the ordinary sense brings into consciousness what has not been understood or truly felt, so something analogous may be occurring in connection with what has in other contexts been referred to as our social unconscious (Fromm 1955). I use the term to refer to all that we do not let ourselves see of the emotional fallout from the social arrangements and institutions about us.

There is no simple way to relate social issues to dreaming consciousness. As socially and culturally conditioned beings, we have to a large extent created our own environment. The imagery that appears in our dreams arises out of the infinite wealth of material available to us because of our historical past. We refashion them to suit our personal needs, but they are there for us because we exist as social beings. Borrowed, as it were, from society, do the images maintain significant connections to society? Can the dream be looked upon as a societal as well as a self-confrontation? What can the images reveal of our social support system and the social dangers linked to that system?

Dreams provide an admirable instrument for unmasking personal myth, that is, the self-deceptive processes that operate to blind or distort the individual's view of himself as an actor in society. When understood, the result is an enhanced consciousness of one's self. The question we are exploring begins where that process leaves off. Can we go back to the dream and get beyond the personal micromyth to the social or macromyth? Can the dream's capacity for truth help us identify those aspects of society that interfere with our connections to significant others, as well as to ourselves, and our potential for self-realization?

The bidirectionality of dream imagery is best illustrated by the appearance in the dream of social stereotypes such as portraying a black man as a rapist or a female as a cow playing out a domesticated role. Images of this sort have a dynamic aspect in their meaning both for the dreamer and for the society that gave rise to the image. Exploited by the dreamer in depicting a current tension, the stereotype is further enhanced. A mutually reinforcing influence is at work. Through the use of metaphor such imagery tells us something about the unsolved problems both of the dreamer and of society. By clarifying the role that social stereotypes play in our dreams and by seeing the way that socially derived biases and prejudices influence our lives, we shift some aspects of our social unconscious into the realm of social consciousness. Where we go from there will be determined by many factors. The point is that, through dream work, we have the opportunity to position ourselves more honestly vis-a-vis some of the social realities we face.

The other indication of this bidirectionality is the appearance in dreams of images that reduce natural human attributes to the status of objects that can be manipulated and made available in the marketplace much as any ordinary commodity. Often this takes the form of depicting sexual organs as objects, hollow or pointed and dissociated from any truly human context. Appearances, that is, the beauty of women and the macho look of men, sell everything from cars to cigarettes. Dream images that are derived in this way reflect forces at work in the larger social scene that are both subtle and strident in their dehumanizing impact.

In the following dream, a successful professional woman is still reactive to her father's male chauvinism.

A woman in her late thirties is about to embark on a new relationship with a man. She senses some hesitancy on her part and has a dream that displays the roots of her ambivalence. At one point in the dream she sees her father sitting on a swing with four female relatives in their heyday, dressed like can-can girls. What emerged from the work on the dream were two powerful images that surfaced from childhood to influence the dreamer's approach to a new relationship. One was that of the male, derived from the image of her father as privileged to flirt and become involved with other women. The other, that of the female victimized by the profligate male, was her mother. These are images the dreamer still struggles with personally but, in a larger sense, they relate to the residues of sexism, a social issue not yet disposed of. The privileged male and the victimized female are still available social stereotypes.

Our dreams usually focus on the psychological dimension of our lives. In the following dream of a professional woman living in the north of Sweden there is an interesting interplay of the biological, the psychological, and the social. A word about world events at the time of this dream is essential to its understanding. It occurred soon after the Soviet nuclear mishap at Chernenko, the murder of Olaf Palme, and when the U.S. invasion of Libya was still a live issue. These events have to be looked at from the point of view of the Swedes who, despite their very strong negative reactions, felt helpless and frustrated in the face of all three events.

The Dream

There is a man in my dream who seems to be a combination of my husband, Bengt, and Per, a man I was with as an activist in the sixties. He is lecturing to a group of medical students. He is talking in a spontaneous and vivid way as well as demonstrating by very simple movements of his thumb what he means. He holds both hands up and keeps flexing and unflexing his thumbs. Then he makes all the students stand up and do this exercise. When they stop different things begin to happen in the group. He then explains the physiology of what is happening.

Then the lecture ends, and I am alone in the room but the exercise stays with me. I write down the entire lecture. It is as if, by doing that, it acquires a whole new dimension. It is transformed from being a medical phenomenon illustrating bodily reactions to a more generalized kind of understanding of the nature of fascism. I have acquired a new understanding of why fascism spreads and have learned something more about the oppression of women, the existence of self-destructive impulses, and why they (women) have such vitality.

The lecturer had indicated that the more you move your body in the way he indicated the more kinetic energy is developed, this being a form of aggressiveness in a positive sense. The exercise he had given the students resulted in the kinetic energy being handled in different ways. Some of the students expressed it directly by engaging in small playful fights. Others made only a slight gesture by touching their right shoulder with their left hand. These students were suppressing the energy so that only traces of it appeared in their gesture. The lecturer then asked the students about the way they experienced the exercise. They were to rate their reactions on a scale of 1 to 5. A systematic difference emerged from this. Those students who were concerned about the social context and who felt that letting out the impulses would not be constructive for that context suppressed this energy. They rated the experience very low. Those who let it out without concern for the social context rated the experience very high.

As I wrote the lecture down in the dream and began to think about it, it suddenly occurred to me that this experiment explains the victory of fascism. Those who live out these aggressive impulses without concern for the social fabric feel better and grow stronger. Fascism is simply the system under which these impulses can be acted out legitimately and freely. On the other hand those with a sense of responsibility for the social context are more discontent, become weaker, and are finally swept aside as the others inevitably win control. The society they strive for is not able to survive.

In the dream I also felt I understood more about the male-female problem. Women, being suppressed, are made unfit for life. I became aware of the self-destructiveness that results when the aggressive impulses are turned against the self. At the end, however, I realize that, in spite of this happening, it will be better in the end and will ultimately bring me more strength and power when I no longer need to hold them back.

This dream was presented in a group, and the process described in chapter 1 then unfolded. After the group had offered their projections and the dream was returned to the dreamer she then responded:

> I awoke from this dream feeling both relieved, as if I had discovered something, and also very sad. In the dream I had the very strong feeling of coming close to the way things are in the world—how something like the murder of Olaf Palme could occur. That filled me with a sadness and anger I felt in my body. Per and I were lovers in the sixties, and we had worked together in the movement. We were very much against the signs of American aggression. Per's reappearance in my dream is connected with my thoughts about the murder of Olaf Palme. Was the CIA involved? Were they trying to create unrest? Palme was a very powerful spokesman for the oppressed and for that reason may have been thought of as a threat. Why is it that those responsible for world affairs create situations that are so disastrous for the common people? In the dream I realize this is the nature of the way mankind has developed and it has come to the point where it

may no longer survive. Why is it that what is constructive is not viable and what is viable is not constructive? Psychiatry teaches us to let our impulses out, which is the reverse of what I say will make for survival in the dream.

When I awoke from this dream I felt it was important to remember it. What was strange about it was that it seemed more like a lecture than a dream. In thinking about the context, I had this dream the night of the last day of a one-week stay at a convalescent home. Being there made me even more sick. The food didn't agree with me, and I lost 4½ kilos in weight. I had headaches, insomnia, and nightmares and discovered that my blood pressure became very high. It was only on the last day that I began to feel better. I had gone there because I had been so sick all winter.

I felt very isolated and miserable at this home. I had forgotten my eyeglasses and couldn't read, and reading to me is like an addiction.

A research project that I have been on for a year was also on my mind. I had been given time from my job to do this project, and where I work time is a very scarce commodity. I was too ill to make any progress with the research. It was at a standstill. I felt I wasn't using the time properly.

Then I suddenly thought of where that strange movement of the thumb came from. I had been to many doctors but none took my symptoms seriously until I came to Dr. K. He was sympathetic and investigated all my complaints thoroughly. For the first time I felt someone was really listening to me in an understanding and respectful way. One of the tests he had me do was exactly the thumb movement shown in my dream.

The way the man in the dream lectured was also very much like the vivid and dramatic style of Bengt, which I admire very much. I would like to say important things to people in his vital way. I have worked in the movement against the war in Vietnam, and I have also been active in the struggle against the abuse of women.

What brought me to this convalescent home was the self-destructiveness I refer to in the dream. Yet, as in the dream, it comes out of something healthy and this represents a contradiction for me that is hard to resolve. The problem is how to mold destructive impulses so as to put them to good use, to allow them to gain expression without harming the social context so that, as they come out, they would be good for both society and the individual. In the dream it was a kind of insight that this was not possible but that the realization of this impossibility might be the useful beginning of some kind of process. Listening to the lecture, taking part in what was going on,

> was a good feeling. I also liked my writing it down and working on it. That was very important to me. It was my way of doing things. It was different from the way Bengt and Per did things, but it was no less effective. The dream is telling me that different kinds of contributions are necessary and that I can be satisfied with mine. Bengt and Per are both nourishing men and both gave me a lot, and now I have the feeling I am putting it to good use. I don't have to create out of nothing. I can use the good things I have gotten from others.
>
> On awakening I had the feeling of having made an important discovery. It almost made me feel embarrassed. I had feelings of both satisfaction and guilt. I even felt afraid to present this dream to the group for fear something would be harmed, that in some way it would be turned into its opposite.

At the end of this rather moving and lengthy response the dreamer expressed the need for more help with the dream and invited the group to engage in the dialogue.

Before any questions could be asked the dreamer herself began to talk more about her feelings around the time of the dream.

> The time at the convalescent home was a kind of breathing space. We had canceled a family trip because I wasn't feeling well. For the week I was away I had no contact with the outside world. The dream group was on my mind.[1] We were very involved in making the arrangements for it. While I was at the home it was such a relief being among simple, common, working people. It was so different from the usual academic atmosphere around me. It felt good. There was a kind of natural warmth and a genuine, alive interest in each other. It made me aware of how worn out I felt by the limited contact that exists among my colleagues. The people I was with that week were content just being and living day to day. Being with them was a healing atmosphere.
>
> Not being able to read, of course, was a problem. Reading is a kind of passion with me. I was touched by the atmosphere of the place as well as relieved at getting rid of the usual poisons I take into my body—coffee, sweets, and the like. I felt stressed at work, and my blood pressure shot up. When that was discovered I was "sick-written,"[2] and that relieved my conscience about taking time off.
>
> I thought about you (M.U.) coming back for this dream group work. I usually have a dream when I'm preparing for the workshop. But this time I didn't want to have one. I had been working too hard

> and felt worn out. And the problem with my research was stressing me.
>
> My dream seems to be pointing out how strong are the self-destructive forces in myself. The dream also seems to be saying that, although they will win in the short run, they lose in the long run.

In the playback the dreamer was then asked if she could say more about the double image represented by the man.

> They are people I love and have loved. Both have touched my heart. Per is always connected to my concern with the condition of the world. It may also refer to Monte who touched my heart. It was the combination of the lecture, the phenomena manifesting themselves, and my pondering about them afterward that seemed so important. I liked what Monte said last night. In dream work we work not only for ourselves but also for our species.

The dreamer was asked about the arm-to-shoulder gesture.

> I wouldn't have noticed the gesture until the lecturer pointed it out. It had no meaning for me.

She was asked if there was anything more she could say about the thumb movement.

> I was so touched by Dr. K. taking me seriously. I have been to many other doctors who haven't taken me seriously. He made a thorough investigation and found a basis for further diagnostic exploration.

The following orchestrating projection of mine evolved out of the dream work:

> At the time you entered the convalescent home you were in a state of despair, both physically and emotionally. It was only on the last day of your stay at the home, a time when you were beginning to feel better, when hope was again entering your life, that you were able to create a dream in which you searched out the root causes of your despair. The result was a heroic effort on your part to explore the connections between what you were going through personally, physically, and psychologically and the way you were experiencing what was going on in the world around you. The clarification of these connections comes through the words you put into the mouth of the lecturer and your pondering over them. They seemed to provide you with an answer that was very important to you; namely, how bodily distress and psychological despair derive from choices made with

> regard to concern over the social context. When that concern is absent the anarchic play of the energies released moves in the direction of fascism and the ultimate dissolution of the social fabric. For those with a concern for the social context the energies have gained expression in self-destructive ways. Just as you felt yourself moving to a state of paralysis physically, as you felt stalemated in your research work, the recent events in the world, specifically the bombing of Libya and the atomic explosion in the USSR (Chernenko), conveyed a message of hopelessness about the world at large. Your dream places this despair in its proper context. There is cause for despair in the short run, but there is hope in the long run. Your physical recovery and the regeneration of your faith in the common man provided the basis for this hope. That hope was also sparked by the respectful concern shown you by the one doctor who really listened to you. This validation of your worth as an individual is the most powerful weapon you can have in the struggle against destructive forces that are coming at you from without and within. This is even more important when it seems as though the external destructive forces are on the move and are invincible. Perhaps that strange little movement of the thumb can take on added significance in this connection. It is a very small movement but it is movement and that is the important thing. It is movement out of the state of paralysis.

The dream plays out a counterpoint between social hopelessness and personal hopelessness on the one hand and social and personal hope on the other. As long as there is a sense of personal paralysis there is a sense of social paralysis. An important point in the dream is the scene where the dreamer has written down the lecture and is pondering about it. This is her style, her way, and she is satisfied with it. It is not the same as Bengt or Per, but it is her own. The sense of insight this gives her, although it recognizes the "impossibility" of changing the social context in any immediate way, provides her, at the same time, with a basis of hope for the future. Contributing to this hope, even laying the groundwork for it, was her physical improvement and her interaction with the people about her at the home that revived her faith in the goodness and strength of the ordinary person.

She awoke with a feeling of discovery and relief. It was as if an oppressive weight had lifted. In part it had to do with the realization that it was not up to her alone to come up with a solution, but that she could take what was valuable from others in her effort to keep alive her hope for a better world. She was feeling the support she was receiving at the physical, psychological, and social levels. Just as the body could get rid of the poisons that harmed it, so could the social organism—even in the face of what seemed most impossible. Reparative mechanisms were set in motion, undermining the congruence between personal and social despair.

Social and Personal Disorder

We are not only individuals—we are also part of a vast continuum held together by mutual needs, by feelings, and by biological necessities. We live and move as part of the whole of our society, our culture, our species. All our lives we are subject to complex social forces which, at best, are only partially understood. We all possess social blinders that screen out or distort those aspects of the social scene which we prefer to dismiss or separate from ourselves. Consider Nazi Germany where so many people kept their distance from what was going on. The fact is, of course, that these forces leave their mark on each of us despite our limited or distorted vision. That mark is often at odds with the aspirations and potential inherent in human nature.

To the extent that social arrangements foster biased or distorted views they are inevitably internalized by its members in the course of their development. We incorporate the resultant disorder within our own psychological-biological processes. However, to make contact with the disorder and to recognize the social myths that envelop us in so camouflaged a manner, we must somehow adopt a position from which our customary milieu can be viewed against a different background. From such an altered frame of reference we may sense the existence of a social aberration or impediment which, under ordinary circumstances, feels natural and "right" and goes unrecognized. The dream is one resource that can offer this different perspective. If there exists within each of us and within society as a whole, as I believe there does, an uncorruptible core of being, there is an opportunity in the private, penetratingly honest world of the dream for this innate, basic mode to assert itself. For this to take on meaning in our lives requires some understanding of how personal and social disorders interweave and interpenetrate.

When emotional problems endure they do so because of their congruence with prevailing social values and because of the absence of countervailing social influences. A neurotic trend to endure must be reinforced, implicitly or explicitly, by the social field surrounding the individual. When a social field offers resistance to its operation a crisis results creating the opportunity for the emergence and strengthening of healthy trends. In our striving for wholeness and self-realization our perceptual apparatus constantly registers, whether we are conscious of it or not, the neurosis-reinforcing or health-evoking aspects of our social milieu.

Our dream images are self-confrontational constructs. They call attention to hidden assumptions about ourselves that some recent event capriciously uncovers. The image selected or created to serve this purpose is often one which, in exposing the personal dynamics involved, also provides us with clues as to the neurosis-reinforcing as well as health-evoking qualities of the social field related to the particular predicament we are dreaming about. To investigate this involves the shift from a concern with the vicissitudes of an individual's struggle with the strictures imposed by the socializing process itself to a concern with the individual vis-à-vis an historically determined but currently existing and specifically identifiable social structure. Fromm is one of the few analysts who has taken this route, but he has had few followers, and certainly the implications for our concept of dreaming have not yet been spelled out.

The private myth or micromyth highlighted in the dream often gains expression by attracting to itself images drawn from experience that carry a congruent social or macromythic valence. This fact generally escapes notice because we are not in the habit of extrapolating from the dream image to the social reality that lies beyond. Both forms of myth are highly resistive to change. In the case of the individual micromyth the distortions and limitations of the waking ego have to be overcome. The personal myth embodied in the dream can yield to the socializing practice of group dream work wherein the emotional thrust of the dream becomes recognized by the waking or social self. It is this process of engagement with one's feelings in a supportive and cooperative milieu that makes for change. While the personal myth doesn't vanish, it is restructured so as to encompass the newly recognized aspects of the self more accurately.

Dream work involves the transformation of an experience felt under conditions of temporary suspension of the social self into a communication meaningful to the social self. The process is difficult, uneven, troublesome, but infinitely rewarding. It is more than the negative process of ferreting out personal foibles and hypocrisies. It becomes a treasure hunt where one can discover an unsuspected quarry of human virtues. Our capacities for concern, courage, tenderness, and so forth confront us in our dreams, waiting to be recognized and validated by our social self. Paradoxically, it is often our obtuseness to the existence and strength of these virtues that serves to perpetuate the very myths that get us into psychological and emotional difficulty.

When the dream image points to problem areas at a more broadly social level, dream work takes a different turn. When individual meaning is pursued the dreamer moves closer to the resolution of the issue. When the focus shifts to the social meaning of the image, we are faced with a somewhat more complex task than if we were to concern ourselves only with the personal meaning. Our dreams then take us beyond the personal unconscious. A two-step process is involved. First, the particular predicament can be seen with greater objectivity once the broader social perspective comes into view. There results less of a personal and more of a shared social responsibility for whatever the issue may be. This approach highlights what Bastide (1966) describes as the use of the dream as a disposal system for social garbage. He is referring to the way certain tension-generating issues that are primarily social in origin are experienced as personal and private. This privatization of what may be regarded as social waste products serves a given status quo. In Sweden, for example, the economic pressure on young women to pursue dual careers as working mothers is even greater than in the United States. This is reflected in dreams by feelings of personal guilt associated with the need to leave very young children in day-care centers and going off to work.

This is not to say that the dream confronts us with social issues explicitly but, rather, that the emotional fallout registers subjectively, and that this is what the dream image objectifies. This pertains to both the good and bad impact of social arrangements, although it is the latter that gives us trouble. Allowing ourselves to be confronted not only by the personal but also by the social referents of the dream leads to a deeper understanding of enduring flaws in the social structure.

The second step referred to above concerns the course of action once social insight occurs. Dream work in the ordinary sense helps people to modulate their behavior. In the framework of this added social dimension the element of social concern comes into the picture, and here effective action takes a collective form and is directed toward modulating the behavior of others as well as ourselves. We become involved in issues that go beyond what the individual can do as an individual. Solutions to social problems require social action (Taylor 1992). Dream work helps us to see and feel the constraints and pain that come from trying to fit human needs into somewhat less than human containers. It can set the stage for some form of action. What then follows depends on the interest and degree of social concern of the dreamer. It is important to bear in mind that, just as personal insight is a consequence of work done against defensive resistance, social insight also requires work against resistance. Not everyone will find it easy to relate to this dimension of dream work. For those who do there are many possible paths into this territory, so that anyone who is interested can find one that is congenial to his or her own style and interests. We can move into the realm of the social unconscious through social science, politics, psychology, the arts, and so on. The important thing is the awareness that there is territory to be explored.

We come now to a rather interesting question of why it is that society as we know it, so-called civilized society, has been so neglectful of dreams. Attesting to the truth of Bastide's thesis is the generally derogatory attitude toward dreams that exists in civilized societies. I have referred to this bias as "dreamism" (Ullman & Zimmerman 1979), and like all "isms" of that kind it connotes a prejudicial attitude. It serves as a defensive maneuver that protects society against the social truths that are apt to emerge if the social relevance were to be given its just due.[3] The only socially sanctioned use of dreams is its use in formal therapy or in laboratory research, neither of which touches more than a small part of the world of dreamers. Neglecting this most honest, reliable, and available way of monitoring our subjectivity, we have gone somewhat astray. Were we more attentive through our dreams to the negative emotional fallout from some of the social arrangements we have been heir to, we might move to greater unity in opposing instead of tolerating and fostering the level of divisiveness that now characterizes the world scene. In our dreams we share similar basic concerns. If dream work developed on a large scale, might we then become more tolerant and more accepting of differences?

From my experience in group dream work I am convinced of the high price we pay for this neglect. Dream work is a natural avenue for unloading personal secrets and moving toward greater personal freedom. This is a universal need which is not yet met in our society except in the limited fashion of the client-therapist situation. The need is not only not met but is generally not even recognized as a need. This might also be said of society as a whole. Society has not recognized the need to have a view of itself from outside its usual perspective. This is what the dream does for the individual and, because of the bidirectionality of the dream metaphors, what it can do for society as well.

Toward a Sociology of Dreaming

Mention has already been made of the seminal work of Dorothy Eggan (see Hillman, this volume) on Hopi dreams where she clearly points to the interplay of cultural myth and personal tensions displayed in the manifest content of dreams. Eggan (1952) further notes:

> If, then, the assumption is justified that dreams are a probable universal form of mental activity, at once idiosyncratic and culturally molded, there follows the inevitable conclusion that their communication is a challenge to the social scientist as well as the therapist. (p. 477)

What Eggan has to say about myth and dreams in Hopi society is equally true of Western society with one difference. In contrast to the relative ease with which myth can be discerned in primitive society, the discovery of myth in one's own milieu involves taking a look at our own insides, a feat even more difficult for a society than for an individual.

In 1966 the distinguished French cultural anthropologist Roger Bastide issued his clarion call for a sociology of the dream. Based on his studies of transitional societies in Brazil and in Africa, he noted the impact of acculturation on dreams. His paper was a stinging criticism of the way sociologists ignore "the other half of our life" and envisage man "standing and sitting but never asleep and adream."

> For sociology interested in man awake, the sleeper might as well be dead. Sociology leaves it to anthropology to study the dream's place in the traditional civilizations, and to psychology to discover in the web of our dreams the motivations of our actions. (p. 199)

In contrast to primitive society where dreams and their significance are institutionalized and serve many different functions, contemporary civilization refuses "to accept any institutionalization whatever of the dream's social function, considering such an institution a 'waste product' not within the competence of a sociology worthy of its name—a kind of social sewer service" (p. 201).

The metaphor of a social sewer service is an apt reference to the corrosive social fallout that finds its way into the unconscious domain of those who are victimized by it and where the only signs of its presence may be intimations of guilt. Personal responsibility and guilt replace social responsibility, and the status quo remains unchallenged. Bastide's call for socially sanctioned concern with the significance of dreams is even more timely today where we don't seem able to stem the tide of moral decay that more and more insistently makes its presence felt. The social referents of the dream can serve as "tracer elements" exposing the social waste that is otherwise swept under the rug.

Coming at the problem from a different perspective, Trigant Burrow (1964), an early American psychoanalyst, wrote extensively on the connection between social disorder and personal disorder. Burrow's starting point was the unity of the human species and the forces at work limiting and corroding that unity. We are phylo-organisms and as such organically concerned with the survival of the species and the maintenance of a level of interconnectedness that will insure survival. He traced the roots of what he spoke of as a ubiquitous social neurosis to the evolutionary development of a symbolic system (language) that mediated between inner and outer reality and that ultimately led to conformance to prevailing cultural values. Unconscious allegiance to the rights and wrongs of a given society entailed a certain risk to all that makes for authentic interconnectedness. This level of unconscious conformance in turn led to what he referred to as the I-persona. In his own words:

> In this universal displacement of the organism's bionomic center of gravity, as it were—with supplanting of the relational function as a whole by mere discrete parts, or symbolically conditioned "I"-persona—the solidarity of man was rudely displaced. Instead each "I"-persona was now a separate and autocratic center of motivation. (p. 113)
>
> In short, it (the "I"-persona, M.U.) introduced the biological extraneous element of self-advantage and morality among individuals in place of relational coordination that rests on the common advantage of the species as a whole. Men did not any longer function in cooperation with their fellows or with their common environment. The solidarity of the species was henceforth submerged in favor of the preeminence of me—of the "I"-persona. (p. 114)

Burrow referred to the general social blindness that accompanies these developments as a social unconscious that exerted a generalized maladaptive influence. His concern with species unity and survival is as timely now as it was a half century ago when he first formulated it. Unless we learn how to prioritize the fact that we are members of a single species, we are not apt to find a way of alleviating the level of social distress that now exists. While not expressly concerned with dreams he too looks to the sociologist for help:

> Thus it behooves the sociologist to take cognizance of the possibility of an order of conscious beings with a new and larger sense of the meaning of life as interpreted in terms of the biological principle of unity man has inarticulately felt but as yet only understood as love. (p. 60)

I think what Bastide has to say about dreams and society and what Burrow has to say about species unity and the social unconscious provide a framework for a future sociology of the dream. There are several tributaries that could nurture an endeavor in that direction apart from the direct contributions of sociologists themselves. One way would involve a greater educational effort to reach the general public with the importance of dreams and their bidirectional ability to disclose hidden aspects of both the self and society. As noted in the first section of this chapter, the social referents are readily discernible.

Charlotte Beradt (1966), a journalist living in Germany from 1933 to 1939, collected hundreds of dreams from people in all walks of life and managed to smuggle her collection out of Nazi Germany. The book she wrote offers example after example of how successful the regime's propaganda machine was in instilling awe, fear, and, ultimately, feelings of helplessness in the face of power that appeared so invincible. All of this was clearly evident in the dreams she reported. In the dream of a middle-aged housewife a Storm Trooper appeared standing by an old-fashioned Dutch oven in her living room. He opened the oven door and out came a harsh voice reminiscent of one heard during the day over the loudspeaker repeating every word she had ever said against the government. The terror generated by the invasive propaganda succeeded in its aim of people terrorizing themselves, "turning themselves unawares into voluntary participants in this systematic terrorization in that they imagined it to be more systematic than it actually was" (p. 48).

Just as dreaming consciousness is sometimes more sensitive to subclinical manifestations of malignant growths, might a population more sophisticated about dreams become more aware of imagery depicting the misuse of social power?

Another tributary to a sociology of the dream might very well come from clinical sources. Andrew Samuels (1993), a Jungian analyst, in his recent book offers a detailed explanation of the political overtures in the practice of depth psychology and inversely of the relevance of depth psychology to an understanding of the political world. In the following excerpt he illustrates the admixture as it makes its appearance in a dream.

> An Italian patient dreamt of a beautiful lake with clear deep water. He said this represented his soul and then immediately associated to the pollution on the Italian Adriatic coast. The image of the lake, and the association to coastal pollution, suggested, in the form of one symbol, the patient's unconscious capacity for depth and his present state of which he was all too conscious—a state of being clogged up by "algae", like the coastal waters of the Adriatic. (p. 62)

He summed up the personal meaning of the dream as follows:

> In this particular instance, the notion that there was a possible "solution" of his lake-soul potential, and the idea that being clogged was a state he had gradually got into over time and was not a witch's curse, together with the vision that depth and clarity and beauty were options open to him were powerful and liberating thoughts for the patient to entertain. (p. 62)

Going on to the political referents he writes:

> The images of the dream can be approached via their individual presence, or via their political presence, or via the movement and tension between the two. In the dream of the lake, the tension between the individual and the political presences of the image was prominent and insistent; after all, the patient was Italian. What, the patient and I asked together, is the role of pollution in the soul, or even in the world? What is the role of pollution in the achievement of psychological depth? Can the soul remain deep and clear while there is pollution in the world, in one's home water? Did the lake, with intimations of mystery and isolation, clash with the popular, extraverted tourism of the Adriatic? Eventually, the patient's concern moved onto the social level: Who owned the lake? Who should have access to such a scarce resource? Who would protect the lake from pollution? These were his associations. From wholly personal issues, such as the way his problems interfered with the flowering of his potential, we moved to political issues, such as the pollution of natural beauty, not only by industry but also by the mass extraversion of tourism. And we also moved back again from the political level to the personal level, including transference analysis. (p. 63)

While there have been earlier forays by psychoanalysts into the permeability of the political and the psychological,[4] Samuels is the most comprehensive that has come to my attention.

Finally, there is a hopeful sign from another direction—the world of industry. In the wake of the human potential movement in the sixties personnel development strategies have evolved in response to the felt need of large corporations to soften their bureaucratic image. A decade ago a unique program was initiated by an Indian psychologist, Anjali Hazarika, working with management in the petroleum industry in New Delhi. In a recent book she gives a full account of her endeavor. What was of special interest was her exclusive focus on dream work both on an individual and a group basis. Her goal was to offer help in working through job-related tensions. Organizational change comes about as a consequence of change in the managers themselves. Engagement in dream work exposed these managers to the creativity embodied in dream imagery while at the same time sensitizing them to the extent to which a healthy working atmosphere depended on their ability to liberate the creative energies of all involved in the enterprise. It was obvious that so much of the subjective distress that came to her attention arose out of the way that bureaucratic structures and the traditional compartmentalization limit the free flow of creative energies resulting in alienation and a lack of a sense of personal fulfillment. Dr. Hazarika's efforts in this direction are particularly timely as corporate structures face the need to compete in a globalized economy.

These are only a few of the ways that our very versatile dreams lend themselves to the exploration of social issues and invite further sociological studies.

Summary

Dreams have a connection to the social scene that is worth exploring. The images we make use of in our dreams are social in origin even though they are idiosyncratically transformed for our personal use. Some of these images are bidirectional; that is, they have something to say about the unsolved problems of society as well as of the individual. Looked at in this way they are pointers toward some of the negative or limiting aspects of society. Social insight derived from dream work can deepen social concern. A sociology of the dream is called for.

Notes

1. She had the responsibility for organizing the dream group on one of my visits to Sweden.

2. Permission given to remain away from work for medical reasons.

3. Even in those interested in dreams, dreamism manifests itself in the disparagement of a dream as unimportant, banal, etc. No dream should be subjected to a judgement from the waking state.

4. For further commentary on this connection, see Fromm (1955), Gruen (1987), Ullman and Storm (1986), and Ullman (1960, 1973, 1993).

References

Bastide, R. "The Sociology of the Dream," in G. E. Von Grunebaum, and R. Callois, eds., *The Dream and Human Societies.* Los Angeles: University of California Press, 1966, pp. 199–211.

Beradt, C. *The Third Reich of Dreams.* Chicago: Quadrangle Books, 1966.

Burrow, T. *Preconscious Foundations of Human Experience.* New York: Basic Books, 1964.

Eggan, D. "The Manifest Content of Dreams: A Challenge to Social Science." *American Anthropologist,* 54, 4 (1952): 469–85.

Fromm, E. *The Sane Society.* New York: Holt, Rinehart, and Winston, 1955.

Gruen, A. *The Insanity of Normality.* New York: Grove Weidenfeld, 1987.

Hazarika, A. *Daring to Dream: Cultivating Corporate Creativity Through Dreamwork.* Thousand Oaks, Calif.: Sage, 1997.

Samuels, A. *The Political Psyche.* London: Routledge, 1993.

Taylor, J. *Where People Fly and Water Runs Uphill.* New York: Warner Books, 1992.

Ullman, M. "The Social Roots of the Dream." *American Journal of Psychoanalysis,* 20, 2 (1960): 180–96.

Ullman, M. "Societal Factors in Dreaming." *Contemporary Psychoanalysis,* 9, 3 (1973): 282–92.

Ullman, M. "Dreams, the Dreamer and Society," in *New Directions in Dream Interpretation,* Gayle Delaney, ed. Albany: State University of New York Press, 1993.

Ullman, M., and Storm, E. F. "Dreaming and the Dream: Social and Personal Perspectives." *Journal of Mind and Behavior,* 7, 2 and 3 (1986) 429–47.

Ullman, M., and Zimmerman, N. *Working with Dreams.* Los Angeles: Jeremy P. Tarcher, 1979.

CONTRIBUTORS

JENNY DODD, M.S.W., was born in Kent, England. Her grandmother was a psychoanalyst and her mother is a psychotherapist. Ever since she can remember, dreams and the psyche have been an integral part of her life. She graduated from Edinburgh University with a Bachelor in Music degree and subsequently spent several years training and working in the field of music therapy and music teaching. In 1991 she enrolled in the Adelphi School of Social Work and obtained her degree in 1993. Since then she has been working with seriously disturbed children and their families in New York City.

SVEN HEDENRUD, M.A., M. Div., is a teacher of pastoral care and counseling at the Pastoral Seminar of the Church of Sweden, Lund. He is a state licensed psychotherapist and supervisor. He served as Director of St. Luke's Psychotherapy Center, Gothenburg and has a background in parish work and hospital chaplaincy. He spent 1978 at Lutheran General Hospital in Park Ridge, Illinois, in their Clinical Pastoral Education program. He is a founding member and the present secretary of The Dream Group Forum in Sweden.

DEBORAH JAY HILLMAN, Ph.D., received her doctorate in anthropology from The New School for Social Research. Following postdoctoral training at National Development and Research Institutes, Inc., she worked on studies concerning the lives of street youth. She is currently self-employed as an editor/ethnographic consultant, and does both artwork and dreamwork.

RICHARD M. JONES, Ph.D., received his B.A. from Stanford University in 1950 and his Ph.D. from Harvard University in 1956. He served on the faculties of Brandeis University, the University of California at Santa Cruz, and Harvard University. In 1970 he joined the planning faculty of The Evergreen State College in Olympia, Washington, where he served as Professor of Psychology. He was the author of *Ego Synthesis in Dreams, The New Psychology of Dreaming*, and *The Dream Poet*. Richard Jones died on January 29, 1995. Prior to his death he had prepared an early draft of a book he was writing on dream as metaphor and the role dreams played in the origin of language.

EDWARD F. STORM, Ph.D., is Professor Emeritus of Computer and Information Science at Syracuse University. He took his undergraduate degree in mathematics and physics at the University of Delaware and received his Ph.D in applied mathematics from Harvard University. Since retiring, his interests have shifted to music composition, performance, and structural analysis, and to the relation between the structure of music, language, and dreams, and the abstract theories of computing.

CLAIRE LIMMER, M.S., is a psychoanalyst in private practice in Westchester, New York. She received her B.A. from the City College of New York, her M.S. in Special Education from the Bank Street College of Education and was graduated from the National Psychological Association for Psychoanalysis in 1988. She is a member of N.P.A.P. as well as the National Association for the Advancement of Psychoanalysis. For many years she was a teacher of emotionally disturbed children at a children's psychiatric hospital in the Bronx. She has led dream workshops in her home community as well as at conference centers. Her current life centers on her practice, her joy in the natural beauty of the world, her friends, and a growing family that now includes five grandchildren.

MONTAGUE ULLMAN, M.D., is a psychiatrist and psychoanalyst who founded the Dream Laboratory at the Maimonides Medical Center, Brooklyn, New York. In the course of his career he has been interested in dreams from physiological, psychological, sociological, and parapsychological perspectives. These various aspects came together in shaping the group work he has done with dreams over the past decade, both in this country and in Scandinavia. He is currently Clinical Professor of Psychiatry Emeritus at the Albert Einstein College of Medicine, a Life

Fellow of the American Psychiatric Association, a Charter Fellow of the American Academy of Psychoanalysis, and a Life Member of the Society of Medical Psychoanalysts. With Nan Zimmerman he is co-author of *Working with Dreams* (Jeremy P. Tarcher, Inc., 1979), the author of *Appreciating Dreams* (Sage Publications, 1996) and numerous other publications on the subject.

JOHN A. WALSH, D.MIN., is currently Associate Pastor of Holy Cross Church, Orlando, Florida; Director of the Consultation Center, Maitland, Florida; and Supervisor of the Mental Health Unit at CENTAUR—The Central Aids Agency in Orlando. His doctoral studies are in the area of the relationship between psychology and religion, and specifically in the understanding and interpretation of dream experiences as a ministerial focus. He is a graduate of Aquinas Institute, St. Louis, Missouri, with a doctorate in ministry, and a graduate of Marywood College, Scranton, Pennsylvania, with a Master of Arts degree in psychology. He is an ordained Catholic priest of the Diocese of Scranton, Pennsylvania.

INGE WIDLUND, M.A., is a psychotherapist in private practice. He is a member of Gruppanalytiska Institutet i Stockholm, Dromgruppsforum (The Forum for Dreamgroups),Sweden and Group-Analytic Society (London). He had earlier been a civil servant, working with organizational development and research. Apart from his clinical practice he is also working as consultant in organizational matters, supervisor, and lecturer. He is the editor and co-author of two books on group-analytic psychotherapy: *Gruppanalytiska Perspektiv* (1989) and *Den Analytiska Gruppen* (1995). His interest in dreams started when he met Monte Ullman in Sweden in the late seventies, and he has been leading dream groups for psychotherapists.

JOHN R. WIKSE, Ph.D., is currently Associate Academic Dean of Shimer College, Waukegan, Illinois, where he teaches social theory and humanities. He first became interested in dreams in the late 1960s while a graduate student at the University of California at Berkeley, where he was studying political theory and psychology. Influenced by Perls, R. D. Laing, Gandhi, and Marx, he started thinking about the relationship between therapy and revolution in order to evaluate the civil rebellion occurring around him. Influenced by the Reichian renaissance, the beginnings of men's and women's liberation groups during the end of the antiwar movement, and the increasing complexity and self-consciousness of "relationships" of that time, he began to perceive that dreams were useful counsel. He left California in 1971 to teach at Pennsylvania State University and published *About Possession: The Self as Private Property* (Pennsylvania State University Press, 1977). During these years he became acquainted with the work of Trigant Burrow, and, under the auspices of the Lifwynn Foundation, met and worked with Montague Ullman, who encouraged him to appreciate his dreams and understand them as social information.

NAN ZIMMERMAN is a writer, musician, and teacher. Her interest in dreams became focused in 1960 when she began keeping a journal. This journal became the seedbed for later work with Montague Ullman with whom she collaborated to write *Working with Dreams* (Jeremy P. Tarcher, Inc.,1979), now published in seven foreign countries. Through her association with Dr. Ullman, she recognized that understanding dreams was a natural, organic process. She has led many workshops based on the premise that anyone can learn to work creatively with their own dreams if given certain skills and support. She is a graduate of The College of William and Mary. In addition to teaching piano, MIDI keyboard, and dream work, she is currently writing a book of personal essays. In it she examines the struggle to overcome the identity of victim and the possibility of transformation through the acceptance of uncertainty.

INDEX OF NAMES